Dare to Ride i...

This is a book about a "Magicka...
magicians from two different eras. Ev.... ....ugit utey never met each
other, they work with energies of a very specific nature.

The first set of magickal diaries are from Christine Hartley and
show what type of magick was performed within the Merlin Temple
of the Stella Matutina, an offshoot of the Hermetic Order of the
Golden Dawn, for the years 1940-1942. This information is important
because it describes exactly how rituals were done and what the participants experienced. Hartley's diaries have been edited, explained and
expanded upon by Alan Richardson, making this one of the most
important magickal documents ever printed.

The second set of magickal diaries are those of Geoff Hughes. They
detail magickal work that he did during the years 1984-1986. Although
he was not at this time a member of any formal group, the magick he
practiced was under the same aegis as Hartley. He worked under
Merlin.

Both Hartley and Hughes were trained initiates of Dion Fortune's. They both eventually went on to follow that archemage of
legend and otherworld reality. *The third section of this book, written by
Hughes, shows exactly how you can simply make contact with Merlin.*
Merlin, the protector of England and a source of the magickal power
behind many British-oriented groups, is destined to be an important
part of the magickal systems of the future—you can find out about
it today!

The Dragon is another symbol that appears frequently in magickal
writings all over the world. Find out how Hughes uses the dragon to
explore this universe, and other levels of reality, and learn to use this
dragon energy yourself.

The magick of Christine Hartley (under her maiden name of
Christine Campbell Thomson) and Geoff Hughes are like the poles of
some hidden battery which lie buried beneath the Earth, and beneath
the years. There is a current flowing between them. The energy is
there for you to tap.

Many people today are looking for a magickal path that is both
natural and yet has aspects of ceremonial magick. Here it is—a book
that shows a path that thousands of people can easily follow.

If you have been looking for a way to tap into the ultimate mysteries, this may be the path for you. If you simply want to learn how
real magicians work their rituals, and the actual results and experiences
they have, this book is a must!

About the Authors

Alan Richardson was born and raised in Northumberland, England. He trained as a teacher, worked as a nurse, and spent a few young and fascinated years wandering about Kentucky and West Virginia. His previous books include *Gate of Moon*, which goes some way toward the creation of a truly Western system of Magic, based upon the Arthurian cultus; *Dancers to the Gods*, which contains the Magical Diaries of Colonel Seymour and Christine Hartley, detailing the Work they did within the Fraternity of the Inner Light for the years 1937-39; and *Priestess*, which is the first full biography of Dion Fortune. He is married, with two children, and lives in a large village in the heart of Wessex.

Geoff Hughes was born January 14, 1943, in Lewisham, southeast London, England. He served in the British Army for 22 years, during which time he was stationed in West Germany, Borneo, Singapore, Northern Ireland, and England. Married to Val, whom he met when she served in the Women's Royal Army Corps, they now live and work in the county of Essex. They have three children, one grandchild, two Jack Russell terriers, and three cats. Geoff started on the Magical Path by initially visiting a Spiritualist church. From this he progressed through a number of esoteric schools before joining the Fraternity of the Inner Light where in due course he was initiated into the Western Mystery Tradition. In March 1984 he was "moved out" of the Fraternity by the Inner Plane Adepti, and thus began the work detailed in this book.

To Write to the Authors

We cannot guarantee that every letter written to the authors can be answered, but all will be forwarded. Both the authors and the publisher appreciate hearing from readers, learning of your enjoyment and benefit from this book. Llewellyn also publishes a bi-monthly news magazine with news and reviews of practical esoteric studies and articles helpful to the student, and some readers' questions and comments to the authors may be answered through this magazine's columns if permission to do is included in the original letter. The authors sometimes participate in seminars and workshops, and dates and places are announced in *The Llewellyn New Times*. To write to the authors, or to ask a question, write to:

Alan Richardson/Geoff Hughes
c/o THE LLEWELLYN NEW TIMES
P.O. Box 64383-671, St. Paul, MN 55164-0383, U.S.A.

Please enclose a self-addressed, stamped envelope for reply, or $1.00 to cover costs.

About Llewellyn's High Magick Series

Practical Magick is performed with the aid of ordinary, everyday implements, is concerned with the things of the Earth and the harmony of Nature, and is considered to be the magick of the common people. *High Magick*, on the other hand, has long been considered the prerogative of the affluent and the learned. Some aspects of it certainly call for items expensive to procure and for knowledge of ancient languages and tongues, though that is not true of all High Magick. There was a time when, to practice High Magick, it was necessary to apprentice oneself to a Master Magician, or *Mage*, and to spend many years studying and, later, practicing. Throughout the Middle Ages there were many high dignitaries of the Church who engaged in the practice of High Magick. They were the ones with both the wealth and the learning.

High Magick is the transformation of the Self to the Higher Self. Some aspects of it also consist of rites designed to conjure spirits, or entities, capable of doing one's bidding. Motive is the driving force of these magicks and is critical for success.

In recent years there has been a change from the traditional thoughts regarding High Magick. The average inteligence today is vastly superior to that of four or five centuries ago. Minds attuned to computers are finding a fascination with the mechanics of High Magical conjurations (this is especially true of the mechanics of Enochian Magick).

The Llewellyn High Magick Series has taken the place of the Mage, the Master Magician who would teach the apprentice. "Magick" is simply making happen what one desires to happen—as Aleister Crowley put it: "The art, or science, of causing change to occur in conformity with will." The Llewellyn High Magick Series shows how to effect that change and details the steps necessary to cause it.

Magick is a tool. High Magick is a potent tool. Learn to use it. Learn to put it to work to improve your life. This series will help you do just that.

Other Books by Alan Richardson

Dancers to the Gods
Priestess
Gate of Moon
An Introduction to the Mystical Qabalah

Llewellyn's High Magick Series

Ancient Magicks for a New Age

Alan Richardson
and
Geoff Hughes

1989
Llewellyn Publications
St. Paul, Minnesota, 55164-0383, U.S.A.

International Standard Book Number: 0-87542-671-9
Library of Congress Catalog Number: 88-45185

First Edition, 1989
First Printing, 1989
Second Printing, 1989

Library of Congress Cataloging-in-Publication Data

Richardson, Alan, 1951-
    Ancient magicks for a new age.

    (Llewellyn's High magick series)
    1. Magic.   2. Occultism.   I. Hughes, Geoff,
1943-   .   II. Title.   III. Series.
BF1999.R456   1989   133.4'3   88-45185
ISBN 0-87542-671-9

Cover Art: Lissanne Lake
Illustrations: Amanda Blake

Produced by Llewellyn Publications
Typography and Art property of Chester-Kent, Inc.

Published by
LLEWELLYN PUBLICATIONS
A Division of Chester-Kent, Inc.
P.O. Box 64383
St. Paul, MN 55164-0383, U.S.A.
Printed in the United States of America

To Michelle,
for helping to invoke
the Dreamtime

—A.R.

Contents

Foreword

This is a book about a Magical Current.* It details the work of magicians from two different eras who never met each other in this world or the next, but who each in their own way have worked (and work) with energies of a very specific nature.

The first set of Diaries were given me by Christine Hartley, and show in a fragmented form something of the magic performed with the Merlin Temple of the Golden Dawn for the years 1940-42.

The second set of diaries were shown me by Geoff Hughes, and detail the Work he did during the years 1984-86. Although he was not at this time a member of any formal group, the magic he practiced was under the same aegis as Christine. That is to say, he worked under the guidance and tutelage of Merlin.

The third section of this book has been written by him with the specific intention of showing, in a very simple manner, exactly how each person can make his or her own inner contacts with this same entity.

Both Geoff and Christine were trained initiates of the Fraternity of the Inner Light, originally working under very different influences indeed before leaving to follow that archmage of legend and other-world reality. Christine left because her personal relationships within the lodge became strained; Geoff left because, as his diaries show, the Grand Master of the lodge passed him on to Merlin—though by no means with his willing consent. In a very real sense he has carried on and developed a line of magic that was originally used in a sometimes crude and often diffuse form within the Order of the Stella Matutina—the Order of the Morning Star—which in itself represented those dissident factions within the now legendary Hermetic Order of the Golden Dawn.

Despite the enormous publicity that the *GD* receives today, and despite the explicit accounts of its inner teachings and rites, very little

---

* The term Magical Current is, of course, a felicitous description of something as indefinable as electricity. We can only really perceive it and analyze it in terms of how it manifests within the world. Using other terms of reference we might analyze a Magical Current in terms of movements in history, or else via the psychological practices and theories in a particular nation during a definite era. For our present purpose we must look for these manifestations among the adepti of the Golden Dawn.

information is available about what these magicians actually experienced. On top of that, books about the essential meaning of magic have been marred by the sort of dense jargonizing that has been termed, and rightly, as "psychobabble"; or else it has been taken to the other extreme and dealt with in the sort of credulous tones that seem to have the exclamations "Gee!" "Wow!" and "Now get this . . . " thrumming at subsonic levels below every breathless and usually empty statement.

There are several reasons for the dearth of such hard, personal information. First, the magicians of the *GD* were enjoined to destroy all such documents in good time before their deaths, or else make arrangements to ensure that this was done afterward. Second, their magical diaries were often unreadable, comprised of the sort of cryptic shorthand and terse comments characteristic of all such documents never intended for publication. But the primary reason that so little personal documentation is available is the very human one of shyness. The inner life of the magician, while being intensely real, can also sound completely incredible to those people with no understanding of the sort of energies and entities involved.

I remember Christine taking very great care to explain to me about Cheiron, one of her main inner contacts. She believed—no, she *knew*—that Cheiron was *a force and an entity that exists within the otherworld*, and who has always had a benign interest in humanity's progress. Being still a young man, too enwrapped in the specious nonsense of modern psychology, I was dubious about this to say the least, but resolved to keep an open mind. Now I have long since thrown away my doubts, and cease to be surprised at the number of others I meet today who have also made the Cheiron contact.

All of which is something of a softener for the surprise that many will feel upon reading Geoff Hughes' account of his workings involving a dragon. As he says, he does not know *what* it is, except that it is part and parcel of the Earth's consciousness—and something more than that somehow. All he can do is get on with using it, and making the most of things while they last. No real magician would do otherwise.

In fact it was the dragon which drew me toward Geoff, although at the time of writing this I have not yet met him. I had written the original draft of this manuscript with no clear idea of theme or direction, intending to pad it out with some of Colonel Seymour's essays and lengthy quotes from own previous books. However I held onto the thing for some time because I felt that more was to come, although I could not have said what, or how. It was only when Geoff wrote to me care of my publishers and asked me some innocuous questions about *Dancers to the Gods* that an inner antenna of my own began to vibrate, and I replied to his letter with a greater care and detail than I would perhaps have normally used. Two letters later, when he made a passing reference to his "dragon magic" as I would term it, I knew why I had been so desultory in my approach to the book. It was the dragon that I had been waiting for—that and certain other symbols which cropped up exactly on cue.

The image of the dragon or winged serpent had bothered me for some time. Originally, some years before, I had hoped to co-write a book on dragon magic with that fine Welsh poet David Annwn, but the project never got off the ground, in more senses than one. And try as I might I could never fit it into the themes of any of my previous books, although I made a gallant attempt in *Priestess*.

So, in brief, the communication with Geoff by letter and telephone, and the study of his magical diaries in the light of those belonging to Christine, helped reawaken certain inner contacts of my own that had been dormant for almost two years.

Of course Geoff will attract a great deal of hostile comment from those people who merely practice magic, as opposed to those who *live* it. He is willing and more than capable of looking after his own psyche in this matter—which is why I have kept my comments, via footnotes, to a minimum. Besides which we have agreed to disagree on many minor matters which we can ignore in this instance for the sake of readability.

I would add that his experiences are not without precedent, as he is fully aware. There are many others working the Merlin contact, and presumably many others involved with dragons of one sort or another. And although I am not a magician as such, I too had an encounter with a dragon long before Geoff's letter ever appeared on my doormat.

The story goes back to the summer of 1986, when I had become very interested in tracking down fragments of the ancient worship that once existed in the valley where we lived. It seemed to me that the whole area was once devoted to those great Welsh divinities of Beli and Dôn, from whom the major figures in both Welsh and Irish pantheons are descended. The focus of it all, I felt, was around a little known conical tumulus that exists within the grounds of a large private house which I came to call, for no very clear reason, "Bel's Tump."

I first began trying to learn the magical secrets of the tumulus on June 30, according to my own diary, and as I reread it at this moment I find that on that same day I received a letter from a young lady in South Africa, who confided to me her own visions of hawk, ruby and dragon which she had gained while meditating upon the pentagram. She made some passing reference to Merlin, too, and asked me what it might mean. As I recall now, I answered in the vaguest of terms, not really knowing too much myself and forgetting about it entirely up until now. Today, in ways that this book will show, it has all become crystal clear.

The entry in question, however, reads:

Lay in the bath, 10:45 p.m., astrally circling Bel's Tump, nine times, calling on Him in the name of Dôn, his wife. Widdershins, drawing out the power. Then one more ½ turn so that I stood at the N., leaning onto the earth slope, and indeed falling in. Images of the other sites along the valley, inter-connected with lines of light. Asked Beli for the Wisdom of the valley.

Very very strong sense of "thereness."

Then, exactly a week later, I went back again:

Monday, 10:25 a.m.
Letters from E.M.G., R.S., and Fiona Clark.
Long dream last night of us three (my family) escaping from occupied France. Now, I interpret this in the Gnostic sense.

But, prior to sleep, approached Bel's Tump in the astral. Had a vision of a broad tree with a whitened bole, and then the Tump itself, a demonic looking creature rising from it. For once, despite the usual frisson of fear, I didn't shut it out and *demanded*, several times, to know its secret.

Then came an extraordinarily long and vivid image of a colossal dragon pouring from the mound, slithering out, vast. Again I felt no fear despite the reality. I knew it was part of me. At my demands to know its secret it crumbled to white powder and bones.

Then I found myself within the mound, looking up at a hole in the top. There was a table there, figures (not clear). There was a sword, too, its hilt *very* bright, blade concealed. I seemed to draw the sword—an act of royalty.

Vivid, strong figure appeared, like an alchemical drawing of a king—Beli no doubt. I allowed him to knight me.

Visions of the wheeling cosmos above—stars, currents in space.

Asked for a good life for us three (or more) . . . offered myself in return.

> All of this last far less powerful than the merging of the
> dragon. The rest *may* have been self-created in a sense—esp. re.
> the sword and my "kingship" of the valley.

So that was that. I tell this not, I hope, for the sake of some ego-boost (if I wanted to do that I'd choose a better way than just churning out an old vision) but to show that Geoff's more spectacular experiences with his dragon are not entirely beyond the pale of human and magical experience.

I am unable to give any clues, even at this remove, as to what my poor, short-lived beast actually meant. I can only say that it was one of the most moving and effective experiences in my life, only matched by two others: the first, when Michelle and I celebrated our own "mystic marriage" on the lower slopes of Glastonbury Tor, with the aid of some bread and wine, and the image of Morgan le Fay; the second when I first held my baby daughter in my arms and knew, beyond doubt that, after her mother, she was the most beautiful creature outside of the Andromeda galaxy.

So the awakening of my dragon was as intense as all that. I cannot say better. And if, as any magician or artist would assert, the vital experience of a single individual can ultimately affect humanity as a whole then it will all work itself out some day, to someone's satisfaction.

Geoff's own motives in publishing these diaries of his is to show that each person, no matter how modest or mundane their lives, can become their own Priest or Priestess, mediating those powers to which they are best suited. In the Practical Section of the book he goes on to show with admirable clarity and directness exactly how we can set about this, and enter the otherworld with surprising ease.

One unique quality of this book is that not only can we learn just what a particular magician is experiencing in this day and age, and learn how to follow similar paths of our own, but we can also check and correlate it all with the Workings of traditional adepti from almost half a century before.

The problem faced by magicians is not simply that they are without honor in their own country: they are without honor in their own *time*. Christine Hartley at least lived long enough to see it all come full circle when young people started to beat a path toward her door after many decades of near obscurity and even scorn. I have my own methods of avoiding or ignoring the worst of calumny, but Geoff is one of those rare types who leads from the front, and is always likeliest to draw the worst of the fire. Nevertheless he feels—and I agree fully—that the old days of traditional magical secrecy have passed, and won't return for another couple of generations. All we need to forge our own trails across the otherworld are simplicity, honesty, self-reliance—and above all the willingness to work—and work *hard*.

The magics of Christine Hartley (under her maiden name of Christine Campbell Thomson) and Geoff Hughes are like the poles of some hidden battery which lie buried beneath the Earth, and beneath the years. There is a current flowing between them. The energy is there for us all to tap.

—Alan Richardson

The
Merlin Temple

Part I

Morning Star

Introduction

This is an account of a group of people who practiced magic. They did so under the aegis of the Stella Matutina, or the Order of the Morning Star. This in itself was derived from the original Order of the Golden Dawn which in its hey-day, at the turn of the century, attracted some of the brightest and most interesting souls of the time.

The complete rituals and teachings of both Orders have been freely available for some time, and in recent years some excellent histories have been written. Despite all this, it is surprising that very little has been published about what these magicians actually experienced, why they performed their rituals, and to what end.

The documents printed herein relate to what seems to have been the Merlin Temple of the Stella Matutina, and were written largely (but not solely) by Christine Campbell Thomson who joined this group after she left the formidable shadow of the occultist Dion Fortune, who ran the Fraternity of the Inner Light. These Inner Workings, as they are called, allow us a fragmentary but extremely valuable insight into the last days of a great magical tradition, as experienced and seen through the spiritual vision of some neophytes and adepti as they link with the egregore of the Order for the first time.

No attempt has been made to give these Workings in any chronological sequence for the reason that they tell a story within a story, and one that is best told by looking at themes and concepts in the light of a greater whole. Beyond this, I have used the material (or perhaps misused it) to suggest a more modern system of magic that can be tailored to an individual's own needs, and based upon what I see as the very essence of the Order's teachings.

Although it will offend many people in the saying, the plain truth is that while the magical system of the Golden Dawn is eternally valid, it is also presently obsolete, excepting those elements that I have attempted to identify in relation to these unique documents.

As with my previous books on magic, I have made little attempt at being objective, and less at being secretive. The time for that sort of thing is past, and won't return for another generation. The opinions

3

and analyses are peculiarly my own, and will stand or fall under the strengths or stresses of my own little idiosyncracies in these matters. My whole intention is to make the would-be initiate think for himself, learn for himself, while at the same time suggesting techniques and attitudes that can prove wonderfully effective in producing results on both outer and inner levels.

If nothing else I would get this same would-be initiate to realize that the word itself simply means "to begin," and that the Great Initiates are characterized less by their cosmic wisdom than by the deep knowledge that they are endless beginners at all times, with an infinity of things to learn.

—Alan Richardson
Wessex, England
1986

On the 25th of November 1954, William Elliot Carnegie Dickson died at his home in St. George's Road, Twickenham, Middlesex. He was 66 years old and had had a distinguished career as a medical doctor, specializing in the fields of neurology, bacteriology, and pathology. He had studied and first practiced his craft in his native Scotland—Edinburgh to be exact—but in time he achieved enough success to have the cache of a surgery in much-vaunted Harley Street, in London. That address alone was as much a proclamation of status and attainment as any of the many letters after his name.

He and his wife Edith were the sort of people who were regarded as pillars of the establishment, yet who lived the sort of lives, which, while noteworthy during their existence, made no apparent impact upon the generations which followed. But there was more to the Dicksons than the profession of healing, more to William's life than his hobbies of fishing and photography. At least once a week, for the duration of the Second World War, he and Edith brought out two pillars from a large and locked cupboard. One was white and one was black, and their bases were cubical to represent the element of Earth, through which we all exist. From these bases rose images of lotus flowers, symbolizing regeneration and metempsychosis. They were known as the "Pillars of the Gods of the Dawning Light," and they rose beneath the high ceiling of the room a little beyond the height of a tall man.

With these in place, along with the double-cubed altar and certain other items of ritual significance, the earthly personalities of that man and his wife dissolved into the ethers as their consciousness changed onto purely magical levels. As *Fortes Fortuna Juvat* and *Dominus Illuminatio Meo* respectively, they opened one of the last Temples of the already legendary Hermetic Order of the Golden Dawn. However empty the room might have seemed to the earthly eye, to the vision of a seer it shimmered with an ancient light.

This was never the most illustrious of temples. It never quite achieved the resonance of the Ahathoor in Paris, or the original Isis-Uranis that had been formed in London 50 years before, nor did it come close to the relatively new but formidable Hermes Temple in

Bristol—that city which the brothers Cabot had left to inhabit the New World. But the dominant force behind it would emerge again with renewed energy almost two generations later, long after the more illustrious temples had died, or ossified. For it was no mere Jungian archetype that they derived their charter from, nor yet some mythopoetic symbol that they vaguely aspired toward. The force behind the Lodge, as they termed it, was a real and powerful and often uncompromising entity which existed and exists within the Otherworld. It had manifested itself in many ways on many occasions, and often in human form: then it had always been seen as an archmage, master magician; and when it did so it became known by the name of a little bird.

It became known as Merlin.

T he various and varied Temples of the Hermetic Order of the Golden Dawn were devoted to the study and practice of magic. Magic was understood to be a particularly religious pursuit, using a body of arcane knowledge that would enable the participants to come a little closer to the Gods. In crude but accurate terms the senior adepts within the Order believed themselves capable of direct mind-to-mind contact with discarnate entities of exceedingly high status. These entities were felt to be far removed from the mere shells picked up by the coarser perceptions and lesser wisdoms of those within the Spiritualist movement. These entities had, and have, an evolutionary interest in humanity.

The importance of the Golden Dawn and all its various offshoots is not so much in the magical techniques taught, nor yet in the philosophies and principles behind them, but in the rays of light which have splayed out from the source and which can be seen, like the veins beneath a dragon's hide, coursing through the darkness beneath the Earth and its consciousness, and thus through the dreams of man and woman down through the years.

T he *GD* (Golden Dawn), as it was always called, was formed by three men and one woman. One of these men was W. R. Woodman, an aging and frail non-entity, a lamb of a man sacrificed to the need for the group to begin with a mystic trinity. Another was Dr. Wynn Westcott, a learned and wise coroner who was nevertheless stronger at administration than practical magic, and whose character provided the sort of lubricant that every large society—occult or otherwise—needs in order to turn smoothly. And then there were the Mathers, who can hardly be considered separately even though it was the husband who has attracted the lion's share of historical acclaim and assassination.

Samuel Liddel Mathers was born on January 8, 1854 at Hackney, near London. Tall and lean faced, hard and handsome, he was the sort of man around whom the air seemed to crackle, and whose magnetism was such that lost and unknown qualities of the soul were drawn to the surface of those who came close to him. His background was uncertain, his profession was always precarious, his sanity often doubted—but there would have been no Golden Dawn without him. No one was indifferent to him. His only passions in life were magic and the art of war, and with his essentially Gnostic view of the world he often saw the two as entirely supportive. Mathers, beyond anyone else, proved the old maxim that there are worlds of difference between magicians, and those who merely practice magic. Westcott and most of the Order merely practiced magic, but Mathers was a magician in every atom of his body, which he knew to be a microcosm of the great body of the God he served.

And then there was Mina, or Moina as she liked to be called. People often forget her. Yet without her influence Mathers would have spun madly off into the cold realms of oblivion. Moina loved him, supported him, acted as his priestess, and made his magic work. Indeed, she was as instrumental in bringing through material from the Secret Chiefs as her husband.

Moina was lovely. Strangely modern in appearance she could walk the streets of London today and no one would guess that her style had come straight from another century. She had what the Gaels would call the "Two Sights," and some of her younger admirers, with the magnified passions that only younger admirers can have, thought that she was the greatest clairvoyant of all time. Perhaps they were right. She and her husband never had sex. They didn't much like it. And they took the escape route that many mystics preferred in that bitter Victorian era, declaring chastity an absolute virtue as far as their own brand of adepthood went. Moina's forte was in working with the elemental kingdoms of Air, Earth, Fire and Water, and she set her heart toward the faery light of the Celtic pantheons with all of their power to charm, hypnotize, or simply annoy. It was through her that the *GD*'s power was originally earthed and made effective, for unless a magician makes some nominal link with the elemental forces, his magic just *will not work*, and becomes no more than noises in the head.

These were the main personalities behind the original formation of the Order. The mundane events which linked them are less interesting.

The basis of the story was that some time in February, 1886, a cipher manuscript was found which presented a substantial skeleton of rituals that were quite unlike anything that Westcott and his intimates had yet encountered within their Craft, as Freemasonry was called. The men in question were all Master Masons within the *Societas Rosicruciana in Anglia*, and what they found excited them all in a way that only other Freemasons with an archival bent might understand. One version of the *GD*'s gestation has it that the manuscript was found in a bookstall in Farringdon Road, London. Another states that it was uncovered in a Masonic stock cupboard, having once belonged to the seer Frederick Hockley. The whole tale is made dubious by its links with a mysterious female adept in Germany calling herself Anna Sprengel who eventually gave Westcott a charter to found his own Order based upon the five rituals that had been delineated. As a Mason this formal charter would have been necessary to Westcott: it would give the new Order some validity; not only in his eyes, but in the eyes of those of his fellows within the Craft. Those things were important in these circles within the final decades of the 19th century.

Really, Westcott was playing games. The saga of Anna Sprengel was concocted by the old doctor himself, the charters forged. Yet the vital thing is that he helped unearth the skeleton in the first place and helped arrange the fragments into some recognizable whole. It was left to the Mathers to put flesh on the bare and rather brittle bones, and between them raise enough power to imbue their unlikely golem with a life of its own.

What they created was a body of magic that took in the best of Theosophy, without its Himalayan overtones, the ceremonial magic of medieval European and English traditions, the best of occult Masonry which harkened back to Frederick Hockley and perhaps beyond, all sifted and shaped through the peculiar and demanding philosophy of the Kabbalah. It was scarcely a native British magic, but in an era which had seen the Goddess driven Eastward, out of the Western consciousness entirely, it went some way toward bringing Her back to the British shores, pausing, so to speak, among these essentially Mediterranean sources of inspiration.

The first temple was known as the Isis-Urania, and was formed in 1888. It was followed by the Osiris, Horus, and Amen-Ra, these being located in Weston-super-Mare, Bradford, and Edinburgh respectively.

The whole structure of the magical progress within the *GD* was based upon a measured climb up that glyph known as the Tree of Life—a climb that was in itself marked by various stages known as Grades. In a way, by virtue of sheer human vanity, these Grades contributed as much to the Order's decline as any internal politics. We might tabulate them as follows:

Malkuth	Earth	Zelator	1-10
Yesod	Moon	Theoricus	2-9
Hod	Mercury	Practicus	3-8
Netzach	Venus	Philosophus	4-7
Tiphareth	Sun	Adeptus Minor	5-6
Geburah	Mars	Adeptus Major	6-5
Chesed	Jupiter	Adeptus Exemptus	7-4
Binah	Saturn	Magister Templi	8-3
Chockmah	Neptune	Magus	9-2
Kether	Uranus	Ipsissimus	10-1

The Outer Order of the Golden Dawn initiated up until the sphere of the Sun; during this time, and in order to prove oneself fit for the next initiation, the student had to master an exceedingly demanding curriculum which took in all aspects of occult philosophy, with especial emphasis on the Kabbalah. When he or she found themselves at the level of the Sun, facing initiation as an Adeptus Minor, they then learned about the Second Order, the Inner Order of the Golden Dawn, known as the Rosae Rubeae et Aureae Crucis.

Here the studies became even more intense and the candidate had to demonstrate to his superiors that he had achieved a practical talent for occult arts as diverse as the consecration of talismans, clairvoyance, the creation of numerous items of ritual equipment properly imbued with power, "rising on the planes," and various divinatory techniques.

Whatever else might be said against the *GD*, those souls who had conscientiously followed the curriculum could never have been accused of sloth, or looking for some easy escape from the cares of the world.

The Second Order was based upon the myth of Christian Rosencreutz. *CRC*, as the name was invariably abbreviated, was a larger-than-human and indeed Christ-like figure said to have been born in the year 1378 and who became the indwelling genius behind the Rosicrucian Order which appeared, mushroom-like, in 17th century Germany. *CRC's* body, it was said, lies hidden in a vault, dead but uncorrupted, like some Egyptian mummy that is eternally on the verge of re-vivifying. Still potent, still aware, *CRC* was felt to be emanating strange forces into the ethers, down through the centuries. A lot of the adepti believed it implicity. Others, with perhaps greater wisdom, simply got on with *using* the myth.

The rituals of the Second Order involved an actual reconstruction of *CRC's* seven-sided vault, marvelously decorated and charged with occult sigils, with the Chief Adept lying in the pastos, or coffin, ready to awaken before the new adept's magical eye, and in doing so awaken something potent within that person's spirit. Even A. E. Waite, who was one of the dullest, most tedious of all the commentators in the occult field, and who had a reputation that we would find hard to accept today, thought this ritual was one of the most sublime and wondrous of all time.

Now all this might have been the end of it but for the emphasis that Mathers began to place upon the Third Order, which he claimed was comprised of entities who were more than human—the Secret Chiefs—who were in fact the real intelligences behind the creation of the whole Order. The question of the Masters is one of the most vexing and contentious issues in any study of magic. Israel Regardie, who in a paradoxical way preserved Golden Dawn just as Martin Luther "saved" the Catholic church from its own inherent corruption, wrote of them in *My Rosicrucian Adventure*:

> That commonly found fantasy ... of being in touch with Masters ... is so evidently neurotic, or even blatantly delusional, that most of those claiming it would have done better to have included some kind of psychotherapy in their early magical training. They would then have become familiar with the meaning and motive of the whole world of fantasy and dream with its manifold distortions, perversions, and aberrations.

While not denying the possibility that such beings may well exist (though he would prefer them on the physical plane), his criticisms were primarily those of a psychotherapist. When he wrote this in the mid-1930's psychotherapy was still a new and mightily hopeful art that seemed to offer the real chance of driving with surety to the heart of any problem. And while what he said was perfectly true—many of the adepti *did* make fools of themselves in their search for Masters—he could not have foreseen how utterly destructive the modern obsessions with psychotherapy have proved to be. The follies and pecadillos of the magi around their cubical altars can scarcely compare with those shown by the men and women with the leather couches. Nevertheless, Regardie was right when he noted: "It is only an enlarged or inflated ego—which really conceals a dismal inferiority and insecurity—that demands such a quest."

The question of Masters, Secret Chiefs, or inner plane adepti really is crucial to the art of magic; but we must learn to look at them in a new way, and one dependent neither upon the manic insistence of the spiritualist medium with his guides, nor yet upon the smug dismissiveness of the psychologist. More of this later.

At a time when the Order was undergoing many internal stresses—as happens to every magical group at some point—Mathers just became tired of supporting the charade about Anna Sprengel and her Continental dispensations. Westcott, he claimed, had never at any point made contact with European source. The real inspiration behind the Order, he went on, was that of the Secret Chiefs. It was they who gave him the wisdom of the Second Order, and no one else. He did not know their earthly names, but only knew them by certain mottoes. He had rarely seen them in the flesh, but had made frequent contact with them on the astral plane. He believed them to be human, and living on this Earth, and possessing terrible superhuman powers.

Many of the magi, for whom magic was just a genteel form of co-educational Freemasonry, were appalled. They resigned, or worse still they joined up with Waite. Of those who could accept the essential truth of their leader's statement, the evident authoritarianism of the man in many little trifles seemed to indicate an approaching madness.

To be fair, Mathers *was* a difficult man to deal with, and one who apparently had spells of instability coupled with the innate self-destructiveness expected of the "braid Scot." Then again the same might be said about any great man from any field of endeavor.

By this time, also, he had assumed the name of McGregor, thus becoming Samuel Liddel McGregor Mathers, and using the motto of that clan which was *'S Rhiogail Mo Dhream*. Moina's own Magical Motto was *Vestigia Nulla Retrorsum*. Magical names and mottoes were usually, but not always, synonymous. Their usage within the Golden Dawn was compulsory. William Butler Yeats, for example, called himself *Daemon est Deus Inversus*, or D.E.D.I., when he signed letters, or when others referred to him in correspondence relating to the order.

These names changed, sometimes, as the magician's perceptions about themselves changed. Thus Mathers, who began his magical career as *'S Rhioghal Mo Dhream*, eventually became *Deo Duce Comite Ferro*. The idea behind it all was that the neophyte was about to build a completely new personality, and one which would enable the Higher Self to express itself more fully during the sublime intensities of ritual. And so John Doe would create a name, or motto, that would express his highest aspirations or deepest insights. This name, fitted firmly within his psyche, would in due course become a key to awakening the highest perceptions, and vivifying what was called the Body of Light.

Effective though this technique was, and profound though the psychology behind it proved to be, in actual practice the majority of the magical names used within the Golden Dawn were simply hereditary family names. If a neophyte lacked imagination or pedigree he need only look up his name, or his mother's name, in one of the many reference books on heraldry and genealogy to find the appropriate tag. Thus *Fortes Fortuna Juvat* was traditional to the Doller, Murray, Troyte and Dickson families; *Deo, non Fortuna*, the magical name of Violet Firth who contracted it as a pen name to Dion Fortune, was common to the Digby, Harrison, and Firth families; while Sub Spe, the name used by Brodie-Innes, was almost certainly derived from his mother's side.

Sadly, with honorable exceptions, the illuminati of the Golden Dawn were not choosing names to express their innermost light: they were just being a little snobbish. On the other hand, this in no way devalues the technique itself. The justification for it all is whether it can be made to work, regardless of personal motives.

The Mathers never had much money, either, yet magic always came first. If it is possible to sacrifice one's soul to the Devil in return for earthly riches, then Mathers sacrificed his to God: he might find his own brand of heaven at the end but he paid an earthly price by never having much material security. If he, as was claimed, charged large sums to initiate Americans he was doing no more than every other European entrepreneur has ever done, for in his case financial necessity rose, as it occasionally must, far above the magical morality of the moment.

While he stayed on in Paris, however, working at his translations of obscure but influential texts on medieval magic, living the sparse life of a mage for 24 hours a day, seven days a week, the brethren back in Britain decided that the time had finally come to rebel.

Foremost among the rebels were Arthur Edward Waite and Robert Felkin, who divided up the dissidents and created little empires of their own. Waite had been born in America in 1857 but had come to England with his mother when he was still very young. Like Mathers, he had been a clerk by profession, and like Mathers he had made extensive studies in a wide variety of esoteric subjects in the library of the British Museum. Waite, however, was guilty of one of the greatest of all crimes in magic: in everything he did, everything he wrote, in all that he said, he was a bore. Incapable of writing an interesting sentence, he nevertheless had a great reputation among a section of the literati who mistook obfuscation for wisdom. And within the *GD* itself a lot of the more dismal elements found his to be the voice of reason, choosing to join his Holy Order of the Golden Dawn after the schism, wherein the rituals were rewritten, and the emphasis placed upon the mystical as opposed to the magical. Israel Regardie was later to describe him as a "Pompous, turgid Roman Catholic masquerading in occult dress." And that about sums him up.

Dr. Felkin, on the other hand, brings us much closer to our present theme, for under him the dissidents with the original *GD* were reorganized under the collective that became known as the Order of the Stella Matutina.

He was born c. 1858 and, like Carnegie Dickson, studied medicine at Edinburgh University, qualifying in 1884 but with a break in between when he worked as a medical missionary in Uganda. He also took a German M.D. at Marburg in 1885, and gained some reputation as an expert in tropical medicine.

It was in Edinburgh that he and his wife Mary joined the Amen-Ra Temple, as run by the lawyer and novelist J. W. Brodie-Innes, although he himself had been a member of a secret group that had operated within the *GD* before the schism, known as The Sphere. He wrote of this:

> The objects of the Group were: to concentrate forces of growth, progress and purification, every Sunday at noon, and the progress was 1st, the Formulation of the twelve workers near but not in 36 [Blythe Road]: 2nd Formulation around London; 3rd, Formulation round the Earth; 4th, Formulation among the Con-

stellations. Then gradually reverse the process, bringing the quintessence of the greater forces to the lesser . . .

Now the original Egyptian Group only lasted from the summer of 1898 to 1901, when we had a meeting and we were told that the Egyptian had retired from the Group and the Group as it was then constituted was brought to an end, the reason being that he was changing his place on the higher planes and could no longer work with us . . . so the second Group was formed having the Holy Grail on the central pillar.*

The Egyptian in question was of course one of those discarnate entities that attracted such titles as Masters, Secret Chiefs, or Inner Plane Adepti, the nature and reality of which we will discuss in due course. But the very fact that Felkin was using such inner contacts, as they are now called, meant that he had reached the stage of development traditionally associated with the Adeptus Minor and beyond. For all his often wayward enthusiasms, for all his later and exaggerated interest in earthly Rosicrucians lurking in mysterious Continental enclaves, Felkin was a *real* magician, and closer to the spirit of Mathers than any of the other heretics who had parted company with their former leader.

He is in fact one of the most underrated characters within the turbulent history of the Golden Dawn. He had enough charisma and natural authority to gain a large following when the empire began to fragment, and unlike many of the other rebels he had no doubts as to the reality of Mathers' comments about the Third Order.

(In fact the insults and mockeries that are invariably—ultimately— heaped upon any hierophant by the very initiates that he has helped to train should rarely be heeded *too* much: it is a sad fact that there is no creature on God's Earth more bitchy, more catty, or more brilliantly vindictive than an adeptus gone to seed—or never quite germinated in the first place.)

If Waite's response to increasing dissatisfactions among the brethern, then, was to form the Holy Order of the Golden Dawn, then Felkin's immediate answer was to create, at the behest of those Chiefs of his own that he termed the Sun Masters, the Stella Matutina, or Order of the Morning Star, the first outer Temple of which was dedicated to the great god Amoun.

---

* Ellic Howe, *Magicians of the Golden Dawn*, London 1972. p250-51. This is in fact the most comprehensive of the histories of the Golden Dawn, superbly researched but marred, somewhat, by the fact that Mr. Howe has little sympathy with magic or magicians. Nevertheless it is interesting to compare this Working with the scheme used by Dion Fortune's group during World War Two, in which the Holy Grail was one of the primary images, and the group itself formulated in a very similar manner.

The taunts that modern historians of the movement direct at Felkin were due to the fact that at this point in time he and his wife traveled Europe in search of those mysterious Rosicrucians who were supposedly behind the Order of the Golden Dawn from the very beginning. To many people's surprise at the time he even claimed to have had some success in finding them, although this was probably no more than a very human ploy to bolster his authority within the still-troubled groups back in Britain. But really, in his search for the sort of earthly Masters who would complement those he had found on the inner planes, he was no more than a child of his time. If nothing else he met a man who had the sort of power and insight that might be expected in one of the Rosicrucian adepts of legend, for within Rudolf Steiner, the founder of Anthroposophy, he found one of the most extraordinary figures in the occult movement this century. Steiner was indeed larger than human. The final judgement on Felkin's harmless little passions must be that he did what so many of us go through life without *ever* achieving: he found what he was looking for. More than that, the rays which shot out above his own magical horizon are the only ones which have traveled down to us today.

In many ways he was indeed the necessary counterbalance to the Mathers, and the name of his Order was no mere random choice. The Stella Matutina is, of course, the Morning Star, or Venus, which happens to be both a morning and an evening star. When it precedes the Sun before the dawn it is known as Lucifer, the Lightbearer; when it follows the Sun at dusk, it is known as Hesperus. Either way it brackets the impulse of the original Golden Dawn and can be glimpsed above the horizon when the Sun itself can no longer be seen.

The main difference between Felkin's Stella Matutina and Mather's Golden Dawn was one of tone. Felkin seems to have brought what we can only describe as Atlantean elements into the group mind—presumably via those entities known to him as the Sun Masters. While the exact identity of Mathers' own teachers is not clear, he told Moina once, who told W. B. Yeats, that one of them was a man of Scottish descent, known only by the initials of his magical motto, E.L.S. On the other hand the Adeptus Minor Ritual names the "Three Highest Chiefs" as: Hugo Alverda, the Phrisian; Franciscus de Bry, the Gaul; and Alman Zata, the Arab. The names were said to be enscribed on the scroll held by *CRC* as he lay in the tomb.

Now judging from the names and the little that is known about them, these Chiefs were not as far West as we might have expected. But magic at the turn of the century was in rather the same state as European learning before the Renaissance. That is to say the Classical and pre-Classical knowledge was preserved and even developed by the Arabs within that golden crucible known as Byzantium. Only slowly was it rediscovered and brought to Europe by a small number of learned and insightful individuals. *CRC* himself was said to lie in the fabled city of Damcar, which seems to have had a Middle Eastern location. This is one of the reasons why there is a resonance between a lot of traditional *GD* lore and the brighter aspects of Islam.

Although it is extremely unlikely that Mathers ever made contact with that entity which concerns us in this book, in a real sense he was, for a time, the Merlin of Britain, the Archmage. His only mistake, if such it was, was that he tried to cling to the role at a time when he should have graciously relinquished it. Yet who can blame him for that? It was part of his romance anyway.

It is also appropriate that he and Moina should have removed themselves to Paris at a certain point. In the workings of any major Magical Current within Britain there will always be unexpected links with its oldest and most cherished enemy—France. We find this within the Arthurian saga (which the Bretons appropriate to themselves) in the figure of Lancelot du Lac, "the best knight in the world," who is the regent of those Celtic aspects of the Aquarian Age. At one time Britain and France were physically united, and even after the Channel had finally divided them there was a regular traffic of young men and women between the countries whose object was to work their own post-Atlantean Mysteries. If the sacred colleges of England were to be found around Stonehenge and Avebury, to name but two, then those of its neighbor could be found at Carnac, at the tip of the Breton peninsula, which in itself drew its charter from Ys, the fabled lost city which had once been an Atlantean seaport and center of the Serpent Worship.

Pick up Ys on the inner planes and you pick up the *GD* at its Stella Matutina phase. Touch on the egregore of the Stella Matutina and you will eventually find Ys. Brodie-Innes once told Dion Fortune that wherever you found the name Coldharbour in Britain, there would be found remnants of this worship. It is not known what he based this statement upon, but it was certainly to Ys that he referred.*

---

* In the light of what follows it is worth bearing in mind Blavatsky's: "Thus it stands proven that Satan, or the Red Fiery Dragon, the 'Lord of Phosphorous,' and *Lucifer* or 'Lightbearer' is in us." And also that Welsh tradition records that Gwenddyd, Merlin's sister, was also the name of the Morning Star.

The break with Mathers complete, we find that by May 1902 Felkin, Brodie-Innes, and one Percy Bullock had formed the Amoun Temple of the Stella Matutina. The choice of this name, too, was not random, for in the great Temple of Luxor (which was itself a massive if microcosmic representation of man), the Sanctuary of Amoun corresponds in role and location to the pituitary body, one of the ductless glands secreting substances which influence the whole human machine. The anterior and posterior lobes of this body contain hormones which stimulate the thyroid, parathyroid and adrenal glands, as well as the sex organs and mammary glands. The lobes of the pituitary deal with the regulation of growth, the regulation of water balance within the body, affect the muscles of the uterus and thus influence childbirth, as well as the pigmentation of the skin. Without the pituitary body, life ceases in days.

Alter the levels, adjust the symbolism, and we can see some of the effects within the influence of Amoun. It *had* to be the first temple within this new Body of Magic. If Felkin did not know this with his conscious mind, then functioning in his Body of Light, under the magical name of *Finem Respice*, it was all a natural part of the patterns he was weaving.

It must be admitted, however, that much of this was due to the peculiar influence of one of his fellow adepts, the aforementioned J. W. Brodie-Innes, a lean, wry and educated Scot who had been born on March 10, 1848. Although he was a lawyer by profession, he was far better known as the author of such immensely popular works as *Morag the Seal*, *The Brood of the Witch Queen*, and *The Devil's Mistress*. As a young man he had spent a lot of time in the Western Islands, off Scotland, picking up remnants of the Celtic magical lore that still survived there:

> Different regions of the astral world are familiar to different branches of the Celtic race. One must go to Brittany for the cult of the dead, and certainly anyone who wishes to find fairy lore as a real and vital faith should go to the Western Islands, and should go with a comprehension of, and love for, the Celtic music . . .
>
> The lore of the fairies and elementals, that defied the colder vehicle of words, was expressed in music on the pipes . . . They said that the pipers would fall asleep on some fairy knoll, and in their dreams would hear strange music underground, and on waking would set the tune on the pipes. But no man could ever compose the fairy music . . .*

---

* *The Sorcerer and his Apprentice*, R. A. Gilbert, London, 1985.

More than anyone else, it was Brodie-Innes who brought the spirit of Celtia into the egregore of the Stella Matutina, and opened up paths that would lead toward the study of the Earth Mysteries, or what someone would later term the "Green Ray." It has been pointed out, also, that once he traveled extensively within the British Isles to study the lost art of witchcraft, and that now, a century later, witches themselves study his Order to learn a little more about themselves and their own Craft. And although he was at home within the non-intellectual wonders of the Horned Gods, he was also able to use the abstruse formulae of High Magic to observe the workings of the planet: Once, setting his raised consciousness upon the center of Draco, which he knew to be the Kether of the starry sphere, his inner self expanded until it seemed that he strode through the darkness of space like a giant, balancing the great forces which swirled round him: "The attention is then fixed on each force in turn, now alive and clothed with a definite symbolic form. In this it is desirable to use the forms of the Gods of Egypt, so as to avoid the chance of illusion through memory creeping in by the appearance of the human officers one is accustomed to see . . ." And he goes on to say: "I now felt every force moved by my own higher intuition, directed by the Spiritual Will. All thoughts of earth were lost altogether, and only the great forces were perceived . . ."

At this point he found that he could formulate the figure of a terrestrial globe in the place of the altar, and that by fixing his attention on any point of the surface he could get a mental picture of what was happening there "recognizing at the same time that it took place by the action and reaction of the great forces which moved by the will of God and were therefore in all things perfectly good. This rendered impossible any feeling of joy or sorrow at any event, any hope or any fear, any affection for any individual, or antipathy."*

Or as another rebel of a very different sort would later put it: "Pure Will, without lust of result, is in every way perfect."

Brodie-Innes was also something of a cuckoo in the nest, moving about between the two Orders as it suited him. He might have been playing a double game, as it has been implied, but on the other hand he might just have been going where the magic worked, for purely pragmatic purposes.

B. I., as they all called him, pursued his own Secret Chiefs in a

---

* *The Golden Dawn*, Israel Regardie, Llewellyn, St. Paul, 1986.

manner that would have been entirely acceptable to Mathers: "Whether the Gods or even the Secret Chiefs really exist is comparatively unimportant: the point is that the universe behaves as though they do." It was, and is, a marvelously effective attitude to take in a complex matter.

Felkin and Brodie-Innes were in many ways (often unwittingly and unwillingly) partners within a rite. In odd ways the magic they practiced has come down to us today, altered by the times of course, but still directly traceable to their innocent invocations in a variety of mundane locations at the end of the Victorian era. The surprising truth is that magic *always works*—although never within the time span you want it to work, and rarely in the manner you expect.

If Felkin can be likened to one of the serpents which wind around the Hermetic caduceus, then Brodie-Innes is clearly identifiable as the other. Symbolically, and also at the behest of otherworld contacts, B.I. made a clean break from Felkin by opening his own temple in Edinburgh in 1910. This was again dedicated to Amoun, but on another arc, and known as the Amen-Ra Temple whose early members included the Brodie-Innes', the Felkins, William Peck, Kate Moffat, as well as Edith and Carnegie Dickson, and some half a dozen others.

In differing ways, perhaps one temple acting like the anterior lobe of the pituitary body, and the other akin to the posterior lobe, these primary temples of Amoun and Amen-Ra, which were seen as situated at the base of the brain, would secrete those subtle forces that would affect the conception, growth, sensecence, death and renewal of the corporate Body of Magic that would be created.*

Felkin, Brodie-Innes, and Carnegie Dickson would call down forces that would carry the spirit of Amoun and Amen-Ra into the other temples they worked with, and because of this there would be aspects of the group mind that would respond to the Gods and Goddesses of the Old Land, as Egypt is called.

It must be remembered, too, that despite the enormous wealth of the native British Mystery Tradition, the adepti of the Golden Dawn were not really aware of it, emerging as they were from the powers of the church on the one hand, and the influence of rationalism on the other. Yet as the Mathers were using trance and/or supra-conscious methods to uncover or create a whole system of magic from the wasteland, so were distant archaeologists at that time bringing back to the Victorian public an endless series of wonders that had been sifted and

---

* Interestingly, if the mythological figure of Brittania is aligned with the geographical land mass, then the city of Edinburgh itself can be seen as placed in the pituitary of the Goddess' brain.

Mut, Cobra and Uraeus

dug from the sands of Egypt. The magi, tired with the insular arrogance of Empire, had never seen anything like it.

Egypt and all its pantheons was inevitable within the *GD*: it was both fashionable (and magic goes in fashions like anything else) and it was necessary. Nowhere else had magic been studied so profoundly and nowhere else had so much survived. The temples, the buildings, the pictures and the hieroglyphs, all built to exquisite proportions with outstanding subtlety, had an hypnotic effect upon the Victorian minds. And more, because a man can only really understand his own country by going overseas for awhile, so would the study and practice of Egypt prepare him for the day when he could look at his own native system with freshened eyes.

(That, at least, is a relatively respectable interpretation of the Egyptian emphasis in the original Orders. But the truth of the matter was that Egypt's magic and the magic of ancient Britain were both derived from the same Atlantean sources, though from different phases. The Egyptians took their magic from Atlantis as did the British; but because they codified it in the way they did, the conscious minds of the Victorian magi were able to deal with it far more easily than the fragmented images of their own land.)

The names of the temples of the *GD* were not, as we have seen, chosen from fancy. They represented direct if unconscious contacts with the gods or goddesses they were named after. The only exception was the Osiris in Weston-super-Mare, where Benjamin Cox, its Imperator, seemed to choose from a wide variety of random names without the slightest understanding of what was involved. The Osiris was an all-male temple. It lasted only a few months.

To the Egyptians, the whole of their country represented a cosmic scheme, the different territories consecrated to the Neters, or cosmic principles, which also patterned themselves within the temple of the human body. The symbol for Upper Egypt was Mut (Amon's consort), or the Vulture, representing—in all its aspects—gestation, primordial reconciliation; while the symbol for Lower Egypt was the cobra, symbol of duality and the creative impulse. And the pharaohs would bear upon their brows the royal diadem, the uraeus, formed from the cobra and the vulture, itself modeled upon the anatomical structure of the brain, and an earthly symbol of the Divine Man.

So it is by using this lateral insight that we can come closer to home. Substitute the vulture for the hawk, and the cobra for the serpent, and bear in mind that the hawk's terrestrial shadow is the dragon—then we can catch a glimpse of the Pendragon behind the veil—that Dragon King and Divine Man who exemplifies the oldest law that the king and the land are One.

All of this is a far and speculative cry from the years prior to the Great War, as it is called in Britain, of 1914-18, when the original Golden Dawn had become as dismembered as Osiris, and spread widely across the nations of Britain, France and America, waiting for the Great Woman to come who would find the missing pieces and join them up once more. The state of the Golden Dawn at that time might be summed up as follows:

There were several temples still loyal to Mathers, among them the Ahathoor, three temples known as Alpha and Omega, and fragments from the original groups.

There was the Holy Order of the Golden Dawn yawning away under Waite, plus there were various temples now working under the aegis of Felkin's Stella Matutina with Brodie-Innes threading about between them all, doing whatever it was he felt impelled to do.

It was at this juncture that Felkin emigrated to New Zealand where he lived at a house known as Whare-Ra in Hawke's Bay. Not only did he practice medicine there, but he also formed another temple, the *Smaragdum Thalasses*, about which almost nothing is known but which seems to have survived in some form even down to the present moment.

Mathers died on November 20, 1919, a victim of the Spanish Influenza which swept Europe and claimed almost as many victims as the War. Moina carried on after him, but a lot of people felt the glory days were over as far as she was concerned.

On the other hand, during what was evidently a low ebb in the powers of the Orders, Felkin returned to Britain and promptly created three new temples, which is not so easy as might be supposed. Magically he needed the charter to enable this, but on more practical levels he needed the actual people to attend. Surprisingly, he found no trouble in doing so. Evidently a new generation had begun to hear the inner call that each hierophant vibrates upon the magical levels in order to attract like-souled individuals.

The first was The Secret College, which we must presume was a men-only group as it only admitted Master Masons from the S.R.I.A.; next came the Hermes Temple in Bristol, which became sufficiently boisterous as to demand its independence; and then there was the Merlin Temple itself, which in its early days had been sufficiently affected by Felkin's contact with Steiner as to attract members with anthroposophical inclinations, although this seems to have diminished as the years went by.

It was from these last two, Hermes and Merlin, that the Magical Current sprang that will form the focus of study of this book. And it is from within these that we will find that missing portion of the great body of magic that will help it all live again, for this is where we can find the serpent-phallus, the winged dragon which vivifies the land.

T he seers of the Golden Dawn, linking their spiritual visions with the machineries of the universe, could sit within their enchanted circles and watch dragons writhing to the Earth. The transmission of the life energies down through the worlds appeared to whirl and gyrate in such a way that Mathers was moved to write: "these formula are of the nature of the dragon, that is to say, moving in convolutions, and hence they are called the *Dragon* or *Serpent Formulae*." Following the convolutions of the constellation Draco, which was supremely important in the *GD*'s system, the energy could be seen in four differing ways: the *Direct* or *Creeping Formula*, "in which the dragon may be wingless but footed as regards its symbolic presentation; the *Looped* or *Flying Formula*, wherein the serpents are seen as footless but winged; the *Leaping* or *Darting Formula* where the serpents were both footed and winged; and the *Revolving* or *Flowing Formula*, in which the beast was neither winged nor footed, but had fins to symbolize its flowing movement."

This was Mathers' perception and analysis of that which had been seen by Ezekiel:

> And I beheld, and lo! a tempestuous whirlwind came out from the north, a mighty cloud, and a fire violently whirling upon itself, and a splendour revolving upon itself, and from the midmost as an eye of brightness from the midst of the fire.

Today, it is hard for the less learned and less technical perceptions of the modern mage to understand what he was really talking about, for the material given in this lecture for the Theoricus Adeptus Minor* is so concentrated and abstruse. All we need to understand for

---

* *The Golden Dawn*, Israel Regardie, Llewellyn, St. Paul, 1986.

Hermes and the Wand with Two Serpents

our present purposes is that man has glimpsed dragons down through the ages, and that the mythological responses which lie below the soil like old jewels are there and waiting for us yet.

We can see dragons in connection with Hermes too, in the twin serpents which comprise his wand: the White Snake of the Wisdom Gods: Thoth, Nabu, Dagda, Myrddin; and the Dark Snake of the Moon Goddesses, such as Nephthys and Isis and Morgana, and the lady Mut, from ancient Thebes.

And we can find them writhing next to Merlin, too, for it was he who perceived them battling under Vortigern's tower, making its foundations insecure. It was Merlin who was instrumental in Arthur's magical conception, then spiriting him away to give him the sort of mystic upbringing that would one day enable him to pull Excalibur from the stone, and prove himself fit to become Pendragon, or the Dragon King.

This is the symbolic nature of the Magical Current: an energy which soars through and interlaces the worlds, arching through the darkness beneath the Earth and therefore also through the cold night of instellar space, chasing its own tail, looking for that moment when it can consume itself completely as serpents and dark stars are known to do, drawing all the Light into itself in the absolute nothingness that comes during the Night of the Gods.

But the Magical Current is like electricity also, in that we as mortals can only really see it and study it by its outward effect upon certain pieces of equipment, or via specialized instruments, which is why the biographies of certain individuals are important, as well as the little histories of their Lodges. We might do worse now than start with the Hermes Temple, for it was the focus of many beginnings and many endings with the Order's saga throughout the years.

The original Outer Chiefs of the Hermes Temple were Hope Hughes and her husband Donald, who was so mild a man that people who knew them both were rather nonplussed when outsiders later whispered that he had caused her to commit suicide by his difficult ways. Being something of a family affair we find that Hope's sister, Mrs. Millicent Mackenzie, was the first Imperator, and the lodge itself may well have been run from Catherine Hughes' home at St. Vincent Studios, Grove Road, in an area of Bristol where ley lines are said to cross like spaghetti.

There were long and strong links between Hermes and the Smaragdum Thallasses which continued for some years after even the Second World War, but the essential force behind the lodge in purely earthly terms was Hope herself. She was one of the "two silly women" who, according to the vitriol of later decades, was duped by a young man called Regardie into giving out the Order's secrets both hastily and not too well. When she later leapt from a high window, long after the glories had departed from the Order, some of the adepti explained it by saying that she had tried to attain a grade of initiation that was just too far beyond her abilities to cope.

Hermes/Mercury is the young god bearing the caduceus, with wings on his heels. He is the god of speech, travel, communication, intellect, and magic—hence the term "Hermetic Philosophy." Moina, in a piece of direct communication with that being, described his nature as: "I am Hermes Mercurius, the Son of God; the messenger uniting Superiors and Inferiors. I exist not without them and their union is in me. I bathe in the Ocean. I fill the expanse of Air. I penetrate the depths beneath."* Hermes is the link between the worlds, he is that point whereby the conscious mind can rise upon the planes. This is the crucial distinction between the tranced oblivion of the Spiritualists and the retention of full consciousness used by magicians: the Spiritualists stay where they are, so to speak, and let the spirits come down the planes to take them over; but the magicians rise through the levels in full consciousness, and make the highest kind of contact that their inner states will permit.

Even so, as they would be the first to admit, errors are always likely.

Now whoever or whatever the Secret Chiefs of the original Golden Dawn might have been, those of Hermes were certainly different. Although Felkin died in 1922 and Brodie-Innes the following year, the contacts in *this* temple were evidently potent enough to keep it going for another 30 years. In fact, to the magical perceptions of at least one of its members, it was one of the only temples to maintain its integrity.

"The glory had departed when I knew the Order," wrote Dion Fortune talking about her time in two different lodges, both of them called Alpha and Omega, but one under the provenance of the Stella Matutina, and the second under the wearied leadership of Moina who had taken the death of her husband very hard. The Orders, like

---

* *The Golden Dawn*, Israel Regardie, Llewellyn Publications, St. Paul, 1986.

everything else within British society, had suffered severely during the Great War when a whole generation had been wiped out. At the time of Fortune's initiation in 1919 the two streams of Light were rather dimmed, and the members comprised mainly of "widows and grey-bearded ancients." Even so, she persisted with her studies because, as she said, anyone with the slightest psychic perceptions could not fail to realize that real power lay behind the ceremonies and formulae.

Later on she gained admission to Hermes, "where for the first time I saw justice done to what is, in my estimation, a very great system."

The story of Dion Fortune has been told in some detail in a variety of other sources, but she is important in that a great number of sidelights have been afforded about the two Orders by virtue of her writings. Unlike other writers on magic, she was not shy about describing her inner experiences either. Unlike most other writers on magic, she actually *had* inner experiences. And although her own personal magical diaries were ceremonially and shamefully burned by her successor, Arthur Chichester, some years after her death, she still has things to teach us.

Once, in a privately published article, she described just what could be experienced in a properly worked temple where the adepti understood their craft.

As the power gathers, she wrote, it is exactly as if one were wading through fast-flowing water, getting deeper and deeper. There are times, indeed, when the power could be so great that it became difficult to keep one's feet, and less experienced ritualists who were treading the magic circle swayed as if they were drunk. To the psychic eye, where the line of the circle was trodden at the start, a band of force could be seen spinning like a rapidly running power saw. Even if a nonpsychic person stepped into it he would be aware of it, she felt.

The next phase was the important one, and consisted of invoking the presence of the cosmic entity or entities who are the *real* priests of the rite. "These are spiritual beings, but astral forms are constructed for them to manifest for the purposes of the ceremony." These presences had their appointed places within the temple as well as the physical plane officers, but they also moved about in the ritual, which was an act of teamwork between visible and invisible participants. "No rite is effectual unless these invisible beings are present. It is the knowledge of who they are and how their presence is obtained which constitute the real secrets of a degree. In some Orders these are Lost

Secrets, for which fellowship and charity are no adequate substitutes."

Dion was a magician, as opposed to a mere practitioner of magic. A. E. Waite would never have understood a word of what she experienced—nor would many practitioners of magic today.

The whole point of magic, she pointed out, was that it brought the worlds together; the sharp divisions between matter and spirit no longer existed; through magic, a man and a woman could become, if only for a time, a little more than human, a little brighter than otherwise, and a lot wiser. This, in various ways, would have wider effects upon the race itself. If nothing else, magic helped to produce extraordinarily dynamic personalities.

Small wonder that some of the lodges seemed to explode at various points in their development.

Although she had formed her own Fraternity of the Inner Light by 1927, she still retained her ties with Hermes in Bristol, just a couple of hours away by courtesy of the Great Western Railway, or a bit longer via the London Road which stretches through the counties of Berkshire and Wiltshire, going within yards of Silbury Hill and the massive stones of Avebury, one of the Great Goddess centers of Europe. She was still attending the rites in Hermes in 1934 when she helped initiate a 27-year old by the name of Francis Israel Regardie, who assumed the Magical Name of *Ad Majorem Adonai Gloriam*, and who became something of a sacrificial priest, stabbing a gold knife into the body of the Order so that a greater vitality might one day flow from it.

Regardie himself has documented what happened next. In brief, he was dismayed by the poor standard of his teachers—the Inepti, as he liked to think of them. Important documents were ignored or minimized; valuable techniques were no longer taught; too much emphasis was placed upon those Secret Chiefs whose existence, he felt, were better looked at in the light of modern psychology, and which he was quite certain had no such independent existence on the inner planes as believed by his superiors within the Stella Matutina. He did the only thing possible. He preserved the Order's teachings by breaking his oaths and publishing the knowledge en masse, in 1937.*

It is interesting to consider that the temple which proved so satisfactory to Dion Fortune was the same one that proved such a disap-

---

* As well as being a brilliant man he was also something of a Romantic: and like all such he would inevitably rail against the laxness and apparent slipshodness of modern education. We hear it today: "In the old days they taught their pupils so much more." Perhaps they did, but consciousness changes from generation to generation. Modern magic has not become less active and more visual because of television's influence: the Television Age began *because* new generations were becoming more attuned to this new mode.

pointment to Regardie. To the former's psychic perceptions Hermes was certainly functioning more than adequately in the early 1930's; to Regardie's intellectual perceptions the lodge was spiritually bankrupt.

Regardie was wrong, even if it was necessary to publish and be damned.

He was in fact a very young man, part of that cursed generation which wanted to explain everything away via the apparent calm logic of psychotherapy. His intelligence got in the way of his psychism, as it often can; he failed to see what was really going on at other levels. He practiced magic, but he was—in those young days at least—no magician. Now, psychology and its offshoots are becoming more and more like Latin: a dead language, but one which has provided us with permanent roots and stems. A century ago it was inconceivable that any educated person could go through life without studying Latin or Greek; in a century's time we will begin to say much the same thing about psychology, by which time something else will have replaced it.

What he never understood was that it is not necessary to play Enochian Chess, make Angel Calls, be fluent in Hebrew, or be sybilline in the geomantic arts in order to be adept at magic at the highest levels. Likewise, one does not need to be able to construct or understand the workings of a liquid-crystal calculator in order to make profound use of one. There are other ways. There are always Other Ways. They are never easier—for there is no such thing as an "easy" way in magic— but they are just as effective.

Yet in a strange way, if Regardie had little time for those mysterious Chiefs with whom Hope Hughes and her fellow magicians would frequently link their minds, he was in one way more surely in the grip of the lodge's otherworldly essence than anyone. His impulses toward publication and exposition were entirely congenial to the highest source of all within the lodge—to Hermes himself. Although he suffered from the abuse of the shocked members of the Order (including Crowley), he was only doing what he was told. He published *The Golden Dawn* in America in 1937. Perhaps he felt, also unconsciously, that by crossing such a vast expanse of running water he could avoid the hostile Magical Currents that would inevitably be sent after him. The women of Hermes consoled themselves by showing the cruel humor and anti-Americanism that is, unfortunately, endemic to the British psyche, and later told each other that Regardie met the worst fate that anyone could possibly have inflicted upon them: he married an American woman, and thus got his just desserts.

But he would have the last laugh as sacrifical priests often do, for he lived to see it all start up again, in a different era, in different ways.

R egardie, in his role as secretary to Aleister Crowley, was some-
times referred to as The Serpent, but Fortune was followed all her lives by dragons, even though she was never quite aware of this. Like the sort of ghosts which flicker at the peripheries of vision, they danced away on those rare moments when she turned to look at them full on.

She was born in the same year that they discovered the tomb of Cleopatra—that "Serpent of Old Nile" to use one of her titles—in the country of Wales, whose symbol is a red and clawing dragon, between the headlands of Llandudno known as the Ormes, which in itself means "dragon," on a site where Taliesin once described a great yellow dragon as having arisen, flown off, and ultimately devastated Europe.

Violet Firth, to give her her real name, came to England at an age when she still brooded about the Atlantean memories she had had from the age of four onwards, and then lived in the flat, once-drowned lands of Somerset, where every year countless numbers of elvers, or small eels (and therefore sea serpents), swarm up the rivers and streams and ditches known as rhines, spawning as far inland as Glastonbury Tor. The elvers come from the very place of Atlantis. She was to marry Thomas Penry Evans, who was himself Welsh, almost the quin-tessence of Welshness in fact, whose profession as a surgeon is best symbolized by the caduceus, and whose Magical Name within her own lodge was simply Merlin. In her past lives she had been a Cathar, a warrior woman of Viking stock, a priestess in ancient Egypt; but in her heart of hearts she was an Atlantean herself, a sea priestess, and it was the Serpent Magic that she practiced although she was never very clear as to how, or in what form. To Dion, as everyone called her, the Serpent Power was something to do with sex, which she never much enjoyed in physical terms, and that great energy which lies coiled at the base of the spine, which was known to the Easterners as the "kundalini."*

The serpent was, and is, a prime symbol for unity, for both male

---

* She would also have been entirely familiar with the red dragon whose image adorned the floor of the vault used by the adepti within the Golden Dawn.

and female were combined with symbolism of the snake which swallows its own tail.

Any magician knows that the forms the nature spirits, for example, use to impinge upon each individual's inner sight, can be reduced to a truer pattern by an act of will—to something more akin to a geometric pattern of flashing light. And so if we can learn to look at the human soul in the same way then we will, at the very heart of all the presentations the human soul can make, catch a glimpse of those dragons that obsess us.

According to Dion the Serpent Force could be made to rise and travel up the spine as far as Tiphareth, as shown on that glyph which places the human figure on the Tree of Life. But she got it wrong in this instance, and for once departed from Golden Dawn lore with poor effect. The force rises much higher, to the sphere of Daath, the "Hidden Sephira," whose symbols are: the Prism, the Empty Room, the Sacred Mountain.

Daath is where humanity could be found before the Fall—the fall to matter as seen by the Gnostics, rather than the more crass concepts within Genesis. Only when man can *know* the world he lives on, in the same sense that a man can *know* a woman—only then will the dragon eyes open and the wings begin to unfold.*

We can make a paper cut-out of the Tree. If we take Kether and place it on Yesod, so that absolute consciousness and absolute subconsciousness are at One, then Malkuth will fall neatly into the place of Daath. If we look at this circle from the side then we can see that its rim divides it neatly into six units, which can themselves be separated into trinities.

This is the formula of the serpent consuming itself; it is the formula of man in full circuit with Nature, and the glyph of the "male-female, quintessential One." The dragon is both slightly more and also rather less than this, as it is the serpent in the winged and footed phase, as Mathers would have described it, for in our journeys through the worlds and life it is only by extension of the wings that we can control our direction. By tilting those extended planes of Justice or Mercy, and all the ethical qualities linked with Mars and Jupiter, we can alter our flight paths. Through this means we can learn to arch enough, and direct ourselves accurately enough, so as to be able to take our own

---

* *The Ladder of Lights*, by William G. Gray: "Lucifer fell by refusing to recognize Man, and can only rise as Mankind releases him. Both Man and Lucifer hold each other captive on different levels. God may redeem Man, but Man redeems Lucifer. It is worth remembering too, that in one tradition the Holy Grail is a jewel from Lucifer's crown."

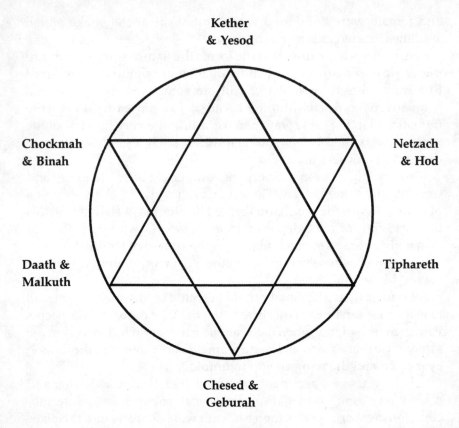

Kether
& Yesod

Chockmah
& Binah

Netzach
& Hod

Daath &
Malkuth

Tiphareth

Chesed &
Geburah

own mouths in search of our tails and bring the innermost consciousness of our Higher Selves into complete union with the uttermost
oblivion of our lower natures.

Dion experienced something of this in 1930, and in 1932 she took
the unusual step of publishing this extract from her own magical diary
in the monthly magazine of her fraternity.

Seated in an Egyptian god-attitude and facing southwest, she
drew the astral circle around herself then projected her astral body to
the center, faced east, and invoked the names of God of the central
pillar of the Tree of Life.

Losing all sense of her physical body she rose upon the planes,
white robed and with the striped nemyss of Egypt on her head, going
beyond the Moon, beyond the Sun, and determined to head for the
blinding white light of Kether "as the going still seemed good." She
became just a point of consciousness without qualities, a "single spark
of essential life." Suddenly she was turned about and then "found

myself backed into the Tree as it were, and expanded to an enormous size, a towering, cosmic figure. Nude and hermaphrodite, very powerful, of a golden-buff color. This figure was the full size of the Tree. Its feet were planted on the globe of the Earth . . . the three supernal Sephiroth were about the head . . ." She re-absorbed down into Malkuth again after having had this tremendous sense of size and power, rising right up through the cosmos, and feeling like an angelic being, and hearing an all-pervading undertone of music and a swinging of spheres in their orbits around her. She was back in her temple now, but with this cosmic figure with her consciousness in it, looking at her normal-sized astral figure, fully robed, with consciousness in it

also, while in the street outside dogs barked and small boys made loud noises. At the end of the Working, after several more raptures, she "spontaneously assumed the dress of an Egyptian priest with uraeus headdress and brightly colored Horus wings." She came back to normal consciousness; her breathing was very shallow. She reaffirmed her entrance into the sphere of Earth with a strong stamp of her foot. "There remained, however, a sense of a scarlet triangle over the root of the nose, full of tingling. It seemed as if the skull had been cut away here, exposing the brain."

The uraeus headdress and brightly colored Horus wings: the snake and the hawk. For a time, for a brief time, she was a Dragon Queen, and all opposites had become at One, and the voice of the Land she loved so much spoke through her.*

---

* *Applied Magic* by Dion Fortune: "Horus is sometimes called the Lord of the Aquarian Age. He is a winged complete being containing within himself his father Osiris and his mother Isis. Isis and Osiris were one being in primeval times and later split in two. Their son represents each on a new arc—joined once more into one being."

Dion Fortune is very good at hinting about Egyptian Mysteries but the most remarkable books are those by Schwaller de Lubicz, an excellent analysis of whose ideas can be found in *Serpent in the Sky*, by John Anthony West, which has inspired parts of the present volume.

T o Dion, Atlantis was to be found *in a new phase*, centered upon the rounded breast of Glastonbury Tor, that great pagan center in the West of England which has the famous abbey at its base—which in itself was once one of the major pilgrimage centers of Europe for the Christian faith. A strange area, once drowned beneath a shallow sea, it is soaked through with pagan atmospheres and Christian associations, linked in a curious harmony by the overshadowing image of King Arthur whose tomb is believed to lie within the grounds of the abbey, and which certainly has a resonance of its own, regardless of the truth of this.

To Dion, the conical lump of the tor was eerily reminiscent of the sacred mountain on that lost island she had first glimpsed as a child. The serpent-mounted Kronos pole that she and Dr. Moriarty had glimpsed in one of the temples had come down to her through chains of genetic memory and magical insight, and showed up now as the tower of St. Michael dominating the top, who is the archangel dedicated to the overthrow of dragons and demons and non-Christian things in general.

To Dion, the Arthur buried in the abbey was just another in the long line of Great Initiates who had come down through the aeons, each of them a Pendragon, each of them personifying the cosmic order on Earth.

It was in Glastonbury in the winter of 1923-24, just after Moriarty died, that Dion received from her own Secret Chiefs a communication that was later published as the *Cosmic Doctrine*, which became the core book of what was her own lodge, the Fraternity of the Inner Light.

Surprisingly, she was not the first to make this contact.

Frederick Bligh Bond was the highly respected Director of Excavations for Glastonbury Abbey who was to cause no little controversy by his use of long-departed spirits in discovering (and physically recovering) lost portions of the abbey they had once inhabited. Although Dion was not the automatist concerned, she was present on at least one occasion when some of the material "came through." In Bligh Bond's own book about the experiences, *The Gate of Remembrance*, we find references to "the merlins" who strode about the land passing on their wisdoms, to the mysterious spirits known as the Watchers of Avalon, to the doctrine of reincarnation, to the westward flow of the Magical Current, and can even see a graphic image and simple analysis of the gyroscopic "Ring-Pass-Not" which was so important to the structures behind Dion's own philosophies.

L ater on, working by herself, she used these Watchers to uncover the sunken temples of Atlantis in much the same way that Bligh Bond used his spirits to uncover the Edgar Chapel. More than that, she had some very definite ideas as to their individual identities.

There was Lord Erskine, a former Lord Chancellor of Great Britain who had once, in an even earlier incarnation, been none other than the sainted Thomas More. He was the real Inner Chief of her lodge. They called him Lord E., or the Unnamed Master when Dion decided that they should no longer talk openly about him. Thomas Erskine was a Scot, from Edinburgh who had been born in 1750 and who died in 1823. After a brief career in the Royal Navy he went on to achieve staggering success as a lawyer. Famed for his wit and his talent for picking popular causes, he became a minor and brief cult figure in his own lifetime, his adoring public unfastening the horses of his carriage and pulling him in triumph through the streets of London after one of his better victories in the courts of law.

Then there was Socrates, about whom little need be said, and who was evidently connected with the late Dr. Moriarty in some way. The Cos. Doc., as they called it, was apparently so dense, and the teachings from a source so deep, that it needed two inner plane communicators working in tandem in order to reach the surface levels of Dion's mind.

And then there was the lodge's favorite, David Carstairs. He had been brought up in the Midlands as the son of a scrap metal merchant, who wooed his girlfriends with fragments of junk that he solemnly assured them were precious Egyptian amulets. Later on he enlisted, as all the young men did, and died amid the mud and slaughter of Ypres, in 1917. When Dion picked him up on the inner planes he gave an address for her to contact. She wrote there, and although it was not *quite* accurate, nevertheless her letter was forwarded on to one of his parents, who confirmed the accuracy of her mediumship. Within the lodge, they called him the Master David. He was witty, earthy, and represented the very flower of that English manhood which had been wiped out during the pointless massacres of the Great War.

Now there are various problems connected with the identities of all three, but these have been detailed elsewhere;* and in any case

---

* See *Priestess*, by Alan Richardson. London, 1987.

Dion was certainly aware of them. In brief, the historicity of these entities is in some doubt—especially as regards Carstairs—but this in no way diminishes their intrinsic reality.

Using the Golden Dawn's system it is possible to "test" the spirits by a variety of methods (such as challenging them to produce another form), but this is not always wise or right. For example, a very young man being interviewed by a very senior employer in a large and initially bewildering organization is hardly advised to ask his interviewer if he really *is* as harsh as he sounds, unhappy as he looks, or clever as he seems. He accepts the job and terms of contract, rather, and only a long while after he has proved himself, gained some measure of security and earned some respect might he choose to try and get behind the facade of the man who employed him.*

"What we are, you can never know," said the spirits of the Cosmic Doctrine, "and it is a waste of time trying to find out." The images they use to present themselves are for the convenience of making contact; they enable the mind to grasp what it cannot conceive, like the blind men touching the elephant.

Dion knew herself that it is often difficult to tell a disassociated personality from a spirit control, and a spirit control from a previous incarnation. But she knew, as Brodie Innes knew, that we must learn to act "as if": Whether the Secret Chiefs really exist is comparatively unimportant, for the point is that the universe behaves as though they do. The historical images that the Chiefs provide themselves with are simple devices, like lenses which are chosen and adapted for the individual. They may well have had an earthly incarnation at some point, and may well be exactly what they seem . . . but we must never make a cult of this aspect of their presentations to us.

This is for the simple reason that in so doing we would be making a cult of our own selves—with all the attendant problems this would bring.

I would insist that all magic is essentially tribal. This tribe can best be visualized as a circle (or even as a sphere). Half of it is in the otherworld, half in the earthworld. It is a circle which links past, present and future and makes no distinction. The tribe contains souls which are

---

* From a practical point of view I regret that I disagree. In the event of an unknown entity showing up whilst I am Working I do challenge, firmly but very very politely. On the odd occasion that this sort of thing does happen I tend to take what is given with the proverbial "pinch of salt" until I am fully certain of who/what is involved. It is all too easy to be led astray by one's own subconscious and desires. The magician is totally involved with a system that requires utter control; should the need arise for others to complement the Work being undertaken we have arrived at a situation where a "known" entity introduces the "unknown," and the link is formally forged this way. (G.H.)

incarnate, souls between lives, souls which have ceased incarnation, plus beings which have never been and never will be incarnate.

Each tribe has a succession of leaders in the earthworld. Their job is to bring through the Magical Current. In their turn they are over-shadowed by tribal leaders from the otherworld—what are termed the "Secret Chiefs." In fact, if we can, think of that as being in the sense "Chief of the Clan McDonald," or "Chief of the Clan McGregor." The tone and the style of the tribe alters according to which Chief and which earthworld priest or priestess is predominant at the time. The tribe might grow, change, or contract, but the center will remain the same.

When a newcomer links with the tribe he can tap the collective wisdom of the tribal mind. Often when this happens he has visions of what may appear to be past lives but which are more nearly tribal visions, or points of collective experience down through the ages. These are not always to be taken personally.

Sometimes the newcomer will feel him/herself overshadowed by a tribal member from the otherworld. A mistake can be made here by believing him/herself to be an actual incarnation of that entity.

Tribes can, do, and should overlap. The Chiefs and the earthworld leaders come and go, but their essence remains within the tribe. The Chiefs, therefore, are not meant to be worshipped, for they are points of contact between the worlds. They are part of us as we are part of them. Each member of the tribe is part of one corporate whole. We cannot worship them for we would be worshipping ourselves.

Whatever intellectual output might result is less important than the personal sense of contact with the otherworld, and linkage with the collective consciousness of the tribe.

What must be remembered is that the initiates of the Golden Dawn were just that: they were beginners, in the strictest meaning of the word "initiate." They made mistakes; they often made fools of themselves as mortals do. But in so doing they brought something marvelous into the world: they brought wonder, and they brought the light that wonder gives.

A mong the bright things, magic also brings a sense of omnis-cience among the lesser adepti. It is the sort of omniscience that is a close cousin to smugness. It manifests in whispered phrases like: "Ah but the trouble with *him* is that . . . " Or, "Where *he* is going wrong is that . . . " And on and on throughout the infinite varieties of destructive support that pupils invariably end up offering their teachers behind their backs.

It was no different in the *FIL*. Dion's problem, as they termed it, was in her choice of husband. Merl was too working class, even if he was a doctor: too much of a rough diamond, when what Dion really needed was pure and clear crystal. Perhaps if they had studied Dion's attachment to the Morgan le Fay tones of the overshadowing Atlantean priestess, they might have used the prophecy of myth to understand that her marriage with Merl was inevitably doomed, and meant to be doomed. Nevertheless they thought that this new man in the lodge, Charles Seymour, who was so much more cultured and urbane than the rough and ready Penry, might be just the new priest their Warden needed.

C harles Richard Foster Seymour was a warrior priest. In fact he had always been a warrior priest. Although he could hide his more esoteric ideas behind some superb and respectable scholarship, his magic and his warfare found their real origins on the upper levels of the City of the Sun, on the island of Ruta in lost Atlantis.

An Irishman, and ten years older than Dion, he followed the Dark Snake of the Moon Goddesses, and perfectly balanced that White Snake of the Masters of Wisdom which Dion had chosen. He was as close to the feminine side within him as Dion had been to those masculine elements within herself—which is why, of course, they were real adepts in the full sense of the word. If neither of them could play Enochian Chess or make the Angel Calls or do much in the way of geomantic prophecy, they could handle the power and the wisdom in a way that few people have ever done.

Seymour saw action in many countries, especially in Africa and Iraq, and by the end of his career he had reached the rank of Lieutenant Colonel and found himself as a senior tutor at the Staff College in India, where he taught men who were to be Britain's generals in the Second World War. Fluent in Russian (as well as Greek, French and Latin), he spent most of 1917 in Russia on a diplomatic mission that is now lost to the annals of time.

In his most pungent incarnation he had been a Priest of Mithras along the Roman Wall which stretched, and stretches, across the width of North Britain and beyond which, according to contemporary belief, only the souls of the dead went. During that life he had attained the grade of Griffin, which was the second of seven grades within the

Mithraic priesthood. His friends within the *FIL* called him, accordingly, Griff. Mythologically the griffin has the body of a lion, the head of an eagle, and wings.

A natural mystic with a rare talent for ritual, his first awakening was in India when he had stood upon the extreme tip of a ten-thousand-foot crag and looked across the blue rain-washed landscape of the monsoon-swept Himalayas and knew that the Earth had a consciousness of its own, and that he had some part to play in giving it voice. He may well have belonged to one of the earlier Lodges of the Stella Matutina before joining Hermes. He certainly worked magic in the basement of the British Museum, where the Egyptian antiquities were once kept, but whether as an individual or as a member of the legendary group that was supposed to have met there, no one now knows. Certainly, when he came to join Hermes he knew that this God was the Graeco-Egyptian name for Thoth, and was the creative word, on a lower arc of Amoun, which he saw to be the Absolute of the Universe.

From our present point of view, however, the importance of Seymour was not that he was one of the most learned and lucid writers on magic this century but that during his time within the Fraternity of the Inner Light he actually trained a succession of young people toward making their own contacts with a completely different set of Chiefs, and tapped a very different Magical Current—that of the Stella Matutina in its mainstream.

It is through him, therefore, that we can get some idea as to the identities of those Secret Chiefs that were used by the early adepti within the Order.

These were as follows:

Cleomenes III, a Spartan king who lived from 235 to 222 B.C. After defeating the Achaean league at Ladoceia in 227 he instituted the cancellation of all debts, the redivision of land, and the return to the old Spartan training. After being defeated in battle by Antigonus Dosun in 222 B.C. he fled to Egypt where Ptolemy Euergetes offered him sanctuary. After imprisonment by the latter's successor, Cleomenes escaped, tried to organize a revolt, failed, and eventually committed suicide. Another story has it that he was crucified on a Tau cross, and that upon his death a small dragon crawled from within his body.

Kha'm-uast, the son of Rameses II, who as High Priest of Ptah in Memphis, became overlord of all the magical and religious ceremonies within Egypt. In effect, he was the archmage of the entire country, no small achievement. He lived from about 1300 to 1246 B.C., and in his youth he had been a soldier. Had he not died some ten years before his father, he would certainly have become Pharaoh. Seymour saw him as a Merlin figure.

Lord Eldon was born plain John Scott in Newcastle upon Tyne, Northumberland, on June 4, 1751. Originally intended for the church as his parents hoped, he eloped with Elizabeth Surtees, by whom he had ten children. A lawyer, he became Baron Eldon of Eldon, in County Durham, and he held the Chancellorship of England during the reigns of both George III and IV, broken only during one year, 1806—and that had been by Thomas Erskine.*

He was a man of great charm, but he was ill-read, untraveled, and with neither interest in nor taste for the fine arts. A great drinker, anecdotalist, and non-attender at church, he was a political extremist of the sort that we would now describe as reactionary. He died on January 13, 1838.

Then there was, occasionally, Cheiron, who according to the classical tradition was leader of the centaurs. Seymour managed to contact him through a careful reading of, and empathy with, Algernon Blackwood's novel *The Centaur*—which in itself might offer an indication of at least one of the contacts behind the Isis-Urania Lodge of which Blackwood had been a member.

---

* Scott chose the title of Eldon himself. The name means "from the Holy Hill." Considering that Seymour saw him as a former High Priest from the Sun Temple on the conical hill of Atlantis, this provokes a wry smile if nothing else.

Now Seymour had no belief in any historical existence of cen
taurs. He knew that the intelligence he was contacting, which belonged
to another dimension, simply presented itself in that form and had
done so since the ancient of days. Perhaps nowadays, fed on a diet of
Star Wars and intergalactic derring-do, and brought up on the possibility
of extra-terrestrial life forms, the young magi of the 1980s and 1990s
might pick up Cheiron as some dweller in deep space with human-
oid tendencies.

Somehow, though, I doubt it.

Nevertheless Cheiron was something of a side effect, perhaps
from an earlier system of magic entirely. It is that different Lord E.
whom we must consider in some detail, for he brings us to an awkward
but unavoidable question:

Did Seymour wrongly identify the Chancellor concerned but
manage to make a contact with the same entity? Were Eldon and
Erskine indeed separate beings altogether? It is even possible that
Dion was herself in error and that the Lord she may have picked up in
her early Work was wrongly identified.

I don't know.

The clue to it must lie, somehow, within that title and role of
Chancellor.

Politically the Lord Chancellor was originally the King's chief
secretary to whom petitions were referred, the word being derived
from *cancellarius*, being one who is stationed at a doorway to introduce
visitors. He is, in a sense, the link between the common man and
royalty.

It is almost like the Hermes-Mercurious who spoke through
Moina: a link between the superiors and inferiors, just as Merlin is a
link between the divine and the human.

Were the political system of the nation to be seen on magical
levels, then the King, or Queen, who is the personification of the land
and all its people, is reached via the Lord Chancellor, who is thus a
direct link between the worldly and the spiritual. Lord E. is not so
much a person, albeit on spiritual levels, as a crystal within the strata of
the national consciousness. Sometimes, if the mood is right and the
power flowing, we can look into this crystal and see beyond our own
reflections. Sometimes, such crystals can teach us things, and can
teach us *marvelous* things.

But getting back to those complexities which are always more
interesting than occult philosophy as such, we find Brodie Innes

appearing again . . .

C hristine Campbell Thomson, who was one of the priestesses trained by Seymour,* had known B.I., as they called him, during her career as a prominent literary agent. She also knew that he believed himself to be a reincarnation of Michael Scot, the medieval wizard-sage with whom Lord Eldon associated himself in a mild, genealogical manner. Indeed, when Christine first made the Eldon contact she was quite sure that he and Brodie Innes were one and the same.

When I spoke to her many years after making and working with that contact, Christine was inclined to give a reincarnational string of identities as explanation, which read chronologically: Michael Scot, John Scott, and Brodie Innes—with John Dee squeezed in between the two former almost as an afterthought.

It would be wrong to reject such a vision completely, especially as I personally saw enough of Christine's odd talents to convince me of her status as a real adept in the full sense of the word. But I cannot help but feel that the tribal concept is probably more appropriate here, along with the idea of overshadowing. Modifying the ideas of R. J. Stewart in his book *The Prophetic Vision of Merlin*,† these entities would be, therefore, aspects of ourselves; aspects of tribal consciousness through time; historical persons who have become attuned to mythical powers. Above all this we must bear in mind the fact that historical personages do, often, come through to us in magic, and are not always to be explained away by even the most sympathetic philosophy.

For all practical purposes it might be better to reduce this curvature of light through time to just one single burst of illumination, to Michael Scot himself, who is sufficiently shadowy and legendary as to allow the energies to come through without conscious worries about the very human failings of both Brodie Innes and Lord Eldon.

What little we know about Scot can be summed up as follows.

He lived from approximately 1175 to 1234. Although the locals of Kirkcaldy claim him as one of their own through the Scot family of Balwearie, he was probably from the Borders, and may even have

---

* See *Dancers to the Gods* by Alan Richardson for a dual biography of Seymour and Christine Hartley.
† R. J. Stewart has written three of the most unusual and influential books on Magic: *The Underworld Initiation, The Prophetic Vision of Merlin,* and *The Mystic Life of Merlin.*

been a Northumbrian—that bleak and utterly lovely county where Merlin was said to go and sink into his magical reveries and madnesses. After graduating from Oxford, and then Paris, he served for a time within the court of Frederick II in Sicily. Patronized by emperors and popes, with a reputation for immense learning and wonderworking, he later moved to Toledo where he learned Arabic and translated many hitherto inaccessible works on natural history and mathematics-particularly those of Aristotle. In brief, he helped revive the lost learning and bring it West. Prominent throughout the civilized world, Roger Bacon regarded him as a direct rival. Dante and Boccaccio described him as a magus of great renown. He made accurate prophecies for kings. At the end of his life he came back to the Borderlands and died from food poisoning, it was said, after drinking broth from a sow in heat.

Like Merlin he is credited with various graves, but Melrose Abbey is the most likely contender for his remains. Like Merlin and Lailoken and Thomas of Ercildoune, he was linked with the same lowland area of Scotland, in that world "beyond the Wall" where only the dead went, but which still, today, slides into faery at the slightest touch of the heart. He is in a way Christian Rosencreutz, but with that creature's wisdom brought fully to the West and earthed within the dark spirit of the Gael.

He can still be touched now, and with surprising ease. Through him, we can come a little closer to the mysteries of the Merlin Temple and the secrets of the land on which it stands.

A s we pursue these lists of inner contacts we can often get a sense of bewilderment, aggravated by the natural human desire to compartmentalize all experience. *What* is going on? How? Why? Where is the pattern? Above all else we try to impose patterns.

As outsiders who study magic from anecdote or incomplete diaries we can only do the best we can. It is like picking on some young boy and following him, secretly, throughout his day in a large and bustling school. Unless we know this school intimately ourselves it will seem as if the wretch moves from class to class with no obvious pattern, influencing and being influenced by an apparently random collection of souls. The old souls, the actual teachers whom we might suppose to provide the major influences, sometimes prove less important in time than the chance meeting in a busy corridor with a bright-eyed girl from another class. To the boy himself, carried by the flow, it all makes exquisite sense—give or take the regular encounters with the unexpected—but to us, well, we must make our own patterns to explain it all.

Clearly there are complexities involved in the study of magic that we outsiders will never really fathom, save by analogy or symbol. The anomalies of different contacts used by Seymour's little circles, and the mystery behind the two Lords E., can be better resolved if we look at the glyph of the intertwined circles.

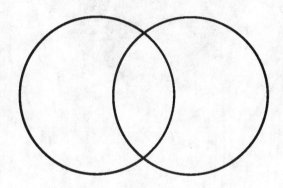

There is common ground between these even if their centers are apart. There are moments when the two lines of light converge, unite, part—and then to all human perceptions travel roughly parallel for awhile before converging once more and then shooting off into opposite realms for what the magus often thinks is for all time. There is an element of this also within the symbol of the caduceus as carried by Hermes himself, in which the two serpents, representing the peculiar Dragon Magic, describe a similar pattern of what Dion would call "flux and re-flux" around a central line. In either glyph Eldon/Erskine (whatever he is) would be found at one of the intersections,

Arthur, Guinevere and Morgan, seen through a Mirror

where all the opposites are resolved. Or else we might encounter, say, Michael Scot at one node and an earlier original, Merlin himself perhaps, at the other. Seymour used to set a certain amount of store in the idea of thesis, antithesis, and synthesis—or in the terminology of the Qabalists, of Hod, Netzach, and Yesod. We can find it within the field of mythology in which Merlin would oppose (but more truly complement) Morgan le Fay, yet find a resolution within the linking concept of either the Holy Grail at one level, or Arthur at another, the two being profoundly associated and even one and the same.

The Magical Currents used by him and Dion Fortune touched upon the Arthurian cycle at that point in which the Holy Grail was the *mysterium tremendum*, the mystic cup which held the essence of the Age of Pisces. Now, in the dawn of Aquarius who is the man carrying water, and who can be named as the great du Lac, who is also Gawaine "the Hawk of May," we can go back like the prodigals we are to claim the best of our birthright from a previous Age, that of Atlantis, and call up that winged serpent which flies below the Earth and above the stars, and set it free again. Thus the spirit of the Aquarian Age will be found in a gradual and quickening return to incarnation of those Atlantean souls who got it so wrong last time. These are the souls who will develop their crystal technologies to unimaginable degrees and either save us, destroy us once and for all, this time, or take us to the stars.

When Kim Seymour and Dion Fortune were working magic and plugging into their Magical Currents it was the Holy Grail which was the best thing. To those who come after, it will be dragons.

S ome time in the early 1930s, probably around 1934, Seymour began to pick up his own Merlin contact, although at first that archmage tended to be on the periphery. In one of his essays he gives a practical technique whereby the individual would imagine himself before an altar, and build up a sense of the two priestesses behind him (or if the worker was a woman, the two priests). When this was accomplished he would turn his attention to the darkness beyond the altar and see the God-Form he was using, as in a mirror. Working the Arthurian system, as he described it, he would thus see the King beyond the altar, and the twin figures of Guinevere and Morgan le Fay behind him and at either side, exactly matching the earthly feminine principles that he had already built up on his own side. "Build that

Merlin with Priestesses

scene until it appears automatically the moment you are seated for your meditation. Now—as the Watcher—see what happens when the priestly figure that is you (as the hierophant) invokes." You may get a surprise the first time you use this method, he warns. And indeed you may. It is always a startling experience when you find that what were hitherto imagined figures of your own creating suddenly come alive, projecting across to you an independent and very marked consciousness of their own.

Elsewhere he gives an image of Merlin in his cave—the moon cave—sitting upon a sacred stool with two female figures behind him, their hands on his shoulders, "in white and silver robes crowned with the crescent moon and silver star." This is the Stella Matutina he is picking up here, for these are major symbols of the Order. It is plain that by this time, 1937, he had made at least a nominal Merlin contact. He goes on to show that Merlin draws all his power *through* these two, who are the white priestess and the silver priestess. "And he loses his rule and his power when he allows the silver priestess to ursurp his divine authority. Thus Merlin fell," he added, perhaps hinting at the subliminal battles he had entered upon with his formidable superior within the *FIL*.

But as far as he was concerned, the real mysteries of Arthur Pendragon and the Inner Celtia were some years ahead. He was still too deeply involved with the Gods of Egypt to give them more than the occasional salute, and the saga of his involvement in and influence upon the lodge took another twist when Dion took possession of the Belfry, a property on West Halkin Street that was described in a disguised way in her novel *Moon Magic*. The work that Dion did here, primarily Egyptian in tone, was presumably under the aegis of Kha'muast and Ne Nefer Ka Ptah, who was the Priest of Anubis. This magic was aimed directly at penetrating the Mysteries of Isis. The exclusively male trinity of her Chiefs seems to have taken second place at this period to her need to become, in a variety of ways, Isis, the Great Mother of the Gods.

For example, on the evening of Thursday, October 28, 1937, after having spent some time working with the mysterious group in the museum chambers, Seymour records in his diary how he and Dion, along with Christine Campbell Thomson, took their places in the lecture room of the lodge with the intention of working the magic of the Old Land.

Three chairs were placed in the South, and the altar was to the

North. Seymour sat in the middle with Dion on his right, as the High
Priestess, and Christine Campbell Thomson on his left. After building
up the power by concentrating upon and invoking Isis as the Primordial
Mother, they linked hands and did some of those tricks in magic which
enabled their consciousness to leave the present world completely.

We 3 went in at 8:10. Invoked Isis. Using the Tatwa method we started
from the House of the Virgins, CCT in black, black litter, black bearers,
went to empty temple where DNF took charge, and to Hall of Sphinxes.
Then into an underground passage and suddenly I shot out and found
myself standing at the entrance of cave where I waited for the other
two. Then all Three went into cave, and past Anubis the guardian at the
curtain. Within was the P. of A. waiting for us. He took over—and spoke
to CCT he set her certain conditions which she refused at first, and then
agreed to them. She then walked to the stone of sacrifice, through the
fire burning on the steps and seated herself between the thighs of the
Black Isis. I am not clear as to what happened then for the image of the
P. of A. and CCT vanished in a sort of red fog. Later I saw clearly and
CCT was leaving her seat, she laid herself on the stone of sacrifice and I
saw the P. of A. bend over her as if sacrificing her (!) Then he vanished
and I took CCT back to the Temple of the White Isis. We returned through
it to the House of the V. where DNF gave the address. Then back to normal.
The power was very great, and my eyes were streaming from it. CCT very
done at the end, and I think a bit scared. Ended 9:15 p.m. Then while
DNF and I were downstairs talking she slept and felt much better.

10 p.m. I found Proctor waiting for me in my rooms and I set to
work to get the Osiris contact. Working on my sanctuary I took him
through the veil and we found ourselves standing in front of the
Ptolemy Gateway and the Temple of Khonsu. We walked through
this—and he described what he saw, and then we went to the shrine of
Osiris which is to the left (West) of the Temple of Khonsu. We went
round this tiny temple and then down into the underground crypt.

Here the whole temple came to life in a blaze of cold soft blue
white light. Then I saw the White Osiris alive—and he turned a ray of
power on to us. Next moment Proctor and I were kneeling before him
(Proctor right). Isis and Nephythys stood behind him. Thoth was on
my left, Anubis behind me. Horus was behind Proctor and a little to his
right. I was looking into the past and at an initiation. A blaze of light and
power came. Suddenly this went and we were back in my room. I was
very tired and next moment the people next door began a row.

Proctor was very puzzled because his shoulder was seized by a
heavy hand, just before we knelt down, he thought I had done it but
opening his eyes he saw my hands on my knees. Anyway I have got that
contact, also the curious impression that then I was a woman!

P. said he saw the place—not as he knew it now—but as it must have
been in the old days. (Very tired but very pleased—both of us.)

Understand that these were no mere pictures in the head. In some way, in some very real sense, they found themselves in other levels of space and time where the Gods of Egypt are still vibrant, and where we can travel today. It seems at first as if nothing of much importance happened, and certainly nothing that could exert much influence on mankind's progress: no philosophies, no wondrous formulae. But in those days, for those adepti at least, it was this actual contact that was important. In linking up with Isis, for example, certain areas in Dion's own subconscious would have been stimulated and awakened: and because she was part of some greater whole then in due course this stimulus would spread throughout the masses. *Whatever happens within the soul and the brain cells of an adept also happens within the collective consciousness of the nation, to be seen in the fullness of time as new attitudes, new moralities, and new ideas.* The same can be said of any artists in the vanguard of a new movement.

Seymour's early contacts with Cheiron, for example, were on the surface no more than an amiable "Hello," set within a cave in the mountain, or else a manic ride across a sunlit plain. Yet shortly after these, suffused with the atmosphere of Cheiron and those possibilities he seemed to present, the old Colonel went home and wrote his long essay which he called "The Old Religion," and forgot all about it. Little did he dream that long after his death in 1943, when the essay was cannily published by Basil Wilby in 1968, a whole new generation of intending pagans used the essay as the very basis of their own magic. The words and ideas came from Seymour, but the impulse and inspiration came direct from the centaur. People affect us in everyday life as much by magnetism as by precept, as much by presence as by instruction. The same is true of those beings that we will, eventually, encounter in the otherworld.

T he middle thirties saw the *FIL* at something of a high water mark, even if the Golden Dawn's empire as a whole had begun to crumble. By 1935 Dion had published all of her best known and most influential books on magic; the lodge functioned at 3 QT, as they all called it, at the Belfry, and also at Chalice Orchard, on the foot of Glastonbury Tor. She still had within her group and under her wing both Seymour and Penry Evans, with the young Arthur Chichester very much her up-and-coming "Sun Priest" as she chose to think of him, with some humor.

But even here it began to go wrong. Merlin—her own marital Merlin—walked out on her for someone younger and more attractive and presumably far more congenial to his own needs than his often overpowering wife. They parted some time around the year 1939, although it had been obvious to everyone that they had been having serious problems for some years before that.

Merl was not the only one to feel disaffected, either. Seymour too was becoming less and less enamored of his Warden, and the Isis Rites they performed together in the Belfry were draining him beyond all reasonable limits. If Dion had drawn him to her in the first place by sounding, on the inner planes, the "call of Isis," by now she could no longer get him to see her as she needed to be seen, which is as crucial in the magical work of building up the God-Forms as the creation of images is in making the inner contacts.

The gossip at that time was of the raised eyebrow and careful innuendo sort that was very popular before the war, a sort of slander with its own codes and signals which basically implied that the Colonel was busy having sex with his priestesses. It was the sort of gossip which had an enormous capacity for giving offense and even ruining reputations in that more innocent age. It was, moreover, completely unfounded. No sex ever took place between any of them (which is not to say that sex was not involved).

The fact is, *all* magic is sex magic. This does not in its turn mean that all magic involves naked bodies contorting themselves into the sort of ludicrous positions which stop just short of hernia and back-strain. All magic is sex magic because each rite, each exercise and projection of power, is also a projection and extension of the magician's very soul. The magic circle or the room he uses is filled with his spirit; and being a creature for whom sex is fundamental, expressions are found on inner levels.

There were entries in Christine Campbell Thomson's original diaries that were excised for the sake of decency during her lifetime, but which I find quite touching:

28th September 1937
And he came and kissed me on the mouth in a way that I did not know anyone could do off this plane, and I experienced the complete satisfaction and relaxation which comes after certain functions have been normally completed.

That was the Great God Pan she was talking about there. Then in the following, after a Working involving Cheiron:

When we got back I felt completely different: my voice was warm and vibrating and I had that sense of complete fulfillment which comes to women in certain circumstances.

Seymour left, shortly after war was declared in September 1939. He did some work for military intelligence in Liverpool and then came back to a modest position in the Home Guard, which was for all those men too old or too young to join the regular army but by no means incapable of wielding a rifle if it ever came to the Nazi invasion which at that time seemed both inevitable and imminent.

When the war did come, with it also came the great leveling, in more than one sense. If the Great War of 1914-18 had had the effect of wiping out an entire generation of young men (and thus robbing the Order of its brightest hopes), then the Second World War almost killed off the Golden Dawn entirely. Regardie's revelations had given the most arcane secrets to a mildly interested general public, while the younger initiates suddenly, and quite rightly, found better things to do for the nation than work magic. The men went off to fight; the women stayed behind to run the factories, or become land girls, working on the farms as Dion had done herself over 20 years before. If nothing else at least a few more cracks were made in the rigid divisions which bedeviled British society then, and which found an odd parallel in the system of Grades used by the original and hawkish adepti of the Golden Dawn. In fact, from this moment onward the system of Grades, which had always been misused and misunderstood in any case, began to die.*

The outbreak of war in September 1939 provides the point of separation from whence the lines of light that we are following began to separate. The story of the schism that occurred between *FPD* and DNF may well be told in terms of these Magical Currents separating or diverging from the unifying point of Lord E. While there seems to have been a mutual compatability in the Green Ray workings of their Lords Eldon and Erskine, there was a marked divergence between the output and tone of Socrates versus Cleomenes III, and Kha'm-uast versus Carstairs—if we can describe the situation in such competitive terms. If Dion had left the Alpha and Omega in the first place because her own revelations of *The Cosmic Doctrine* failed to square with the scheme within that lodge, then she may have felt that the Stella Matutina contacts used by Seymour no longer had any place within her own

---

* Very few Magical Groups in Britain today use the old Grade system. The best groups are those which come together of their own accord, and have no formal structure on outer levels. They simply exist to do Work.

carefully guarded temple.

Inevitably, with the departure of her major priests, the *FIL* began to change. Because of the war her pupils no longer met at 3 QT but instead rendezvoused within the Hill of Vision on the Isle of Glass. At a certain time every Sunday they built up the image of a cave set within Glastonbury Tor, and therein began to work on equal terms with the remaining seniors, aiming at the reawakening of Arthur, the Divine King, said to lie sleeping until such a time as his country needed him again.*

With German aircraft dropping their bombs with apparently unstoppable might, with the unprepared British expeditionary force in retreat from the beaches of Dunkirk, now, if any time, was he needed.

Dion, apart from awakening her own portion of this Arthurian magic—albeit in a specifically Christian aspect—would spend long nights in astral levels patrolling along the mine fields in the North Sea, or else calling up archangelic forces to keep watch and ward along the shoreline of Britain. Elsewhere Seymour was teaching some of his coworkers how to enter the crystal and indulge in magical combat with those malign entities that were felt to have been released and energized by the Nazi enthusiasms.

Everywhere, in every field of occult belief and practice, people were devoting their powers toward guarding that island which had been known since the Dark Ages as Merlin's Enclosure.

It was not until 1941, however, that Seymour secured admission to a new lodge. This new group had, by all accounts, been dying on its feet for some years; however he liked the old mage who ran it, Carnegie Dickson, and was fond of the good doctor's wife, Edith. He knew too that they had at least retained the original contacts used by their particular portion of the Stella Matutina.

For awhile, for a very brief while, the wings of the Merlin would flutter in its dreaming . . .

W e can see Merlin standing in the heart of his enclosure. His robes trail upon the ground and indeed blend into it. He carries a gnarled staff which he holds at a peculiar but specific angle. Were the light that the staff symbolizes to project itself upward, into space, it would head outward toward Thuban, the one-time Pole Star

---

* Arthur's full name was Arthur Pendragon, the latter being a title which means, strictly speaking, the "Head of the Dragon," but which I have chosen to translate here as "Dragon King."

found within the constellation of Draco. Were it projected downward it would scour through the underworld, into the Earth's core. This, to the cosmologies of the magi, would be the world axis, and Merlin would be seen as the one who keeps it firm.*

Merlin, of course, has many aspects. Many people touch upon these in many ways. At one level we can aim our consciousness upwards as the link between the human and the Divine. While at another level (but by no means an inferior one) we can use his aspect as the Horned God and make that other journey down from the human world to the natural world, and explore the deepest recesses of the Earth Mysteries.

Either way, through absolutes of consciousness and sub-consciousness, we end up at the same place.

Merlin is the Great Initiator of the Western Tradition. He teaches us, whether we set our minds toward the stars or the soil. According to one source he was born of a devil which finally succeeded in forcing itself upon the third of three sisters. Being thus only half human, he was brought up by the wise and goodly monk Blaise in a lonely tower amid the wastes of Northumberland.

He managed to avoid infanticide. He proved himself to kings. He had a vision of two fighting dragons—one white and one red—which helped to establish his power. Much later, he used his own talents for shape shifting to help Uther Pendragon mate with Ygraine, the wife of Uther's enemy. The resulting child, Arthur, he spirited away at birth and used even later magics to ensure that he was recognized as the Pendragon, the rightful king of all the Britains. And toward the height of the Arthurian epic he was instrumental in bringing the Round Table to completion. Then at the end of his days the young Nimue used her wiles to learn his deepest secrets before entrapping him in a crystal cave.

Contrary to the story, however, he has never stayed in his cave for long.

That, in brief, is a grossly simplified version of the story of Merlin. Many occultists give an Atlantean gloss to all this, an example of which will be given in the final section of the book.

W hen CCT joined the Merlin Temple in 1942 she was more concerned with bringing her three friends and coworkers through the Grades of the traditional Golden Dawn system than in

---

* This is an image of Merlin in an ante-diluvian phase. The axis today inclines toward Polaris.

living within Merlin's aura daily. The archmage, in those early days, always appeared more as a guide than as the *ne plus ultra* of contacts. This is the way it should be. Whatever else the Chiefs might be they are certainly not jealous. They are more than happy to let their earthly assistants use the contacts of other days and other realms, as long as the Work progresses.

Regrettably CCT never kept up a detailed record of the main work done by the seniors. When she had a clear-out of her documents in anticipation of her death, she handed me the bundle of papers which are largely reproduced in the following pages. For a long time I refrained from doing anything with them as I felt them to be inferior to the juxtaposed Workings of herself and Colonel Seymour that I was then editing.

It was, really, a cocky attitude to take. There is no such thing as "inferior" or "superior" spiritual experiences any more than there are inferior or superior colors. The truth is, there are only different ways of writing them up. But it did gradually become clear to me that there was a story within a story to be told, and that even the apparently unsatisfactory "far memories" can be used to show how newcomers (in this case the Daw family) link with the egregore of a magical Order, and of the sort of things that we can all expect when we come to do so ourselves.

In a sense, the crucial Working of the group is to be found dated the 8th of November 1942, when three members of the temple gathered with the intention of learning what they could about the links which seemed to bind them. CCT was the only experienced magician, and she was being used by the other two, Barbara Daw and the unidentified V.V. as a seeress. The working was a simple one, and very brief, done while the others within the lodge were getting on with more technical matters relating to teaching and study. It begins with the almost throwaway line: "Had a little trouble at first getting rid of an undesirable who looked very like Socrates. Disposed of him and then went on to work under the aegis of Merlin," and then goes on:

> Found ourselves somewhere on the coast near Orme's Head, and watching a boat coming in. There were several boats, native constructed, with square sails (one to each) and rowed by oarsmen in the waist. In the first one was T. clad as a young Roman, and with him was a young man whom he consulted and whom we knew though not quite sure who he was. T. wore the ring. We understood that the fleet was coming to the mouth of the Dee and that T. was bringing reinforcements and help to Chester and that there was trouble on the Western end of the

wall: the tribes were out between Chester and the Wall.

There was a conference in the camp. There was an elderly commander, with a hawk-like face, consulting with T. and with a British guide to whom we took a great dislike. We did not trust him—but we thought that T. and the commander would do so because there was no other way. T. decided that he and the other young man would try to get through the rough country on ponies and on foot in order to scout out the land.

They had just started when the telephone bell rang and I was brought back with a frightful bump.

"T" was Anthony Daw, Barbara's brother, and the elderly commander with the hawk-like face was Seymour. The substance of the far memory is unimportant, although we might notice that the Roman Wall appears in it, with all that it symbolizes. The interesting lines are the very first ". . . an undesirable who looked very like Socrates."

CCT had no inkling of the part played by Socrates within the *FIL*, nor yet of those parts played by Thomas More or Carstairs, of whom she had never heard. Although she was trained up through the Grades with everyone else, up until that point where she was supposed to make her own inner contacts, and although she worked with Dion during the Egyptian and Pagan rites generally, this shows just how far she was removed from the center of the lodge, and how much more closely involved with the Stella Matutina. On several occasions the Chiefs used by Seymour (and who used him) referred to CCT as the Priestess of the Morning Star, without CCT having any particular inkling as to the significance of this.*

And so in banishing Socrates from within their psyches they were in effect making the final separation from a previous line of light. This leads on, with supreme irony, to the fact that once they had done so they immediately found themselves at Orme's Head—that is to say the Dragon's Head—at Llandudno, where unbeknownst to them or anyone else Violet Firth had been born 52 years earlier. They banished Socrates, but they found themselves between those winged serpents that Dion had so often pushed aside.

The comment: ". . . then went on to work under the aegis of Merlin" is also significant within the context of this book, and leads us on to consider the use of the term "The Merlin Current," which seems to have gained some currency within modern occultism, without anyone being particularly clear as to its nature. Naturally if there is a

---

* There are two interim Workings given here in Appendix A which took place at Latymer Court, London, where CCT had her offices. Here we can see a clear and conscious use of the Merlin contact and its serpent/ Atlantean associations.

Merlin Current then someone, somewhere, will eventually be found to be working its corollary, the Morgan Current, which is even older in fact, as Morgan le Fay and her two sisters were well established as Witch queens when Merlin was still learning his spells. Seymour would equate this Current with the Dark Snake of the Moon Goddesses, for they channel the life-force which flows from the Great Mother, down the twisted, double-stranded snake known as the umbilical cord, into that fetus which will one day become the Child, and then the Priest-King, and then the Sacrificed God.

It would be facile to state, blandly, that the *FIL* was working the Morgan Current at the same time that Seymour's own little portion of the Stella Matutina used the Merlin Current. Quite simply, no one really knows, and these are terms of convenience in any case. Also, these things tend to go in phases; positive one moment, negative the next. Dion was certainly overshadowed by the image of Morgan le Fay during the mid-1930s when she worked the subtle magics of the Moon. Seymour was quite as busy with this too, although by the time that war came he seems to have moved ever closer to Merlin himself, perhaps because that archmage has an active and particular mandate to protect his nation in times of acute national peril. The role of Morgan, on the other hand, is to sit still and hold the power steady.

Again, no one will ever really *know*. We can only push those few details that we have into the realms of myth, where fact can be ensouled by fancy, and therefore made fertile.

The only certain thing that can be said is that the link between the two Currents is that of Arthur, the Once and Future King, acting like the central line of the caduceus, who was (and is) an exemplar of the Earth's consciousness, the Great Bear who revolves with Draco, and who can be found in the northern quarter, bright within the darkness. It is only by going to the highest levels, to the Visions of the Chiefs, that we can begin to orient ourselves, which is why it is better to look at the following diaries in terms of theme rather than sequence. So it is that on October 27, 1942, during the middle of a storm at the height of a Full Moon, we find K(im) Seymour, Frere ayme Frere (the magical motto of Christine Campbell Thomson), A(nthony Daw) and the unidentified Mme. meeting at the lodge for a rite that would contact them with some of the Inner Chiefs of the Order.

> K. controlled the levels of power and left me to do the work. We found ourselves in a black temple, reminiscent of the one we had known before but of a later date, for it had been fitted with pillars, the

altar was more elaborate and the figure was seated and male. The altar had been turned at right angles and was now something of a shelf below the figure. On the altar were from end to end—beer in Egyptian jars: corn: grapes: the white cakes and milk in the center: grapes, fish and beer. In front of the altar stood S.R.M.D., who had come there from the northern end where he had been grouped with two other priests: at the southern corner of the altar were three priestesses, of whom I only recognized his wife. The other priests were B.I. and one of whom I was not sure.

Standing in the body of the temple were a group of the Order. We were all there and I saw various others whom I knew such as Sp.D.D.I.M., etc. Led by K. we went up to pass in front of S.R.D.M. [sic] He was in the robes of a magus and was as it were transfigured with light: I saw the symbols of the first 6 Degrees blazing in his centers, terminating at the Ajna: what lay above I could not see. His hands were outstretched in blessing and from them poured light in a great beam: we were all to pass through that light. K. went first and then T. and then myself, the others following (this order is not necessarily clear except that we three went together as stated). When we had passed through the beam and had absorbed the power, T. put his arm round my shoulders and drew me close to him and we stood together facing S.R.D.M. and T. said "Look, I have got my priestess and my queen," and S. smiled and blessed us with great power.

Then the visions faded and we found ourselves floating in the air and looking down at the lost land of Lyonesse and Ys. Back again we went and I found the boat on the sea and again endured the horror of the loss of Atlantis, then back to the pre-Atlantean island where K. and I first found our lives, and then back again to Lemuria, where we were a yellow-skinned, small race, and had our worship in the temple where the gods were totem poles as in Easter Island. And K. recognized that they were always the same—Osiris, Isis, Horus. Before we reached the Lemurian temple, we climbed up a hill and found the entrance was again through a cave—deep and dark, and within we found the Dark Mother. The whole experience seemed to be to show to us that throughout the ages the basis of all the faith is the same and that one must always be born again.

N.B. When we were in the temple with S.R.D.M., K. was particularly conscious of the elemental spirits which came around.

'S Rhioghail Mo Dhream . . . so here he was again, Mathers in his innermost glory, but transmogrified, raised to the level of Magus and by now a genuine inner plane adeptus, a Secret Chief in his own right. Moina was there too, and Brodie Innes, their consciousness returning to that of the tribe. Whatever the tensions between the lodges on the outer planes, all was resolved and made whole upon the inner, long after their deaths.

It is interesting, too, that this meeting with the Chiefs should tail off into a series of visions of Atlantis and Lemuria, before going to Earth, quite literally, in a cthonic contact with the Dark Mother who was approached via a deep and dark cave, and that the elemental contacts were so very strong. Even more than the trinity of Osiris, Isis and Horus, it is the Earth-links which are the most vital. Without them there is no magic. Without them there is no life. Somehow, in some way, we must all find that cave at some time in our lives and make the same kind of silent communion that they did.

They took up on a similar theme two days later when once again the elemental forces were extremely strong. The Su. mentioned in this Working is a nickname for Barbara Daw.

> 10/29/42. Present Su. V.V. F.A.F. Stormy.
> Su. did careful banishing first. We sat in almost darkness. V.V. was most anxious to see Ys, so we asked if we might go there. We spun round in the air and saw it below us through water. Then we went down but it was most curious for the city was empty—a mere shell. We were not very happy in it—it was hardly dead—more as if it had never had life, and we thought we were looking at a dead astral shell. We walked through to the main square where there was a big temple, etc., but the inference was that there was nothing there for us, and we turned with some relief to the open country beyond. Here there were rolling hills and a winding white road—pleasant country. And one came to meet us in a dark habit rather like a monk's. We did not at first recognize it as being K. but knew him later. He made us turn and go up the hill behind him (T. had joined there—brought by Su.). We five then went up to what looked like a small Stonehenge*—and in the center of the stone uprights was S.R.D.M. again. He was as before transfigured and gold and white light. We knelt in a semi-circle before him Su. and V.V. at the horns, then T. and K. and then myself in the middle, and the power came streaming out of him as before. There was a tremendous sensation of peace and power—positive, active peace. And then we were aware of the elementals. The gnomes were running all over the place, and the grass at the foot of the stone pillars turned into flames and the sylphs were everywhere—though I could not quite pick up the undines. There was a great aura over us, pouring out of his hands, and then we raised our eyes and saw a gold chalice outlined on his breast and from it there rose a transparent pillar of white light, in which poised the dove and in the mouth of the dove was the rose. And the great shaft of light seemed to go up into the ether where we lost sight of it. The power and the blessing were tremendous: gradually the vision died away and we came back.

---

* I strongly suspect that this was St. Carnac in Brittany.

And the following night Mrs. Dickson and Christine Campbell Thomson, functioning as D.I.M. and F.A.F., took the contact with Mathers once more, entering the temple which existed on another plane, and going out into the garden behind it, "going through the courtyard in the usual way."

"SRDM came to meet us," she wrote, again getting the Motto wrong, "and greeted D.I.M. as an old friend whom he had not seen for some time. He was glowing and robed as a priest of Fire. He took her by the hand (I followed) and led her to a waterfall among the trees in a kind of wild garden and seemed to be asking her if she remembered it. Then, hand in hand they went to the long temple where we went before with I(rene) W(ilson). D.I.M. was by now clothed in silver and blue and typified Water. He and she walked up the aisle (the temple was full of people in the Order) and stood in front of the altar facing the people, and then appeared to give a blessing; there was tremendous power radiating from them both. Then the vision faded and we came back."

It is plain from the notes that the group had been to that particular temple many times before, although the records have not survived. It is plain, too, that by this time it had taken on actual form within the unconscious minds of the operator, where it is best visualized as being located as the Sanctuary of Amoun, at the site of the pituitary body. The temple that "is not made with hands" does in fact become an actuality within the rolling billows of the astral light, and thus the tribal mind. Individuals can travel there freely if they have the right of entry. When it is properly formed within the mind and, in your imagination, you push against the walls, there is a curiously solid response—as tangible within the head as if you were pushing against the inside of your teeth with the tip of your tongue.

Such occult architecture, however, should be regarded in the same light as the masks and images used by the inner contacts: the lines and forms are means of enabling the mind to work, and to grasp the idea that at the heart of every tribal mind there is a place of Sanctuary.

On the 7th November Seymour, "H," and CCT worked "with the Order method on the triangle."

> Went through to volcanic region and met the guide who was M(erlin). With him we went over the road which appeared to be glass over fire, and in front over the hilltops was a vast Sun: our guide typified astral fire. We went up the hill and then the scene changed and I

found myself in the inner room which was last being used as a board room. They had taken away the long table and had put up an altar at the far end, in front of which was S.R.M.D., B.I. and F.M., the first of the three being in tremendously bright robes. Accompanied by the guide, who walked between us, we went up to the altar. In front of S.R.M.D. was a shaft of light with the cup and the dove illumined in it. Lines of power ran between the six of us and we formed the two interlaced triangles, our guide being the lowest point and S.M.R.D. the upper one. The lines of power were first gold and then changed to blue and red. An aura like a rainbow was built over the six of us completely enclosing us and the power and peace were very great.

Then we returned by the usual route and through the triangle.

While that same night at 10:00 P.M. the indefatigible CCT, along with V.V. and Susan Daw, did some work of a slightly different kind when they built the archangels round the wall of the temple "in the astral," and saw them glowing in their colors, flat like reliefs, with the astrally glowing insignia of each one placed in front of them.

Then, standing round the altar in a square, we saw that the roof was the Milky Way, with the signs of the zodiac in gold clearly printed in it. As we watched, the signs took the forms of their names and these forms materialized down and came round the circle of the altar, being then approximately knee-high, golden and very clear and solid. The A.A.s at this time also became three dimensional and stepped from the walls, making an outer ring of power. The four elemental signs in the corners of the temple also became three dimensional and advanced, filling in the gaps between the wing points. The gold zodiacal figures then started to perform a slow dance round us. There was a cone of white light pouring on to the four of us on the altar and from it the power was tearing into our fingers and right through us (I could see that we were almost transparent) and out at our heels (we were barefoot and I can remember noticing the golden light coming from our pink heels). This light went in bars of power to the figures and it was by its force that they moved. We were aware of the most tremendous down-rush of power that we were storing in these figures. S. understood the symbolism of it and she pointed out to us that we were making a great storehouse for the use of the forces fighting for good. Then the figures went back to the ceiling and the strength of the power died down.

We came back rather tired for a moment but conscious of having been definitely contributing to the war effort and to having had a very wonderful experience.

But it was on the 24th of February, 1943 that CCT, working only with her beloved Kim, picked up the really dominant contact, and understood something of her relationship both with it, and Seymour.

Almost before I had settled down the figure of the great magician of Egypt came up, about ten feet high, in front of me. And then I picked out K. and myself in front of him. K. was very old, wearing a linen robe of some kind and an apron. The apron was that of a man of very high rank: it was the triangular kind shown in Leadbeater* and it was borned with R.A. colors. There were many signs on it: at the bottom was a circle with an eye in it: under the point was a triangle surmounting a square and between the two was the 'oldest sign in the world' with the double crossed bars. On the right side (facing) was a level and on the left a snake. He had a fillet on his head with the uraeus. I was wearing a white robe of something very thin like chiffon, rather cloudy and loose, with silver sandals and half moons at the heels, like little spurs. On my forehead was a crescent moon lying on its back and I had a scrying circular convex crystal round my neck, and a silver belt with a clasp form of two half moons, like the 2-9 symbol.

We seemed to be just standing there in a tremendous astral bell and behind Him I could see the outline of a pyramid with a big astral shell over it all filled with zodiacal and other signs. He was standing on some shallow steps (K. said there were eight of them) which made him even taller than usual. He gave me an ankh.

K. asked if I could pick up the relationship. I puzzled a lot saying that I had not as it were personally contacted him before and trying to fit my priessthood to him as with Merlin. And he kept smiling and saying "It's a wise child that knows its own father," and then I suggested very diffidently that I had been his daughter. It was true: K. was his father: that was quite clear. So that I am the daughter of Himself and priestess in an even bigger way than I thought before.

K. gave me a book to see his own death mask and it was quite clear who he was: for years I have been trying to fit him into an Indian face and could not but I knew there was something familiar about him. Now we know not only those two things but also the identity of the Princess who came from Iraq to be his wife just before Himself died and when I was just growing up.

---

* Charles Webster Leadbeater, the leading figure behind both Theosophy and Co-Masonry during the period of Mrs. Besant's presidency.

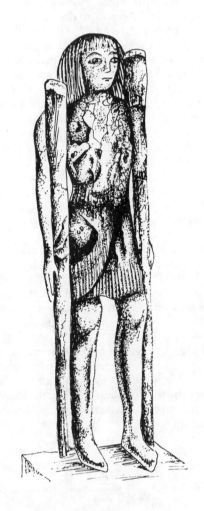

Kha'm-uast

Here is the archmage figure of Kha'm-uast again, confirming his status as one of the innermost potencies within the Order. Strange, that in Seymour's day they had to sneak down into a dusty corner of the British Museum's basement when they wanted to make contact via the intensely magnetic statue of the High Priest, while now, as if symbolic of the way that all these things have come out into the open, Kha'm-uast's figure stands proudly in the main hall.

It is interesting, too, to note the range of Masonic symbolism via the scattered references to the apron, the strength and beauty, the appearance of the master from the North, and the royal arch colors. Kha'm-uast, remember, was High Priest of Ptah, in Memphis, and that God has always been associated with the craft of Masonry in all its forms. Someday a high grade Mason who is also familiar with the rites of the Golden Dawn, Co-Masonry, and the esoteric section of the Theosophical Society may come along to unravel it all.

But in the personal references to that Egyptian magus we find Seymour being unusually shy. When he mentions the death mask he is talking about the well-known and oft-photographed features of a particular mummified pharaoh. He is in fact saying, very quietly, that in a previous life in the 19th Dynasty he had once strode among the courts of the land bearing the crook and flail, and wearing the Double Crown of the Upper and Lower Kingdoms. Worshipped and feared and often loved, he had once been known as Rameses II.

It is easy to sneer at this point. It provokes the old jest that every magician has exalted past lives and no mundane ones, which is the sort of comment made by those who have never actually come close to real magicians. Seymour had, in fact, a number of *extremely* ordinary far memories; plus it must be remembered that no one but CCT was ever intended to read of his magical workings and his past lives. He would have been horrified. So the question needs to be asked: Was Seymour's character, his inner status, his vision and wisdom such that we might regard him as a genuine reincarnation of such a formidable figure? All things considered, even bearing in mind the convenient escape clause offered by the concept of a tribal overshadowing, I think the answer must be yes.

To do him justice, he would have said that it is not Rameses II, or Mr. Smith, or Colonel Seymour who reincarnates: "It is the High Self of each one of us that seeks reincarnation by incarnating *a little bit* at a time." Thus the non-incarnating portion of Rameses, Smith, or Seymour is "the Watcher, the Observer, the Guardian at the Gate, etc."*

The outsider can find it easy to mock magicians generally because of their penchant for finding past lives in the land of Khem. Yet if we can accept the concept of reincarnation in the first place, and if we bear in mind that during its vast history the number of initiated and presumably illuminated priests and priestesses would be numbered in tens and perhaps hundreds of thousands, then it would be surprising if a genuine magician did *not* find any links with that narrow world along the Nile.

Rameses was the pharaoh who oversaw the building of Abu Simbel, and Karnak, who may well have overseen the Exodus too.

Seymour, just as strong within himself, oversaw the creation of a system of magic based, in part, on trinities; and he would one day watch from the inner planes while a whole generation of would-be initiates took a different road, wending away from the mainstream of Judaeo-Christian traditions and making toward the High Place of the Moon, and the pagan contacts. Only today, after 40 years, has the end of the journey been glimpsed.

Kha'm-uast appeared again the following month, on March 26 when V.V., who by this time had taken her initiation in the 4-7 degree of Netzach, joined with CCT and Susan Daw. She was the first to sense his arrival within the temple after CCT had first performed the obligatory Banishing Ritual, designed to scour the psychic atmosphere of any unwanted presences—much as we would sterilize an operating room. Kha'm-uast led them on the inner planes toward a temple "which seemed to be arranged like a lodge." He sat in the East, while the three women stood before the altar. They each had a sense of Kha'm-uast giving them some moonstones to hold, which he held also. The seats in the West and South were occupied only by astral forms that were not clearly definable. At first the North was empty.

One of them knelt before the very sacred light and the other two stood at right and left.

> The S[tar] and the C[rescent] were displayed. The power started to rise and we could see three great lines of light pouring out of Kha'm-uast's third eye to our own. Then the power began to pour in from the North. The shadowy shapes in the other two seats grew clearer and more colorful—indigo and gold. I turned my head to the North and saw

---

* The socialist Mage (and there are a few) would have no problems here. He would argue that, comparatively, Seymour's was the more exalted life, and that his karma was to realize that Rameses' attainments were made possible by class and privilege alone, and that the pharaoh himself was nothing special. Seymour would probably disagree, however.

a rainbow: it seemed to be essential that there should be a rainbow because otherwise the white that was pouring in would have blinded us all: as it was, it caught up all the rays from the Seats and from us and blended into the rainbow through which the power could come without killing us. It stretched out like a great aura over us and the altar and out to the South side of the lodge. The beauty and the strength were tremendous and the reviving power seemed to pour through us. We closed down fairly soon, and my skin was irritating all over and V.V. had a painful sensation in the top of her head.

One noticable thing was that we all seemed to be changing places at the altar: it seemed as if there were three astral forms and we could occupy any one of them at any given moment, because we checked up where we had seemed to be and each of us was aware of having occupied more than one position.

In many ways the making of an inner contact is like falling in love. Perhaps not like the original act itself, but rather the remembrance of the same. Sometimes, at the height of our experience and vigor we can sit perfectly still, the mind relaxed and easy, and through a trick of reverie can bring back some portion of those light and golden days when First Love made its first swirlings in the heart. Full consciousness is there, as also a full awareness of present circumstances, even if this is pushed to one side for the moment. The link is only really broken when the rational mind decides to shove its clumsy foot in the door through the gate of dreaming, and ask questions.

That is a crude analogy, of course, and there are more explanations than this as to what was going on during these contacts with Kha'm-uast, for example. Some of these far memories may be ascribed to a simple case of overshadowing: magicians picking up events that were resonant within that priest's lifetime. But it may be something more dramatic altogether.

Imagine that we are priests in some 19th Dynasty temple; imagine that our inward senses pick up some entities that appear during our rituals; and imagine further that these entities are actually future incarnations of *ourselves*. It is an extraordinary thought, and not one to be shrugged off easily.

Another variation goes as follows: if the magicians of the Golden Dawn could call up Kha'm-uast from those lost days within the Old Land, then Kha'm-uast too, in his own era, could evoke the magicians of the Golden Dawn and bring them back into his place of Working.

In brief, there is not one simple answer as to the mechanics of each rite. No one can say for certain which is pure far memory, which is a ritual of ancient simultaneity, if we can coin a phrase, and which is a mixture of both, but with a bit of mind wandering added.

It must be admitted that the latter did take place, despite all the precautions that each participant took against this happening. On the other hand I have never met a senior magician yet who made any sort of cult out of his own visions, nor have I met any who would have been devastated had their apparent far memories been proved to be inconsistent with historical fact. In fact, very few of them have "cradle to grave" far memories, and none of them have been particularly interested in tracking down their occult histories. The truth is they tend to accept what comes through in that line, act "as if" when it is necessary, but generally are too busy getting on with their Work to get hung up on magical genealogies (which is to say that when we start to experience such things of our own, we must not be dogmatic about their exact nature).

One of the first examples of Egyptian Workings done within the Merlin Temple by CCT and FPD took place on February 18, 1941.

Moon. Waning: 6 days after full.   Weather: Cold and damp.
Self. Very tired—worried.
        Could not get off at first: top consciousness of worry kept on coming in between and preventing me from dropping through. Eventually got away, restlessly, unable to focus but helped by F.P.D. Came to rest finally opposite the great temple in Egypt and saw the Nile by moonlight.
        Crossed the river and was just inside the House of the Virgins. I was aware that there was a new ceremony, something I had not done before. Found myself walking, not being carried, to the lotus pool. It was surrounded by priests and priestesses and in the middle of the water the full moon was reflected quite clearly. It was very dark round it and I assumed that the pool was lined with black tiles or else that the water had been chemically darked for the ceremony. The lotuses were in bloom.
        One of the priests gave me a fishing net—or rather a landing net. I had to "catch" the moon in the net without breaking the reflection and on the smoothness of that catch depended the fertility and success of Egypt for the next year. It was called the Ceremony of Catching the Moon. I knelt down on the marble rim of the pool and slid the net in very slowly, without a ripple, guiding it between the lily pads. Then I lifted it high, holding the stick at the extremity and caught the moon reflection perfectly. There was great happiness.
        Then someone took the net away from me and I walked up the great steps to the Hypostyle Hall. One side of me was the High Priest of all High Priests and on the other F.P.D. The Hypostyle Hall has a por-

ticoed front with a pediment like the Acropolis: parallel with it are two long narrow wings, one of which is the Hall of the Mummies and the other the Hall of Thoth, leading to his chapel: this hall is used only by the men.

We went up the great hall to the altar, which stood about three-quarters of the way up in a dim moonlight effect. I stood before it with F.P.D. opposite and the High Priest on my left and his right, between us. It was a cubical altar. On it were certain objects, which it was most important I should see. One by one I picked them up. They were: a string of moonstones: grass: the plumage of a pigeon (breast plumage of an archangel from the look of it): a bunch of white flowers like ox-eye daisies: a flat bread cake and a low chalice, like a bowl, filled with milk.

Feeling very tensed and keyed up, I first of all took up the moonstones and put them round my neck: then I took the grass and gave it to F.P.D.: next I picked up the flowers and placed them in my robe and gave him the bird plumage: then I broke the sacramental bread, and handed some to him and offered him the milk and we ate and drank in communion.

All this time there was power radiating, which seemed to be centered in the High Priest and spread out to both of us.

Someone in the background gave F.P.D. a little lamp. I took the plate on which the bread had lain and placed it in the center of the altar: then I took the chalice and placed it on the plate, and then I took the lamp and placed it inside the chalice, so that it glowed with a soft moongolden light through the semi-transparent bowl.

We waited a moment, in adoration and then at a sign from the High Priest, we all laid our hands on the altar and felt the power magnetizing it. Then he stamped with his left foot and we followed suit and cut the power.

Next I walked out of the hall to the steps and there I turned to my right and F.P.D. and the High Priest to the left: the priests followed them and the priestesses followed me. I went to the Hall of the Mummy and there was the astral figure of the goddess lying on the floor. I stood beside her: the priestesses took off my robes and left me in nothing but the moonstones. Then I laid myself on the astral body of the goddess and began slowly to absorb her. Little by little she was melted into me until I found myself lying on the bare stone floor. Then the priestesses raised me and robed me again and now they set on my head a silver and moonstone horned ornament because I was now the actual shell in which the goddess was personifying herself. I went down the hall but instead of going to the chapel of the White Isis behind the curtain, I turned to the right and went to a small temple behind behind the Hypostyle Hall and facing two thrones. F.P.D. and I sat on the thrones and after a moment someone from the background brought a model of the child Horus and stood it between us so that the land might be fertile.

I did not know who the High Priest was but F.P.D. knew him and called him by name and asked him about the four boxes. And he answered to his invocation and spoke to me and blessed us and again emphasized the fact that I am of the blood.

And that, so far as I remember, was the end of it.

The four boxes is a reference to the story told within Seymour's article "Children of the Great Mother," via which we can identify the High Priest almost certainly as Kha'm-uast again, or perhaps as his coworker Ne Nefer Ka Ptah, who was a Priest of Anubis.

Her reference to being "of the blood" harkens directly back to the Fraternity of the Inner Light again, with the ideas of the Atlantean "Sacred Clan." Whether she was of the blood or not no one can really say, but she was certainly proving herself to be "of the Tribe," and a fit member of the Stella Matutina, of whose symbols the Star and Crescent she was intensely aware.

Another encounter with the spirit of Egypt took place on August 2, 1942, when CCT joined with the three members of the Daw family.

Hesitated a little, unable to find locality but fell into Egypt where T. said he was already waiting.

The Great Hall of Audience belonging to a very early Pharaoh. It was a very large, bare room, with pillars and stone walls—cool and almost empty of ornament. There must have been one side open to the sky, for there was no sign of artificial light but it was well lit with a cool greyness. The Pharaoh and his Queen-Sister sat side by side on a dais— she on his right. Their thrones were alike—white marble chairs with arms which ended in lions' head arm-rests, and the same ornament was on the basal corners. (The seats were thrones rather than chairs, cut out of solid stone.) The only difference was that the Pharaoh's lions' heads were gold and the Queen's silver. Over their heads was a sort of canopy—of silk, I think. There were servants behind them with peacock feather fans and on the dais further back were the matrons of the Priestesses and the Higher Priests.

The Pharaoh wore natural colored linen robes with a double crown in white linen with the uraeus: he had the formal wig and beard and wore gold sandals on his feet. In his arms were laid the flail and the gold sceptre; his hands were noticeably beautiful with very long, slender fingers, and he kept them over the tops of the lions' heads, at any rate at the beginning. He had a golden girdle and a breastplate rather like Urim and Thummim. He had very attractive eyes (brown) and his mouth seemed very sweet but of course it could not be seen clearly. He was quite young. He wore the sign of Ra on his neck.

The Queen Sister was much younger—very little more than a girl—and it seemed to us that she had only just been old enough to assume her place on the dais. She wore cream linen with silver sandals. She had a very lovely necklace which was made of silver gold and ended in a beautifully worked kephra-beetle. Round her hair was a silver-gold fillet with a star in the center and it was worn over a very light silvery gauze veil. She was dark and the formal wig seemed to suit her. Round her waist was a sash of dark blue and dark red silk made in the form of triangles. In her right hand she held a silver ankh and in the crook of her left arm was her sceptre—a square ebony, with the sides outlined with silver stripes, and a dark orb on the top of it.

It was the Hall of Justice and Audience and there was a case being heard by the two on the dais. The petitioner was a little bald man with a strong suggestion of the Mongol or Tibetan about him. On the steps of the dais, at the Queen's right hand, was the Lord Chamberlain of the household, who acted as interpreter and who was being paid by the other side to act as his advocate. The little man could not speak court Egyptian and the Chamberlain was misrepresenting the case. The Queen suddenly leaned forward and spoke to the little man in his own tongue. At that moment a tremendous wave of hatred went out from the Chamberlain to the Queen: the Pharaoh picked it up immediately and though he hardly moved his head, his eyes never left the Chamberlain for a moment: he insulated the Queen immediately with a ring of power. When the little man had finished speaking, the defendant came forward: he was an extremely broad-shouldered man, very rough looking, with a great quantity of black hair: I got the impression that the whole of his chest was covered with it. The Queen heard him and then gave her judgment in favor of the little man. The Pharaoh made a sign with his hand and two of his household took the Chamberlain from behind and led him away.

The Queen turned slightly in her chair and raised her eyebrows: it seemed to be her first independent judgment and she was very anxious. The Pharaoh looked at her very seriously and gravely, and intimated that the judgment of Pharaoh was the judgment of both Pharaohs and that she must remember she was on the Throne and not unbend in her official capacity to her personal one.

Just then the procession of tribute came up the hall. It was very lovely: first came people bearing huge bunches of grapes on poles, and other fruits: rather like a harvest festival: and then came the animals, little lambs and pigs . . . and then came the children who were to serve in the temple and in the palace—the "first-born." We recognized a number of them, including G., who was aged about 6 and clutching a mud model of a water-buffalo. When they had gone by there was a hush for a moment and the Queen moved slightly as if the audience were finished, when there came a frightful screaming from the end of the hall and a woman rushed up. We all recognized her as S. Her hair was wild and her eyes staring out of her head. It was horrible. She flung herself on the steps of the dais and Pharaoh put out his sceptre for her to touch as permission to speak, and to keep back the officials who would have taken her away. It seemed that her husband and her other child had died of the plague and the first-born who had come with the temple children was the only one left. The Queen seemed to withdraw into herself all at once and to be almost inhuman. There was great sorrow on Pharaoh's face but he could not break the laws of the priesthood and of the State and he had to explain this to her. Then she drew herself up and cursed him and the Queen shrank back and grew a little smaller and slighter and the Pharaoh's eyes grew harder and he signed to the officials to take her away.

Then, after a moment or two, he took the tips of the Queen's fingers in his and led her very slowly down the hall between the ranks of people, looking neither to right nor to left. And I could just see the tips of the Queen's fingers fluttering the slightest amount as they rested in his so that he held them a little more firmly than usual to conceal it from the people. They went through the hall and turned to the right and through a long gallery and through more doors and into a courtyard, which they crossed. Beyond this were more doors and inside were the private apartments. And there Pharaoh left the Queen's hand drop and turned straight away to the left (T. says he went to the private chapel of Thoth) and the Queen went to her own rooms. She had a huge cool bedroom, stone-floored, with a bed on a dais covered with soft green and blue silks and a great white fur rug. And she had a polished steel circular mirror set in turquoise matris, and a low painted table with pots and jars of ointments and paints, all in lovely pale white and green and pink alabaster. For a long time she walked up and down the room, her hands clasped in front of her and the most terrible expression on her face.

After a little while she sounded a small gong and her maids came in and disrobed her of her royal robes and put on her a sea-green silk robe, very thin, with a tracing of gold embroidery on it, and green rush sandals, very cool. And they combed out her own long dark hair and made up her face again, and clasped gold bracelets on her arms and a thin gold chain round her neck, and then she went out of her own rooms to meet the Pharaoh for the mid-day meal.

There is a quality about this Working, however, which just does not ring true. It is almost too dramatic. Christine once told me that Seymour (who was not present) had brought her up short on more than a few occasions, telling her that she had not really *seen* a particular series of events but was using the faculty of a novelist rather than that of a seer. She was quite aware that this dramatizing quality may have crept into several of the far memories, even after all the checks and tests had been been made. The Daws, after all, were newcomers to the field and not as likely to have Seymour's acumen in these matters. But there comes a point, as Christine pointed out, when you either have to remain a deliberately blank screen rejecting every-thing out of fear of making a mistake, or else you let the visions through, and make of them what you can.

The fact that the human mind is capable of visions at all is intrigu-ing; that these visions seem to represent accurate scenes from the past is extraordinary; but that these same visions can be used positively by acting "as if," and add toward the wisdom of the soul, is something that is wondrous. It is undeniable that many people have deluded themselves over reincarnatory sagas that have not stood up against the acid light of respectable historical research. Indeed we all make mistakes of this kind in our early magical careers. The answer to the problem is to hold everything lightly, which is by no means the same as *taking* it lightly. Hold it lightly, and act "as if," but never cling to such experiences—*never*.

If CCT was "going through a phase" in dredging up such images for the benefit of the Daws, the next Egyptian Working has an altogether different tone. Not only is her aged but vastly experienced Moon Priest present for this one, but she herself takes on her full Magical Personality. It is not Christine Campbell Thomson who delves into the treasurehouse of images for the sake of friends, but *Frere ayme Frere*, Adeptus Minor, taking her vision back to some halcyon days.

10/13/42. Present. F.P.D., A., F.A.F.

A. was told to take the lead. She began by picturing the Nile with a dying moon on the land but leaving the water in darkness. Down-stream was being propelled a boat or barge, with about four or six men plying sweeps. On the barge was a sarcophagus and seated behind it were herself and F.P.D., wrapped in cloaks. Both were men, she much the younger. She described her feelings later as being of intense horror and fear: a risky project was being undertaken and she was very doubt-ful if it would come off. At this point she asked F.P.D. if he knew who was in the coffin and he answered in the affirmative, but no more was said then.

During this period, I was completely out of the picture and found it almost impossible even to picture the scenes A. brought up. I supposed that I must be pumping out power for her so much that I had no "sight" left, but yet that did not seem right. I came to the conclusion that this was a picture for her and F.P.D. only and did not touch my own life: they had both recognized the opening scenes and said they had met them before.

The boat went on down the Nile to a temple which was described as looming very large and black against the night sky. There was a hid-den water entrance to it, through a sort of backwater between under-growth, which terminated in an arched and locked door. It was as the boat came to this that I woke up and was fully conscious. It was horrible for I was in the sarcophagus and the blackness and the sensation of fear were terrible. I heard F.P.D. give a word at the door—Mar-det n and it swung back, and I knew we were in a great hall filled with water and still in the barge. I could hardly control the agony of mind that I felt.

They lifted the coffin off the barge and carried it to the foot of a great god-figure, which was black, and before which they lit great braziers that gave off red fire. It was at this moment that A. decided she was not going to witness a sacrifice or a ritual: I think I had known it ever since I woke. They took the lid off the sarcophagus and then the inner shell and there I lay, with the blessed light on my face, my body bound round with the grave clothes and no strength in me. I was still dizzy from the drugs I had had to simulate death so that my own pictures are hazy but I was able to see myself as A. described it. The priests of the temple and F.P.D. bent over me and unwound the wrappings very gently, and lifted up my head and gave me fiery drink, and then rubbed me with oils and ointments so that the life came back into my limbs and I sat up and then was helped out of the coffin and to a heavy stone seat at the side of the god. It appeared that I was the sister of a young Nome who had been killed and that I was the only one of the family to be saved and (according to A.) I was going down to the South to revivify the old faith. F.P.D. hunted up some facts afterwards and it seemed fairly clear that we came from Thebes and that we were the followers of the Moon gods, who had been persecuted by the Hyklos Kings. A. insisted that my twin brother had been killed and that I was intensely miserable: I think this is true also because when I came to consciousness in the sarcophagus I looked all round the priests for T. and he was not there, and yet I was somehow aware of him on the astral and was confused and frightened because he did not materialize. I could not understand his not being there at such a time to protect me.

Presently they brought into the temple an old man with a high, bald forehead and a white beard: he seemed to me to be a captain of armies and to be someone I had known well. It was to him that I was being handed over for safety: A. and F.P.D. had brought me out of danger to a place of comparative safety—one of the old temples outside the boundary, and now this soldier was to escort me to the new living place in the South, where I, the High priestess and Princess was to keep the true worship alive and to teach it to the people.

It was about this time that the picture faded and we all came back. It is a difficult one to write about as I saw nothing of the first part and had to take A.'s word for it, and for the second part, after the first active horror had worn off a little, I was in a rather dazed condition, and though I remember bearing myself royally, I was really confused and only partly conscious. F.P.D. saw the Priest with the Big Hands in the temple and as he once before told us he had come to restore the Isis worship and give it back its old dignity, it is interesting, as the period which F.P.D. assigns to the episode would bring out all this.

Memo. It is curious to see that I was brought from Atlantis out of great tribulation to bring the Mysteries to the West: that I was smuggled out of Lower Egypt for the same purpose and in this life I have been brought to the Order at this difficult time after great personal tragedy and some danger.

Note the comment in the second paragraph about CCT "pumping out the power." There was far more involved in these rites than the simple passivity which allows pictures to float aimlessly before the mind's eye. Below the surface there was a great deal of delicately controlled psychic activity which each individual would have experienced very clearly. This activity would have been as tangible to their senses as, say, the changing of gears in a car and with much the same purpose.

I remember once listening to CCT, in her 80's, chatting with the magician Dolores Ashcroft-Nowicki who was herself trained within the Fraternity of the Inner Light. They discussed the technical aspects of ritual magic with such meticulous agreement as to the inward mechanics, and such exact personal experiences of what could and could not be done, that they might have been talking about some internal combustion engine that they had once taken apart and rebuilt. And this from two women of different generations, who had each left the *FIL* to do work of their own, and who had never met until then. If I had had any doubt before then as to the precision of magic, then that conversation alone was enough to convince me.

The concluding memo is also of interest: she saw herself (and rightly) as something of a Lightbearer, bringing the Mysteries safely out of doomed Atlantis, and likewise out of Lower Egypt. Now she found herself "brought to the Order at this difficult time" with much the same task ahead of her. As shown elsewhere, she was one of the few people to keep the spirit of the West alive, and who lived long enough to see the essence of the Golden Dawn arise once more, and all this quietly, without fanfare.* Indeed there would have been times when she herself wondered what it was all about. Certainly, by the time she gave me these diaries sight unseen since the day she saved them, the prophetic comment in the memo had been long, long forgotten.

However by December 1, 1942, this little Priestess who had brought the Mysteries from Atlantis achieved something of a *summum*

---

* See *Dancers to the Gods* for a biographical assessment of both CCT and FPD, and their own juxtaposed magical diaries relating to the years 1937-39 when they belonged to the Fraternity of the Inner Light.

bonum via the Egyptian Mysteries.

Present F.P.D., V.V., C.C.T.

Just before we started the invocation, F.P.D. gave me the Thoth necklace to hold. It immediately vitalized in my hand and I saw the Great Priest at the end of a long corridor, robed in full dress and standing in a blaze of light. Between him and me, at the side of the corridor was T., who said, "That's my necklace, you know, and the necklace of all those who have served Tehuti."

As the invocations went on I saw the Great Goddess as it were on the top of a high cliff with outspread arms (wings) over the cliff and within them two god forms. The top of the cliff seemed to be a great river and the water poured down in a thick black curtain, rather like the Falls of Niagara.

Then the scene changed. I was seated in the chair by the Nile, a chair made of three crescent moons. At my left hand was T. and at my right another priest, whom I also knew. The call of the water was very strong but I resisted it. Then I went up to the bridge and along the dark path and beside me were the blue men and mermen and mermaids and great grey clouds seemed to envelop us. And then I was asked which path I wanted to tread and I looked round and found I was on the dark one and on the light one was T. And he looked across to me and laughed and said "You know we always have to do these things together!" And I realized that he was now on my right because we had changed the levels of consciousness again. I as the feminine element must climb by the dark path of bringing light out of darkness. And though I chose the dark path when I was asked, I knew why I was doing it; together he and I reached the God at the summit. I cannot detail anything of it; it was beyond sight or words but I have never known more power pouring through.

When opening the centers this time, I was (a) conscious of extremely quick response all through (b) the Daath center was the strongest. (c) the center on the top of my head opened to an unusual extent and tremendous power poured through it.

At first I was shivering cold and damp and later on glowing with warmth and light.

It is not clear who the Great Priest was, other than that he served Thoth. Nor is the reference to the blue men an obvious one—it presumably refers to the water elementals. "I cannot detail anything of it," she wrote. "It is beyond sight or words but I have never known more power pouring through." Here, we might suspect, she was touching the level of the Greater Mysteries themselves, for she was beyond logic, far beyond mere words. But before that point she reached an understanding which can hold true for *all* women: "I as the feminine element must climb by the dark path of bringing light out of darkness . . . " That was her role: that was the role of the Stella Matutina.

Although she had strong Christian elements within her psyche, these were always able to coexist quite happily with the sort of energies that came through via Egypt, Greece, and the Norse contacts. One of the last of the recorded entries into "astral Egypt," if we might invent such a psychic/geographic/historical region, was dated March, 1943. This particular account was apparently typed up by the unknown woman "A." K. is Kim Seymour of course; Chris is CCT; S. and Titi refer to Barbara Daw and Margaret Daw respectively. I do not know if Chaim was a co-worker on the inner or outer planes.

> We found ourselves with Chaim . . . who had been present from the moment we sat down, and were in a room off the big temple. In the middle of the room was a sarcophagus—enormous, made of red sandstone or something similar. The room was quite bare otherwise, sand colored with a tiled floor in a rather deeper tone than the walls. There were big windows on one side through which the sun was streaming. In the sarcophagus lay CH, who was dead. At the head stood K. with Chris at his side: I was at the foot. It was a terrible tragedy. K. was completely bowled over and I was troubled and fearful of what was being laid on me. In the room opposite the windows and with their backs to the temple were the other priests and priestesses—S., Titi, etc. Then beside the sarcophagus came the Ka of the Great One. He lifted the blue necklace from the body and handed it to K. and he took a ring which was engraved with his cartouche and put it on the third finger of my right hand, and I was still more troubled. The sun crept on until it touched his face and then the Ka vanished and the bearers came in with the great lid that was painted with pictures of him and laid it over the body. I led the procession out into the temple, between the rows of priests and priestesses, with the thin high notes of the reed instruments cutting into my heart. Behind me came K. and Ch. and then the great coffin. We walked through the temple to a ramp, leading down to a canal where the funeral barge waited. K. saw the emblems of the gods on the great black sail, and I saw them standing by the catafalque. Then the great coffin came on rollers to where we were waiting and I stood a little in advance of the others and had the task of pushing it over the end of the ramp. As it slid down to the barge the orator behind began to recite his high estates. Then the barge moved off very slowly with the rowers using their great sweeps in the narrow canal and we saw it turn round a bend and then went back.
>
> There was a blank then and we came back to the balcony of the house: Kim was lying on a couch with Ch. beside him and I was on a stool: it seemed later. *He* appeared to us and seemed to be laying the burden on me and to tell me what to do: we got the impression that our work was to wait and pray in patience: it would be shown to us but the weight and the power were bound about my forehead.

Once again, with the appearance of *He*, the Master, we find what is ostensibly a far memory giving way to a contact of the purely magical kind.

Whoever *He* was, he was right: their work *was* to wait and pray in patience. It would take two generations before the Magical Currents worked within the Golden Dawn and its offshoots would begin to resonate again.

The very last purely Egyptian working took place on June 15, 1943, and this was in the form of an initiation for CCT. In fact it was one of the last pieces of Magical Working that her old priest, Seymour, ever did.

> K. decided to invoke O. rather than I. this time and we sat facing the shrine. I called on Himself and he came to support us; we were sitting as usual, side by side. We found ourselves in the big underground water temple, where the barge went before; K. said it was the temple of the dead Osiris. There was a huge statue of the god on an island and the priests were dragging a barge or barges round the island and intoning as they did so. Then I saw the light radiating on the God and at the head of the altar (N. side) stood Isis and at the foot, Nephthys; and then there was a pause. Up a kind of aisle leading to the altar came three people. K., Himself and myself in the middle; I was wearing a plain white robe and no ornaments and my hands were bound with a chain of alternate links of silver and gold. There were silver and gold anklets round my ankles. The two men, K. on my left, led me up to the altar and I knelt down and placed my wrists on it. There was chanting and I was presented to the God. Suddenly a blinding flash of light came from the statue and the links of the chain were severed. I knelt on and the two priests chanted— K. saying to this effect "Behold the daughter of the gods who was as a slave is now free," and Himself took it up as "Behold the freed daughter of the gods lives to serve." And then they raised me to my feet and took me to each end and to the middle of the altar, presenting me to the priests as the accepted daughter of Osiris. Then, they laid me on the altar, with my head to Isis and my feet to Nephthys and it seemed as if I were to undergo a great test. Passes were made over my face by K. and I seemed to shrink into nothingness; my body was dead but my soul lived and went down a long black tunnel. At the end there was a tiny pinpoint of light and it seemed essential that I should reach this and not turn back. As I went on, it seemed as if everything was being stripped away and I was reaching the ultimate core of all. I am not sure what happened then but I survived the test and came through and back again, very slowly and almost painfully, having 'received' the god. And they lifted me off the altar and I knelt at it again and was given the symbol of the Degree I had just taken, the Eye in the aura, and we walked down the aisle with the symbol standing out bright and golden over my forehead.

In their diaries relating to the *FIL* when they were working, at least nominally, under the aegis of Melchisedeck of Salem, "Himself" refers to that entity's lower representative, Lord Eldon, whom CCT was inclined to identify with Brodie-Innes in some sense. However, in this case it is almost certainly the High Priest of Ptah to whom she refers.

The Eye symbol emblazoned in the aura may well have been the Eye of Horus. Let Crowleyans make of that what they will. The idea of symbols being emblazoned in auras is a purely subjective thing, of course. Not every magician can see them, although a few evidently can. On the other hand initiates really do seem to have ways of recognizing their own; some see these symbols in the traditional manner: by pure clairvoyance. Others might find that an internal recognition chord is triggered off on clairaudient levels, while others just *know* they are in the presence of their kind.

If this Working saw CCT die and be reborn under the cosmic pro-genesis of Osiris and Isis, then this rebirth of hers took her, on June 22, into areas that were more truly Rosicrucian, and more closely attuned to what Felkin might have described as the Third or even Fourth Order. This is not a matter of Felkin having extended his "ladder of light" into the realms of extremity out of purely megalomaniac motives; it was simply a matter of different demarcation lines, and terminol-ogies.

> June 22, 1943. Present M.P.D., S.D., C.C.T.
> S. banished quite successfully, but there was a curious feeling when we sat down. M. spoke first, talking of darkness, S. said trees or a deep valley, and I detailed pines and a heavy storm overhead. The blackness grew greater and we all knew that something very unpleas-ant was going to happen. S. felt shivers down her spine and I felt very near fear, wondering how I would tackle a situation alone and feeling responsible. We all called on the A.A. of Earth and he responded, but that only lightened the blackness a little: M. said she saw wolves or leopards with green eyes, slinking in the trees and felt a wall of evil round us. I was impelled to join hands instead of just sitting touching, for I knew that something pretty nasty was around but I could not focus it. Then S. said, "We must call on someone, who do we want?" and into my subcon. came M.S. So I called on him, invoking him three times, and he came and stood between us, in his red robe and black velvet bonnet. And with his coming the whole place got lighter. And he created a triangle of golden light, about breast high, and instructed us to hold the bars of this as it lay between us, with himself standing in it. So we did this and it gave us great strength and the evil drifted further and further

away. And I got the impression that we were in some small danger since we had become helpers on the other side and that we should naturally be more liable to attack, notice having been drawn to us. Then M.S. changed under my eyes to C.R.C. and called me by my name and I felt that we had the protection of the Order. The darkness went right away, the light came like sunlight and we found ourselves in the hall on the mt. with the gold light coming through the gothic windows and the table spread as before and the big people in their chairs under the banners and Tony sitting there, laughing at us. He greeted me by saying that we had been in danger and reminding me that that was why he had sent back my spurs. The power and the beauty grew and grew and down a shaft of light came the cup and the dove and a hand above, and a voice that proclaimed the presence of God. And we took spiritual Communion by the piercing of our hearts by a shaft of golden light that rayed out from the cup, a ray to each person present. Then the vision faded and we came back very slowly and carefully by the mountain.

The "MS" referred to was, of course, Michael Scot, in his "red robe and black velvet bonnet," and the comment is so matter-of-fact that they had obviously made this contact many times before, although the records have not survived. As one of the inner Earth mages it is fitting that he should have taken over where the unhuman Archangel of Earth should have left off.

Significantly, the rite ends with what seems very like the coming of the Holy Grail to King Arthur's Court, at Pentecost—an occasion which was both the very height of Camelot's glory and its end. The cup, the dove, the hand, the voice and the presence could have come straight from Thomas Malory, but here it is *CRC*, Christian Rosencreutz, who makes his presence felt.

And, on consideration, it *was* the ending of a cycle. Seymour had by that time worked out a complete syllabus of study and work for the next few years which would take the lodge ever deeper into the Mysteries of Celtia, with special reference to the Welsh traditions, taking up the Merlin contact more surely and purely. Yet to everyone's astonishment and grief, the old Colonel who had taken them all into the emerald depths of the Green Ray died a couple of days later, following a routine operation. The revivification of the Merlin Temple slowly ground to a halt. Like the knights at Camelot, they all had to go out on their own and discover their own quests, and find their own Gods.

Some of them actually did.

All of this was unknown to them in that previous year, though, when on September 8, 1942, there was a very clear Rosicrucian-style

Working involving CCT, MPD and Margaret Irene Wilson, whom they called Weeny Wilson.

After a few moments there was a conviction of another presence in the room and it was apparent that a very substantial crystal wall was being built round the three, sitting in a triangle and all in personal contact.

A curious "departure" took place because, while conscious of the material bodies, C.C.T. saw the magical bodies in the temple with F.P.D. in the East, herself in the West, M.P.D. in the South and I.W. in the North; leaving them there as shells, the inner bodies (that is, the third layer) proceeded to the temple and gardens where the inner members of the Order reside. I.W. took over here and gave a very interesting description of the garden and of a new temple, built on the edge of the paved rose garden (scent of roses and sweetbriar very strong). All three described the temple subsequently and though perhaps C.C.T. led the work it was no more than leading.

The temple was long and narrow with tall pillars and arches making a very long and high central aisle; this was largely filled with unknown members; in the "choir stalls" sat some we knew, such as B.I. At the altar was a hierophant in scarlet robes whom I.W. thought she knew, though neither of the other two had seen him or could pick up his features. I.W. appeared to be leading the other two, one on either hand, up to the priest on the altar steps. He held up his right hand and in it was a kind of lamen—a red rose symbolically drawn, coiled in the center of a golden frame that was circular, and from which flames and light emanated. The quality of the vibrations running changed amazingly as he came forward. The "lamen" grew not only larger but acquired a solid depth so that before long it was enveloping all three of the "candidates," all in white robes. They turned to face inwards making a circle with the hierophant, and the golden frame surrounded them. Then they separated as the vision died away and were standing once more facing the altar. In the heart of each was the Rose (the bodies seemed to be transparent and it was quite clear to see, the only color in a clear glass-like body), and the three auras were gold and very much defined. The hierophant spread out his arms in the form of a cross, so that he included all three of the candidates. From his third eye came three shafts of golden light, each of which penetrated to the third eye of one candidate, and a shaft of white light poured down on his head. (The change in the vibrations was again most marked; the vitalizing of the entire aura was tremendous.) Then the light died away and the three women walked down the long temple to the west door, over which was a rose window in marvelous colors, which made a rainbow to the floor.

As they were going down the aisle there was the sound of singing and a great chant from all the order members. (Earlier the hierophant had spoken, but though at the time it was possible to give his words, they have gone.)

It seemed that the rainbow was the symbol of closing the ceremony; we walked through it and out into the courtyard and back into our magical bodies in our own temple and then back into our material bodies without any difficulty.

As this sitting was held with the express intention of experimenting with I.W.'s inability to "see," and in a lesser degree that of M.P.D., it might be considered to be extremely successful; both of them played a full part in describing what was going on and the positive power shifted between the three sitters almost equally.

If we see them here practicing their magic within the last days of the Merlin Temple, during the twilight of the Golden Dawn, at a time when Britain was fighting for its life against the Nazi evil, we must not think it all a purely escapist pursuit from the rigors, the terror, and the omnipresent demands of the war. The Order, by and large, consisted of people who were eminent in their professions, and they were all extremely active within these professions. Indeed they had to be to support their families. Unlike today, there was no such thing as a magus on social security. On top of their professional work they were all, in their various ways, involved in the war effort, as it was called, offering their skills, energy, and spare time within the multitude of civilian and military organizations that existed solely to prosecute the war as forcefully as possible. On top of *that*, after they had seen to the needs of their family, clients, and nation, they practiced magic. It was not whim, but necessity. Often, as any real magician can testify, this was the hardest of all.

Responding to the inner needs of the nation at this dire time, there were also Workings specifically devoted to battling the Darkness:

Present. F.P.D., M.P.D., S.I.R., F.A.F., A.

At the beginning M. was aware of T. coming and seating himself between her and S. so that he was in a direct line of contact with me. As it turned out this was for purposes of protection. During the "seeing" S. took over with her experiences which seemed to us to be definitely on a different plane; she broke the thread rather badly and added to the danger by calling on me by my own name, bringing me back to earth with a jerk. Had it not been for T. the shock would probably have been serious; as it was, it was sufficiently bad to be a warning but she was unable to break the picture up entirely. When she took over we were working in the complete astral; her vision seemed to be only on the emotional astral plane and therefore neither really suited the other.

We began by seeing the sea and the west coast of England; I was conscious of Merlin. K. had spoken of the nature spirits, but I got a very definite warning to keep away from them—a warning from T. And I was quite sure that that was not what we were meant to do. Then K. saw drowned men . . . sailors . . . quantities of them, which was rather sad but it was much sadder to go further out and find the drowned ships because the sailors had just left their bodies but the ships only had group souls and could not leave and they were all very unhappy. I saw the Victory the most clearly and some smaller ships and then I realized that what I was seeing was the port of drowned ships—the ships that had fought for England in the past. And there seemed a great stirring among them and we realized that they were being woken by Drake's drum, which was throbbing and beating through us all. The sailors came back to the ships and they rose to the surface and I saw Drake and Nelson on the bridge of one ship, discussing the campaign and who should be the leader.

And then I saw very clearly Merlin and K. saw the Woman Spirit, which came riding in from the sea in a chariot drawn by sea horses, and we realized that this was the spirit of Britannia, the presiding Goddess of Britain and the water. And above and over all was Gabriel.

Then astral contacts grew stronger and stronger; Gabriel in blue with his great wings overshadowing everything from horizon to horizon, turned and "floated" up the Channel, followed by the other two Great Ones and behind them came the fleet, spread out in a long crescent moon. And I saw a great flat sword, like a Crusader's sword, with its tip in Norway and the hilt about Dieppe, lying all along the coast, and it was guarding the line for us. Ahead of Gabriel went three "water spouts" (K.) but it seemed to us more like the three concentrations of power from the inner planes called down by the three leaders. Everything was ether and mist and billowy grey clouds. Gabriel took the sword and with the point of it he cleaved a way through the clouds which were veiling the sea, and through that lane came the ships of the line, one behind the other, and their wakes made a golden pathway that ringed us with protection. They went up the coast of Scotland, just as they chased the Armada, and round above the Orkneys and down on the outside of Ireland and so back to Plymouth Sound, and the gold ring was clear and bright everywhere. And then, while the ships sank to rest again, Gabriel took the sword and I saw him make four crosses, one on Iona, one on Holy Is., one on Glastonbury and one on the hidden Isle of Brendan. And then he took the sword again and made a last cross on Orme's Head, so that we had all the holy places made sacred.

Then the vision faded and I was left with Merlin and myself, Morgan, on the hill, with the turf altar between us and the wind in the long grass, and over the whole of the country was the blue light from Merlin's stone as a token of protection and blessing.

The reference to Drake's drum seems like mytho-poetic fantasy, but there is in fact a long tradition in England which has Sir Francis as another of those individuals who, in times of national distress, once donned the mantle of the Pendragon. Many serious and sober people have testified that they have heard Drake's drum, which is said to start beating in times of grave danger, do exactly that during the First and Second World Wars. The old adventurer has even been associated with the legends of the Wild Hunt, and linked with that as its actual leader. The whole saga is an analogue of the Arthurian myth in which that King sleeps in his cave until similar moments of national emergency. Drake and Arthur are not separate entities: they are parallels. They vibrate to the same note but in different octaves.

Oddly enough Dion also had a very similar vision of a great sword stretching across nations, but lying over into France in this case, down into her African colonies.*

And odd, too, is the comment: "And then he took the sword again and made a last cross on Orme's Head, so that we had all the Holy places made sacred.' This brings us back to the dragons again, and the energies of the Earth that they embody.

Another of the workings which was intimately involved with the Spirit of the Land and the composition of the nation occurred earlier, on August 2, 1942. The "Fire of Azrael" referred to is an example of witchery once taught within the *FIL*, and described in *The Sea Priestess*. Such a fire was intended to stimulate the sight, when the aspiring seer peered deep into the glowing embers.

It is significant that the oak, ash and thorn should appear for these trees were sacred to the ancient cults which worked magic in Britain in megalithic times. Puck, meanwhile, is something of a king within the realms of faery, a pranksterish version of Herne, and it is interesting to see the concept of "seizin" appearing here just as it would within the magical workings of Geoff Hughes, forty years later.

> 8/2/42. Moon waning.
> 2nd sitting. Present as before.
>   Talking about Fires of Azrael: T. suggested we might do something with oak and ash and thorn as we could not get juniper. General discussion and C.C.T. offered to see what could be done next day. Suddenly a big oak tree grew in the N.E. corner of the room. An ash sprang up in the S.W. corner and a thorn in full bloom between them. Almost before we had taken this in, the power came down in full force.
>   *C.C.T.'s memory.* I seemed to grow about seven feet high and to be entirely slender, like a birch tree. I could not move my feet. I was standing upright by this time, physically as well as astrally and the power was pouring through me. I turned to T., who was sitting on my left (my eyes were closed all the time and turned right round on my waist muscles

---

* See *Priestess: The Life and Magic of Dion Fortune*, by Alan Richardson.

only, my legs being rooted). Green light was pouring out of my fingers which were proportionately long and very slender, rather like twigs. I heard a voice from my throat saying "By oak and ash and thorn, I consecrate you: by oak and ash and thorn I fortify you: by oak and ash and thorn I protect you."* Then the power seemed to stream through me: I had also looked for Puck and knew that he was near me and I had mentally invoked by the Kipling charm. I turned back after pouring in the power and raised my arms high above my head, and then spread them out, turning my left hand down so as to disperse the power. Eventually I sat down.

T.'s memory. T. says he saw the power pouring out of me into him and that he too was mentally using the Kipling charm and then his own. *Retrospect.* He saw the Saxons, Danes, Normans and others who make England and felt the oak and ash and thorn stuck fast into his aura. He also saw Puck materializing through me, and the green light pouring off me.

M.'s memory. Very thick etheric mist through the room: she saw me veiled in black but with long green arms and hands. She saw dryads and other earth elementals over the place. (All this in addition to the other general impressions.)

S.'s memory. The shadows of the fairies in the corner and the tremendous overcrowding of the room with the elementals. (All this in addition.)

If these magicians were involved with bringing starry energies down to the Earth, as in the Working described on page 83, then they were equally bound to raise the underworld forces to the heavens. If CCT lived in the Earth and via the Earth, then that planet also lived via her—and any other priest or priestess who links with its energies. *The Earth needs to experience human life just as much as we need to touch on the elemental.*

This power is very clear during the 4-7 initiation of V.V. relating to the sphere of Netzach, and thus "inner Earth."

2/7/42
Present K.H., D.I.M., C.D., K., F.A.F.

A curious ceremony in which the only power was in the invocation of the elementals and in their banishing, and they were very polite elementals. The power otherwise was almost all in the astral. Felt it once during one of the pronouncements, but otherwise the God-Forms never came down. Could not give much to it myself as the actual ritual required a great deal for an unpracticed person. Saw the symbol of the grade burning with intense solid brilliance on V.V.'s head during the last part of the ceremony. Pushed the power into her myself as I felt it was not going from the H(ierophant) Very strong wind around the T(emple) at the beginning but not later.

---

* "By oak, ash and thorn I give you seizin of England."

Work was done in a more intense fashion with a particular element on August 11 that same year.

8/11/42
At Kim's. Present F.P.D., D.I.M., S.MP.D., C.C.T.
    Before any business began I was in the T. by myself when T. came looking very pleased with life and robed in the manner of the High Priests of Egypt. He called me over to the altar and I said, "What do you mean?" And he replied, "Come along, we have some work to do." I found myself with hands raised opposite him over the altar and he was giving me an initiation—I was surprised at receiving it from him but just as I was getting down to what it meant K. came in and I had to replace the blue chalice which I had just picked up for a mutual drinking.
    When we settled down to work on the last path I realized that as K. wanted us to remain seated and yet move round that I would be too busy to deal with S. She was seated in the North and I got her to move a chair so that a second one was placed beside her and between her and me. I then summoned T. and told him that as I was busy I would put S. in his charge. I had already sealed her. I saw him pass a ring round her and left him to get on with the job.
    The power was tremendous when K. began invoking the elements. When he came over to me and invoked I had more awareness of water than usual. I suddenly choked and got a mouthful of salt water. I was standing in my magical body in a sea that was so deep that I had to tread water to keep my mouth above it. Then I realized that I could and must control the element and I so established myself that I was swimming lightly and the great rollers were under me. It was wide and wonderful ahead and I had a great desire to go far out. I heard the sea women calling me, saying "Morgan, sea woman, come back to your own:" and "Morag, little seal, come out to the ocean." Suddenly T.'s hand clamped down on my left shoulder and pulled me upright and he said, "Morgan, have you forgotten your solemn promise! What on earth use is a dripping mermaid to me as a priestess?" And then I remembered and came back to land and dealt with the matters in hand. When K. finally closed, I held myself very tightly together and just saw the golden Temple of P. at the back of the wall.
    After the bulk of the work K. gave us an instruction-dissertation of what he had seen and what we were to do. As soon as this began S. crossed her left knee over her right and her right hand over her left one on her lap and went off to sleep. I did not mind her going to sleep— one can be tired—but she ought to know better than to cut the currents and short-circuit in that way. I considered that as she was deliberately cutting herself off there could be no danger and I had already sealed the door and had been sitting with my sword gripped in my hand.
    I don't understand this water business because it has never had any attraction for me before. ? T. in re Morgan and polarizing.

S., like so many people who make the elemental contacts, lived to a ripe old age but her interest in magic seems to have died with the Merlin Temple. T., who was taking over more and more from Seymour with that man's full permission and encouragement was soon to lose his own heart for the topic while finishing the war in a Japanese P.O.W. camp.

There is an interesting if rather strange account in T.'s own words in which he describes a series of events whereby Su, who was obviously a tiresome young woman at times, became the link through which the dark forces could attack the lodge.

He gave a timetable of events:

Day 1. Sunday	Discussion on S. Decision to act. Course of action not decided on. (M.P.D., C.C.T., Self)
Day 2. Monday	Course of action decided on and checked with B.I. Eleven o'clock sessions to insulate S. from shadow. 1st effort undertaken with immediate and powerful backlash. Assumed success. (Sue, M., C.C.T., Self.)
Day 3. Tuesday	Eleven o'clock again. Decided to return shadow whence it came. Operation successful. Sue remained for night. (Sue, M., C.C.T., Self.)
Day 4. Wednesday	Battle considered won; feasting and rejoicing. C.C.T. and self returning Latymer Court solo. Found on arrival letter from S. which we ignored. 11 o'clock. Checked up on S. O.K. Commenced blackout. Thought of letter and decided to destroy by fire. During this operation vile smell to physical level and attempted materialization. Dealt with. Banishing ritual and room sealed. Became fort for night. Fort held. (C.C.T. and Self.)
Day 5. Thursday	Decided matter must be cleared up. Checked B.I. Orders hold fort for night. Strong temple built for . . . Held just. Nasty incident M.N. Just got C.C.T. back. General unwillingness to stand *fast* till dawn. Managed just. Had reached almost end of my tether. (M., C.C.T., Self.)
Aftermath	Astral hangover having bad effect on physical plane. Overcome by earthing and careful banishing.

On a separate sheet one of the participants goes into greater detail, although it is not certain if this is CCT writing, or T. using her typewriter.

Report of conversation with B.I. on 7/17/42 and action taken. Duration—approx. 45 min.

Held magic mirror very still and was able to have long conversation, all in regard to the experiment with S.

The awakening of the forces against us is due to the fact that the lodge has suddenly become militant and active: while it was merely passive, religious and intellectual it was not worth powder and shot. Now that K. has woken it up and the ranks have been swelled by active members it is becoming a danger to the black forces—especially in view of K.'s work. Primarily, it is K. they want. He has been too careful for them in his personal work and has guarded the rest of us too carefully—neither are we open to the opposition, never having put ourselves in their power. S. had the contact for which they had been waiting and watching and using her as an instrument they were planning to get inside the lodge and wreck it and K. Our job was to prevent that—which it seems that we have done. Our present work is to keep the place clear and to be careful that no entry can be made.

I inquired about the show and my instructions were to insulate S. with the S.S. on arrival. When I got there I found she and K. were already there but that the personality I feared had not arrived. Long before she came I had thrown the S.S. over S.'s s.p. It was glowing and fiery—bright gold and subsequently red and blue. I kept on renewing it but it was obvious that there was no opposition. We had truly cleared the path round her. She seemed utterly drained and though this can be largely attributed to physical and mental reaction to her troubles, at the same time I think one can allocate a good deal of it to the destruction we wrought. Her eyes are clearer but she looks like a shell—animated but subdued.

When the exhibitor arrived she showed little if any interest: I renewed the S.S. promptly and firmly but it needed little strengthening: it was extraordinarily clear. We left soon after and I put a banishing pentagram on S.'s back behind the seal as she left, so as to stop anything from trying to follow.

Later on we remembered she had bought a catalogue so while she was out of the room I found it and exorcised it so that there should be no possibility of contact.

The pictures were magnetized and all wrong in their inner selves.*

The "S.S." is presumably Solomon's Seal of interlinked Triangles.

---

* It would be interesting to learn when Crowley gave the first public exhibition of his tarot cards, as painted by Lady Freida Harris. Seymour went with CCT and pointed out the Great Beast to her. They even bought a tarot deck but Seymour was very careful to "de-magnetize" it before use, making some comments about Crowley's tricks as he did so. The catalogue referred to might just apply to this exhibition. Certainly the magnetizing of such literature is an old and greyly magical practice.

Another sheet is appended in which an actual magical battle is described in which they fought, one presumes, for the very safety of Su's being.

8/3/42. Meeting. 6 p.m.
Present. F.P.D., C.D., D.I.M., A.F.D., V.V., B.M.D., F.A.F.

Quite unprepared for meeting when we arrived for a tea and talk and all very irritated and annoyed. F.P.D. insistent. F.A.F. in bad temper and practically refusing to play. A.F.D. insisted that in the end it was the best solution of the trouble and in any case it was definitely intended as the extra backing up was necessary.

Started badly but the place settled down a little, though it was impossible for F.A.F. to get the usual contacts. Suddenly realized that to allow any loophole would be to play into the enemy's hands and therefore set up and determined to pull down all the power in the world if required.

Waited rather tensely for S., who came in, looking much better and rather "hollow." Did all possible to knock her out during reaffirmation, done with deliberate intent in order to get the matter definite once and for all so far as that ceremony was concerned. S. went through with it, but looked a bit shaken up. Became aware that there was trouble brewing outside the door and there was no one on guard. As soon as long work had been finished, shot outside and found the enemy sneaking up the staircase. Pushed them back and knew that as the Keeper of the Door of the West no one else could do the job at that particular moment. Sword in my hand for a purpose. At first interval sent S. out with an S.S. round her and hoped. Went out all the time in my God-Form—and how!

During second part, spent all time not actually working out on the landing, having a grand scrap with a bayonet fight with a sword. Sent umpteen things down the stairs. When necessary to dash back for reading, formulated a huge Michael and asked him to hold the door. Most of the time we were scrapping together—he in gold and red and I in black and silver—just in my robes, couldn't keep on putting on armor and taking it off again. Was outside the door so long that I thought F.P.D. would realize I was missing from my seat but apparently he did not notice.

At second interval, spoke to A.F.D. and asked for help. Got told off good and proper for not realizing that (a) he had been doing it all the time and (b) that I should not try and do things like that alone. He had been formulating a better M. than mine with all sorts of extra trimmings and decorations. He had put our sword through the door. He said my job was to be inside and to guard S. there. So I retired rather ungraciously and for the third section remained in the T. and left him to have the outside activity. Probably wise as I was completely worn out by then with the power on both sides of the door; we had pretty well burnt S. out with cleansing by that time, and it was a question more of holding her steady than of pouring in power. The show was a great success, so far as we could tell: we brought her in clean and we purged and purified and sent her out as filled with new power as we could and beyond that we cannot do anything. Throughout the ceremony there was a great howling wind round the T. Horrible wind—expected to hear the hounds at any moment. B.M.D. did hear them? (She thinks it was a physical dog-row; A.F.D. and I not sure but no one else seems to have heard it.)

Difficult moment when C.D. knocked my lamp over and it went out: had it been broken should have been troubled. A.F.D. held it burning astrally (full marks—I didn't think of that) and fixed it again—but it made one anxious. He reported stairs very unpleasant indeed. Wonder if the seniors know anything. Curious emphasis on certain points of the ritual and exhortation, giving one to think. Tried to contact B.I. after supper; not very clear, but pretty certain of his presence; A.F.D. saw him in regalia. He was satisfied with us. Spurs very bright.

Quite realize now why the whole affair had to be unexpected. No time for opposing forces to gather and most important that V.V. and I, being the only two with knowledge, should have all the help we could in active warfare. Don't care to think what might have happened had we been alone. B.M.D. coming on magnificently.

Wearied but apparently triumphant, AFD and CCT jot down their separate conclusions about what the former described as "the weird days":

Conclusions from A.F.D.
1. Be sure of your fort and do not quit it on any account.
2. Never lose confidence but avoid the ostrich technique.
3. Magical images will keep and gain strength if "fed" at intervals.
4. Real opposition largely on fickleness of mind. Boredom, unbelief, apparent lack of happenings, etc.
5. Do not be tempted to visualize opponent.
6. Alertness must happen in turns.
7. Remember an image is the instrument of the will. Any image is better than none. The greatest danger is blankness or a formless outgoing of power. The latter especially may be used by an opponent to strengthen *his* image. Make your image and *believe* in it and it will be real and alive.
8. The Ban. Rit. clears a space for a fortress to be built. That space should *not* be left empty.
9. While not overestimating or underestimating the enemy, it is wise to plan clearly and calmly for all eventualities which you can perceive, and run over one's magical armory, for by thinking of it, one vivifies it.
10. Above all, only take on an opponent when ordered by those in command and then only in the knowledge and surety of their protection.

They know, we only guess.
They act, we only build the forms.

Notes and Conclusions (CCT) 7/8/42.
  Before embarking on warfare make sure that the fortress is secured in every direction and in every possible way. The enemy is able to enter by *every* aperture. The strongest defense possible is the S(olomon's) S(eal). (ref. Westcott.)
  While not underestimating the enemy, do not overestimate his strength; complete confidence is the greatest weapon.
  Do not send out a scout while the attack is proceeding. The benefit of news brought back may be entirely counterbalanced by the damage to the personnel and the need for immediate first-aid at a time when all concentration should be on the enemy. It is opening a door for the entry of the opposing force.
  Conclusion. Fools may be protected once but have no right to expect it twice.

  So far it is possible to divide the diaries into fairly distinct sections: There are the visions of the Chiefs, whereby the more experienced members make their contacts with the inner hierarchies; the Egyptian Workings, which often slide into the realms of what may be called far memories; a sub-group which comprises inward initiations, plus one account of someone's entry into the 4-7 Degree; two examples of magical warfare—one for self-defense and one for the defense of the nation; plus a few elemental Workings. These categories often overlap.

  The rest of the entries are far memories pure and simple. Chronologically speaking, almost all of these occurred in the early days of CCT's and FPD's entry into the Merlin Temple. As noted, this sort of thing is invariably one of the first spin-offs when a person comes to link with the collective consciousness of any group. As we have reiterated time and time again they are to be used and eventually outgrown. In this case at least they do fit rather neatly into the concept of the tribal vision, and can tell a story within a story if you know where to look.

  Not all of them are worth reprinting, however. Like youthful poems or bad rituals, they are of interest only to their creators. They include memories of Atlantis, of the Cathars, the Romans along the Wall, two contacts with the Sacred College of the East via the Most Precious One (the Dalai Lama), two more fleeting visions of Drake after his return in the Golden Hinde, two of Bonny Prince Charlie's era where Masonic connections come up quite strongly, several episodes among the Norsemen; and a couple of insignificant memories of obscure lives in medieval France and England.

What is striking is the similarity in era and locale to those far memories hinted at by Dion Fortune in her various novels: she had been burnt at the stake in Avignon; she had left Atlantis before the final cataclysm; she had had at least one life as a Viking princess, and had been something of a virgin priestess in ancient Rome.

CCT's visions never quite go into Rome itself however. Whatever Roman influence existed within her psyche was intimately connected with Hadrian's Wall. (Long before I had ever heard of Dion Fortune, Seymour, Magic, or the Western Mystery Tradition, I too picked up something of old FPD's essence at the still-resonant Temple of Mithras which lies on the bare green lands overlooking the South Tyne. Once, I dared to take my wife into this male-only sanctuary and found that when we got back to the car the entire electrical systems had failed.)

This particular Roman/Viking memory reads as follows:

Date—Uncertain—late June or early July.
Present. A.F.D., B.M.D., C.C.T.
　　Found ourselves in Scandinavia. There was a long ship in a fjord and a little cluster of houses on the shore. The ship was making ready to go to sea. T. came out of the largest house and went up to the gangplank: he was wearing Viking armor, with a huge helmet with horsehair, and carried the sword. He turned at the foot of the plank and went back a step or two to embrace a woman—apparently his wife. She was large and ample in shape, with long plaits of hair and very red cheeks and blue eyes—a full armful of a woman. He kissed her boisterously, shouting with joy and hurried up on board, where his men were already waiting.
　　We followed the ship through the water till she came to the coast of Scotland (N. Britain) and then I recognized the place and the whole story. It was the Viking ship that came to the Wall after I had been taken prisoner by the Romans and was there with K. and N.N. T. was my brother who came over to fetch me back. They beached the boat and sent a party ashore—one very fat man fell in the water and T. laughed uproariously.
　　The "mission" went up to the Wall. That was when K. would have let me go but I refused because I liked him and I liked the Wall. The Vikings thereupon determined to attack and they did so after dark. It blacked out a good deal then, but when the sun rose, the longships were on fire and only one or two of them were left. There were dead

men all along the foreshore and at the foot of the Wall. T. escaped and took his boat back to Scandinavia but the attack as a whole failed completely.

The point that struck us all was the complete absence of any personal affection between T. and myself: I was his sister and therefore he went to try and get me back but he did not mind in the least my refusing to come: I think he preferred it because had I gone he would have had no reasonable excuse for fighting—which was what he wanted. I had no desire to leave the Romans—I think I liked the higher standard of civilization and I was definitely intrigued by their gods (K. and N.N. were Mithras worshippers), and I had a great admiration for K.

Actually it is something of a "re-memory," a recall of something that had been picked up some years earlier, in May 1938. Seymour's vision, taken here from my *Dancers to the Gods*, is worth looking at.

Tuesday May 10th, 1938

Weather fine and much warmer. Self fit. CCT worried over private affairs. Began at 8:30 ended 10:15 p.m. Moon 4 days after First Qtr.

Banished with Pentagram beforehand, room felt very peaceful. Odin came up very strongly and gave CCT a message. His image was very clear. Then as usual as we began to open the centers, but I suddenly found myself standing on a wet cold afternoon at the tower by the Eastern end of Hadrian's Wall. There was a wild red cloudy early sunset behind me, and I was looking at a headland. I was a Roman officer but I think of Germanic birth or at any rate born on the Rhine and Germanic in ideas though an initiate of Mithra. Beside me stood my subaltern, a fair boy about nineteen and I recognized him for N.N. and I was very fond of him. As I watched I saw the long galleys come round the headland—about twenty of them. And I knew the Roman fleets that used to protect the Wall by sea had gone. Our flank was being turned. Then our commander joined me—I recognized him for General Orton whom in this life I had known in India. A very fine soldier (CCT I did not see).

The trumpets went and in the afternoon drizzle and mist the men fell in and we hid 'en echelon' in the heather and mounds just above high water mark, with the light troops and slingers, and a few bowmen in front on the beach and out covering our right flank. We had about 400 men in all. The tide was far out over the mud flats.

The ships came in rather carelessly one after the other and beached in a long line. They had perhaps 300 men, and they were led by a huge man with the design of an eagle on the sails of his ship. Their crews jumped into the mud and directly they landed we charged and in five minutes the raiders' right wing was smashed.

Then the raiders' center and left wing got on land formed at right angles to the sea and charged our right. When they were well into the attack our reserves echeloned behind right charged, took them in flank and that was soon over and the remainder of the raiders ran for the ships, leaving their leader dead. We then set to work to kill the wounded and strip the dead of weapons. N.N. discovered beside the dead chief a girl of sixteen dressed as a man. (CCT had now come into the picture.) She was senseless from a blow on the head (I had a hell of a headache after this,), and at N.N.'s suggestion she was carted up to the tower. The dead leader we found was a celebrated pirate and raider. His name I think was Wolfmar. The actual fight was very short and quick and was over long before dark. N.N. wanted CCT for ransom.

We tried to get information out of CCT and learned that the other half of Wolfmar's fleet was near at hand and they were under the impression that the Roman legion had gone and had expected to find only a few native British troops. I promised CCT swearing by Odin, that if they came back I would give her her liberty if she would be quiet. N.N. tried to take CCT's dagger from her and I watched with considerable amusement a scrap between the two in which the big boned Norse girl scratched and smacked my tall slight good looking subaltern thoroughly. I laughed but N.N. wanted to cut her throat, and for some reason seemed jealous of the interest I took in the girl. Then he and I went to the Mithraic chapel under the wall where I took the silent meditation as the senior Initiate. The night went quickly and at dawn the alarm was given that the complete fleet was coming back. I made CCT put on Roman armor and a helmet and we formed up again in the same place. But before their attack began reinforcements came into view and we were more than stronger than the raiders who drew off out into the bay.

Then a small single ship came in. They asked for the chieftain's body and his daughter. I was on the tower with CCT and N.N. and fed up with the fighting between them told CCT who reminded me of my oath by Odin that she could go.

She went about half way to the shore with N.N. when he suddenly brought her back and said she was too valuable a hostage. I agreed and kept her in spite of my oath, and her reproaches.

Finally I went down to the beach with CCT and the interpreter and met a rather crafty looking raider who had come off to parly.

FPD

The N.N. in question was very probably Dr. Felkin's son Laurence, whom Ithell Colquhoun gives as one of the original initiates of the Amoun Temple.

The memory of the Cathars is also an important one, although more for the implications than the content. Today, the pursuit of those medieval French heretics has become something of a fad, and one begun in part by Dr. Arthur Guirdham's series of books on the topic—notably *The Cathars and Reincarnation*. This is, in fact, one of the very few really convincing books on reincarnation and one which manages to fling up at the same time some radically different insights into the human condition.*

In brief, the Cathars were a sect of Dualist-inclined Christians who lived in the south of what is now known as France. Over a period of time they were persecuted and all but wiped out by the righteous forces of Roman Christianity. Even today, even after the great amounts of publicity given to Dr. Guirdham's extraordinary experiences, the Cathars are hardly household names. In 1942, when this particular memory came through (which is also a re-memory like the one about the Wall) the number of people interested in them must have been minimal. It is curious therefore that in this year, almost 30 years before the long-dead revenants appeared within Dr. Guirdham's own inner life, he should have taken some novel manuscripts to the offices of Christine Campbell Thomson to try and get them placed. The novels in question had nothing to do with the topic, nor did Dr. Guirdham know anything of CCT's own current Cathar preoccupations. Neither did she guess at the saga in which he would one day become so profoundly involved. Somehow, with no apparent consequence throughout the years but the retelling of this anecdote now, those two unique wayfarers were drawn together. Even more, Dr. Guirdham had once worked in the same hospital as Penry Evans, who was no doubt as involved with the heretics of Avignon and Montsegur as his wife.

7/24/42.
Sitting; M.P.D., A.F.D, C.C.T.
Moon in third quarter. Weather dry and fairly warm.
Sat down with the deliberate intention of finding if possible the Templar connection between T. and S. The picture came very clearly and quickly—a young knight riding over a hill between trees; behind him were twenty-four men at arms in half armor, riding in six rows of four. Just behind the knight rode his squire, carrying his helmet. There was sun on the road, which was very white. They rode down the hill and then it seemed clear that they were going to Avignon; I could see the bridge at the bottom of the steep hill by the market place and the horror started to come down. They rode up the hill very slowly, pushing among the people until they came to an inn where the men at arms stopped and the knight and his squire rode on alone to the Palais des Papes. There the squire dismounted and held the knight's horse; in the courtyard an elderly man came down some steps to meet him; he was

---

* Ian Wilson's *Mind out of Time* refused to consider Dr. Guirdham's experiences as worthy of detailed analysis—for reasons that are not at all convincing. Nevertheless this brilliant and often harrowing analysis of reincarnatory sagas should be compulsory reading for all would-be far seers.

grey-haired and worried. The knight (he was in purple with a flat cap with a badge in it) greeted him with a smile but there was a great atmosphere of trouble. Then the knight turned to the squire and drew a big blue ring from his finger and gave it to him and said something that could not be heard. Then he and the other man walked up the steps and into the palais. They passed through a big hall (the one where there is the fireplace and the painted ceiling) and there were a lot of people in the corners of the room—I saw myself and K. among others. But the knight went through to a little room where there was a man sitting behind a table; small and swarthy with a short black beard (just a tuft) and very keen black eyes. He had parchments in front of him and he handed one to the knight. He read it and started to tear it across and said "Je m'en fiche." But someone (either the man at the table or the grey-haired man) said "Il vent mieux signer," and he signed it after reading it again.

Then everything blacked out for a bit and when it came again there was the procession to the stakes in the square at the bottom of the hill. K. and I went first . . . I remember wearing white . . . and T. behind with Su . . . there were a lot of people. K. was passing the word back that we were not to be afraid. There was a very hostile crowd in the streets and they shouted and threw stones. I did not like it at all. We seemed to stumble down the cobbled hill to the square at the end and there they had built stakes in a semi-circle. They put me at the head of it with K. on one side and T. on the other. T. was talking to me out of the corner of his mouth; I could just see him if I twisted round and I told him to watch the crowd beyond the soldiers. Suddenly I saw O.* in the crowd as before and though I knew it would happen, the shock was almost worse than the first time. Then the other horror began because we found S. standing in a group of monks (T. saw this, not I, as I was too shaken for the moment). And someone (he thinks I did) said "Mais, c'est Jeannette!" And she came forward with a horrible look on her face (wearing dark, sage green) and herself lit the pyre. I think the wood was damp because I seem to remember awful smoke but my mind was concentrating on finding the man at the back of the crowd and I made T. look for him. He stood there, as before, and raised his hand and made the sign and gave the word and all pain ceased and the picture blacked out as we died.

All rather shaken, especially T., to whom it was new. The picture of S. was horribly clear and though we had set out with the intention of finding if possible how she fitted in, neither of us was quite prepared for the horror of finding that she had actually been in love with T., had betrayed him in the hope of getting him to recant and be pardoned through her good offices, and had then justified her own bigoted outlook by herself acting as firelighter. Her face was terrible.

The Templar connection often crops up within the compulsions of British occultism in particular, but Western occultism generally.

---

* Oliver Cook, her first husband.

Like the Cathars, the Templars were dualists, believing in a perpetual war between light and darkness. Tradition has long had it that Scottish Freemasonry, of which Seymour and (probably) Anthony Daw were initiates, derived from Templar sources. If nothing else it left these people with a profound belief in the very real existence of evil. Although Fortune was to try and categorize the types of evil and analyze them accordingly, few of the magicians within the Golden Dawn would deny its existence. Indeed, it is only because modern psychology has largely managed to "explain it away" that belief in the power of darkness has waned. While Dion herself might well have debated such dubious concepts as "positive evil" and "negative evil," she was under no illusions that people existed on this Earth and within the Otherworld who were utterly, utterly malign, without the slightest sense of order within, or the least spark of light. Some modern magicians believe that the balance of the perpetual war which exists between the light and the darkness has been upset by atomic experiments. These experiments, they feel, have punctured the fabric of our universe in such a way that entities from other dimensions have appeared which should *never* have entered our realms, and which would never have done so in the pre-atomic era, hence the peculiar barbarisms that are becoming almost everyday events within this post-Hiroshima world.

Of course it all harkens back in some ways to the concept of Atlantis, which was supposedly destroyed by the priesthood of that land misusing the stellar powers they had learned to harness. Sometimes, these visions of the past are often prophecies of things to come.

The Atlantean vision in this case was an essentially charming one however, if completely lacking in the convincing intensities of vision achieved by Dion and privately printed within her lodge. On the other hand these are memories of a childhood in that land, and have no need to detail the rites, powers, and social structures of the lost continent.

Really, Atlantis is something of a key vision to this particular tribe. It is something that seems to be picked up from the onset of linking with the group mind. Atlantis to these magicians is the dreamtime, the Golden Age—though not one that all magicians can accept.*

---

* The best descriptions of Atlantis are to be found in Dion Fortune's *The Sea Priestess*. Incidentally, she had none of the visions of Atlantean super-technology that the more excitable writers insist upon today. There is, I have discovered, a near-infallible guide as to the value of any technical book on occultism: if it contains more than four exclamation marks in the entire text it can be safely thrown in the wastebasket.

Atlantis

8/4/42.

Present. A.F.D., M.P.D.?, B.M.D. C.C.T.

Prepared for anything; contacted B.I. who gave his one-sided smile and then granted A.F.D.'s wish to "see how it all began."

Went back to Atlantis. We four were in a small boat, rather like a broad dinghy with a sail like a Yorkshire Billy Boy—purple. The sea must have been very smooth for the boat had a remarkably shallow draught. M. and I were lying around, S. was hanging over the stern playing with a basket of fish we had caught and T. was doing the work. S. remarked on the tremendous height of the island one. I reminded her that it was the first time we had seen it from the water and level and that we were under the peak itself with the Sun Temple on top and the cliffs there went sheer down into the water. We were at the extreme north (?) end of the island. T. said there was a way up the cliff and that he knew of a young priest who had once done it; we all protested against making the attempt. He pulled the boat round the point and we found a shallow stream running into the sea. We decided to go up it and explore instead of going to the proper landing-stage.

(N.B. We were all young—M. about seventeen and T. the same. I was about fifteen and S. a year younger; we were T. children waiting to grow up. I was just about ready to take on the new life of a priestess. M. was senior and already a priestess and more or less in charge of the outing. T. and I were, I think, known to be about to be mated in the mysteries, though I am not quite sure if we ourselves knew this at this stage or whether it was so natural that we took it for granted. Certainly it did not enter our ordinary consciousness.)

We pulled up the stream, which was little more than a backwater and through a tunnel and came out at the little beach where the Death Ship of the High Priest is launched. There was a sharp bend in the water there and though I had been down once to the launching, I had never seen that backwater. All I knew was the swiftly flowing stream under the tunnel where the Death Ship went. The devil entered into all of us (I think M. and I were the ringleaders) and we agreed to take the boat down the sacred stream. The current here was pretty swift and we went down at a good pace: suddenly M. said she heard falling water; we listened and there was the sound of a very deep waterfall. We did not like it at all. Our little boat swept round a bend and we could see the stream falling over the lip of a tremendous chasm and then we knew what happened to the dead High Priest in his barge. T. took command; he saw something in the shape of a guardian of the waterfall and he knew also at that moment that that was the most sacred place of all, where the new High Priest took over the Apostolic Succession just as his predecessor went over the fall. There was a chain fixed across the river which catching under the flat-bottomed barge, swung it round and tipped the sacred burden into the depths. T. was instructed by someone on the other side that we were to jump for it to a little ledge on the left hand bank. We scrambled ashore somehow (I was not very clear about it) but we all got very wet and managed to save our lives by hanging on to the chain. The pressure of the water was terrific and of course the boat went over like a stone. S. kept complaining how wet she was (she wasn't any wetter than anyone else) and we struggled up footholds in the cliff side— seemed to be metal footholds like steep steps. As we went I knew where we were coming out and didn't like it at all. We came to a door in the rock and T. opened it with the magic word of the priests—which I liked still less. We went up a more regular staircase, up and up and round and round in the rock. There was a door at the top and I knew that it led into the priests' room at the temple—a very "grown-up" place. T. said he didn't know how to open the door and I said very tartly "Turn the handle, of course," to which he replied that he didn't know "it was that sort of door." We were all very wet and very cross and very frightened of the consequences. Even M.'s buoyancy and continual remarks that it had been worth it seemed to have dried up a bit.

We opened the door and filed in. As we expected, the room was not empty. It was a circular room and at a desk or table in the middle was K. He was one of the senior priests. He looked at us and never said anything and we seemed to grow smaller and smaller. Then he told us to go and get dry clothes and then to report back. We seemed to slink out of the room and went to our separate quarters.

A little later we found ourselves back in the round room. There were three or four senior priests there as well as K. The whole thing was so horrible that it is difficult to get it into words because it was so much on the astral and it was so much in a sense a moral scolding. I think I would have preferred to have been beaten and done with it. We had our sashes taken away and we were shut off from all our magical contacts for an unspecified period while the elders considered what to do with us. We went out on the terrace and I started kicking stones about and S. hung over the wall and fingered the roses and M. started to be bright and helpful about occupations, and T. went off to the priests' quarters in a furious temper. I know I hung over the wall with S. and said that as we were shut out of the temple working nothing mattered and why shouldn't we go down the mountain and explore the soldiers' and craftsmen's quarters on the second shoulder, as nothing could be worse than what we were going through. I think T. came back then and we quarrelled about it, but I am not sure. The picture got a little blotted at intervals.

After a time (weeks, I think) I was sent for by myself and had to interview the High Priest. It was very sticky. I got the biggest dressing-down I have ever had because the worst of the fault was mine. I was of the blood, I was supposed to be growing up and on the point of taking on my priestess estate and I had helped to lead S. into committing sacrilege—that was our crime and the only thing that really saved us was that (a) it was not deliberate and (b) the powers had saved us and therefore the priests felt that it was intended that we should live because otherwise we should have been swept over the abyss.

Eventually we were told to appear before the full council of priests and we arrived—very nervous and very ashamed. I think T. had been working in the priests' quarters all the time for there seemed to be no contact between us and we reckoned the time as about three months. The roses on the wall were dead and the wind seemed colder. S. says that she thinks we were put on to some sort of fatigues but I can't remember—nothing mattered when one was cut off from the magic power. There was a very grave homily from the High Priest, and it was not possible to hear it because it was in Atlantean. The gist of it seemed to be however that M. was to be sent to the other island to do new work there and that S. and I would be reinstated at the next zodiacal transit (in a day or two) but that we would probably have to work it out in some form of karma—this certainly for me, if not for her. T. was I think to be sterilized so that he could not function as a High Priest in the fullness of the mating.

There was a very unhappy meeting on the terrace; M. was heart-broken at leaving us (incidentally she had a short vision on her own during the interview, when she went down into the bowels of the mountain in the astral and saw pain and suffering spread before her—it must have been something to do with her new work). T. and I were not really on speaking terms—only on spitting terms. S. who seemed curiously plump and placid, was making the best of things philo-sophically.

Then I took the matter into my own hands and I *demanded* an inter-view with the High Priest. Why I got it, I don't quite know but I did. I marched in with my chin up and seemed to tell him that if I could not be mated with T. I wouldn't carry on as a High Priestess . . . that it was both of us or neither and that I was as responsible as he, if not more so. He had been sent for and was standing there, saying he would rather undergo anything than be mated with me. The High Priest just sat there at the table with his chin on his hand and looked at me with a crinkle of amusement. I remember stamping my foot (which shook T. a bit) and generally carrying on magnificently. I think the High Priest was a little amused; I seem to remember his saying to T. that he thought probably the worst punishment he could inflict would be the fact that he would have to have me throughout the ages as his opposite number and that we should have to sort our karmas together. I know he agreed to what I demanded and waved us away.

When we got into the courtyard, T. boxed my ears in public and flew into a frightful temper, saying he would never go through with it. I dashed into our own room and told S., who was sitting by the dressing-table. I know she was irritatingly mild and cool about it all and I took my gold sandals off and threw them at her and hit her twice. That was when she got up and flung me down on the bed and refused to put up with it any longer. I remember drumming my heels on the bed with tem-per . . . I think I was rather proud of having stood up to the High Priest and got my way and I didn't at all see why T. shouldn't be pleased. Besides, it was most unflattering.

I am not sure what happened to him because it was then that the picture started to break up.

In fact the picture began to break up in more senses than than one, for regardless of the endless cyclicity of life as promised by these and other visions, the death of Seymour marked the effective end of this particular temple. It almost certainly struggled along for a few years while Carnegie Dickson was still alive, but when FPD left this bourne his younger coworkers left the lodge. In CCT's case it was to concentrate almost wholly upon the differing demands of Co-Masonry, within the Ma Kheru Lodge.

Yet if this priest of Merlin died before his Work was fully completed, the years following saw various developments which remedied this: In 1968 CCT, writing as Christine Hartley (she had remarried, to a man who had already made contact with Michael Scot on his own initiative) published *The Western Mystery Tradition*. Part of this was completed in full trance, under the direct if discarnate control of the Colonel. Coming out as it did when the Western world did not know or care that it had sources of wisdom of its own, and believed that all things Eastern were spiritual, and all things spiritual Eastern, *The Western Mystery Tradition* helped to keep one small flame burning—a flame which had been taken from a fire started by Mathers, a century before.

Appendix A

These Workings took place in the interim period after leaving the FIL and before joining the temple of the Stella Matutina.

Notes 11/21/40.
1. Invoked the L. of U.

In a dark wet pine wood very boggy underfoot, with bright blue sky beyond the tree tops. Then L.E. appeared, melted back into a Druid, and again into an Atlantean priest.

He showed us a great egg-shaped crystal, pink, standing on a tripod, and told us to go through the crystal, which we did, leaving the three bodies seated on three stones in the wood, and connected with us by a light ray.

We saw Iona, Glastonbury, and then in very vivid green, Eire! Then we were over Cornwall and Devon and saw a lovely land, where now is the Channel, and over toward Brittany a great city and its port built of immense stone blocks, with truncated pyramids built on stone steps. (I had been to this drowned city once with Paula). We came to the port and saw the curious sailing boats with high prows; went to the square, and into a low truncated pyramid built of very large stones through a pylon-like doorway. We found ourselves in a fair sized hall. At either end were flights of steps leading up to a stone altar, above which in the East was a great golden sun, and in the West a great silver moon.

In the center was a tall tripod with hanging chains, holding a blazing brazier. To the south appeared the figure of a priest—standing by an altar on the top of a flight of stone steps. He said the key to all magic is in this hall if you can find it. We each threw a handful of incense into the fire and the whole hall was filled with a sweet smelling smoke. As this cleared away, a big snake like a cobra was gently swaying above its coils. It was silver bellied, with a golden-green back and deep purple spots, and wonderful gold and violet eyes.

C.C.T. stepped behind me, but I knew him to be the serpent that guards the hidden wisdom, and that the serpent is the key to all magical power. So I opened my heart center and invited him to enter—and slowly I absorbed him into myself, and then I knew that I had within myself the key that unlocks all magical power, (CCT felt as if she was just an empty crystal shell) and I had within my being the potentiality of the cosmic hierarchy.

I knew that as an initiate of the Serpent of Wisdom I had to share this power with my syzygy. And turning to the priestly adept who gave me this initiation I saw that he, as an adept, was himself his own syzygy. He had polarized the higher and the lower natures, and so was a complete self-polarizing entity.

I thanked him for what he had given me, and then we went to our thrones, mine in the East, CCT in the West, and we stood beside the altars, the three forming the Triangle of Power, with the Master at the apex.

CCT was then told that the Sacred Isle of the West is not on this plane as an actuality, but in the heart of the initiate, and with others we were to search for it and to rouse its power in "actuality."

Then back through the crystal into the three waiting bodies. Sounds of gunfire made the last bit rather hurried.

Under the crystal roof we exchanged magnetism from the three higher centers, then built the coloring purple—blue for the head centers, gold for the heart, green for solar, pink the two lower centers. Very invigorating.

Thursday, November 28.

CCT very tired—I was fit. A blitz (mild) was on. Built up her aura which was rather upset. And then picked up the Irish Fairy Folk.

We found ourselves standing on an immense overhang of cliff looking across the Atlantic. Probably it was in Co. Clare. Behind us was a fortress of great stones built into low, thick walls and without cement. I had a sword and round shield. CCT was in a girl's kit—short skirt. There was a sort of roped path down the cliff. CCT went first. I left weapons and followed. Went down to a cove with a spring about 20 feet above high water. CCT was then very dark with a sort of breastplate of golden topazes. Looking out to sea we noticed that the bay was like a horned moon, and looking into the golden glow of the setting sun I saw an island with two peaks at the side and a smaller peak in the center. It was dark blue in color. It was the Holy Isle of the West which is only seen at sunset and thus Mael Dun came to us.

Then a crystal canoe sped over the waves and I saw in it CCT (now wearing long golden hair) dressed as a high priestess with a crown of crystal. But CCT saw Merlin in his blue cloak, while I saw him in red and gold. On reaching the beach the canoe up-ended and became a huge cobra with CCT under the crystal hood. Then I saw in CCT's hand a green and gold serpent. It wound itself round my forehead in several coils and crushed itself into my brain—this was agony—the serpent then became part of my brain, and I knew that I had once taken initiation in the ancient Snake Cult of Phoenician Eire. It gave one a tremendous surge of power—and both CCT and self were a blaze of light.

Then it faded out slowly, and we returned by another, easier way to the cliff top.

I finished strongly elated and full of the life force.

Perhaps, but compared with the exquisite clarity and directness of previous Workings, this one appears confused and jumbled. For what it is worth, my overwhelming impressions when typing this up from the original were that Seymour was, at that time at least, a very ill man.

A.R.

The
Merlin Current

Part II

Return of the Pendragon

Introduction

With Seymour dead, and Christine Hartley and Anthony Daw gone on to other things, the Merlin Temple effectually died. The Pillars of the Gods of the Dawning Light were stored away, the robes and nemysses destroyed, and likewise the magical records, except for those fragments given here.

This was inevitable. Throughout the endless history of ancient Egypt, for example, the seers of each temple always knew when cycles were ending and beginning. Not national or global cycles, necessarily, but the lesser sweeps of spirit and function that could be associated with their own Places of Work. Temples, like batteries, could go flat. New energies were needed, and new structures to contain them. This was why particular temples were taken down stone by stone, and completely different edifices built up again on the same site, yet always, somewhere, containing in the foundations some portion of the old. The same thing happened in Britain when Christianity appeared; sites devoted to the Great Goddess gradually becoming linked with the Virgin Mary. Contrary to the venomous assertions of modern pagans, this was not *always* a forced imposition. The people themselves knew that other times had begun.

By and large the Order of the Golden Dawn—in the broadest sense—died some time around the Second World War. Because the temples it used had no permanent foundations in this world, but rather existed on other levels entirely, and only found earthly expressions via the sort of arrangements made by Carnegie Dickson and others, we can still get in touch with them today. If the two pillars of the Merlin Temple have themselves long since been destroyed, we can create others of our own—gateways if you like—which can enable us to gain a rightful entry into those Currents of Light which once reflected between the Adepti of another era.

In brief, the egregores of the temples are all still there, waiting to be used again—*needing* to be used again.

What happened was that the two World Wars, the Great Depression, the massive influx of Orientalism in the dreadful years of flower power, all stopped the Magical Current from being "earthed." The Work done within the Merlin Temple, for example, can be viewed like one of those Yeatsian gyres, or Mather's dragons, spiraling inward and down toward the world of form, beginning with great and general sweeps that take in the cross-currents of time and far memory, narrowing down to matters of earth-consciousness, but being stopped just short of that point whereby the inverted cone penetrates the land.

In a sense, this is where Geoff Hughes's work begins as a natural development of that Magical Current once worked within the Stella Matutina, although he himself has no particular interest in, or knowledge of, this Order. Nevertheless the symbols keep appearing: Wales, the sword, the hawk, Atlantis, Puck—except that Geoff works exclusively with the Merlin, and has experienced no need to sweep around the starry heavens via CRC, Kha'm-uast, or any of the others.* He is concerned with England and Wales (the country of the Red Dragon), and none other. There is even a curious parallel between the Stone Circle like Stonehenge visited by CCT and others in October, 1942, and the one he uses in making his Merlin contacts.†

His magic is different to that once practiced within the Stella Matutina but, like those rebuilt Egyptian temples, it is the same thing but in a different phase.

Time itself will be the judge of how it will all work itself out within our own psyches.‡

---

* If we could imagine a center line within that downward and inward spiraling gyre, then the first curves are very far indeed from the core—from the Merlin. Only later, as it gets nearer the Earth, does he get more prominent as the curvatures of magic come closer. We could say that in one sense the Magical Current was actually earthed when Geoff Hughes, as will be described, stabs his sword into the ground at the height of his own Working.

† Information on making your own magical contacts will be found in Part III of this book.

‡ Which brings us to a convenient moment to confess that the Temple described in these records may not have been named the Merlin Temple after all. Neither Christine Hartley nor either of the surviving Daws would tell me its official title, and would only add that it was part of the Stella Matutina, and that it had a sister-Temple in Bristol, named the Hermes. However, they both affirmed that they worked under the aegis of Merlin throughout. It may well have been a revivification of the Amoun Temple, changed over to this new contact, and accepting members surviving from both Amoun and Merlin lodges.

DIARY
PHASE I

Initial Contact
March 7, 1984

During my daily workings I was required to "make a journey" and "visit" a certain temple, to carry out various actions, etc.

I "entered" and went to acknowledge the symbols upon the altar. As I did so, it tilted away from me and the symbols disappeared from my view.

Suddenly, I found myself outside watching the collapse of the temple. I was informed that it was no longer necessary. Shaken, I found myself back inside.

I paid my respects to those present, and, in doing so, seven of them each gave me a sword.

Returning to the altar, the Grand Master took them from me and melded them all into one sword in a blaze of light. He thrust the glowing sword into my hands.

As I moved to carry on with my Working, the Grand Master stopped me with the words that my task was done and that there was another task for me to carry out.

Comment

This threw me into a complete panic. What had I done wrong?

I tore myself apart, mentally and emotionally, trying to find a reason for being thrown out of the temple and, obviously, the *FIL*. I had spent a number of years with the organization, served as diligently and as faithfully as I knew how.

I just could not understand why. I decided, at the time, I wasn't having it and resolved to return again.

Meditation
March 8, 1984

I returned and saw a pile of rubble.

In visualization I rebuilt it, but it was very ghost-like and lacked substance. The slightest bit of mind wandering brought the sight of rubble beneath the floor.

Comment

I found this very alarming and withdrew.

Meditation
March 9, 1984

Rebuilt the temple, very insubstantial and fluidic.

When the Grand Master appeared he carried the sword, which was very substantial and gleamed in its own radiance. He thrust it into my hands, repeating that my Work was done, to take the Sword, use it.

I turned to Merlin. He told me that I had pledged myself to him and that I had his blessing. I had been accepted for Service and must now carry it through.

Having received the blessing of all there present I left.

(I discovered, much later, that the presentation of a sword is symbolic of the Initiation of the Grade of Arthur, from Gareth Knight's *Secret Tradition in Arthurian Legend*.)

Comment

Still not happy. I was still adamant I was not going to be thrown out. The *FIL* had been the center of my life. It did not matter that the Merlin wanted me. I was dedicated, and under allegiance, to the Grand Master. I didn't care about the Merlin, I wanted the Grand Master!

I wrote to the leaders of the *FIL* with a complete description of what had occurred and was advised to lie fallow for a year, see what happened, then decide what I was going to do.

A fortnight later I was reading Gareth Knight's *A Practical Guide to Qabalistic Symbolism* when I came across reference to the Nights of Purgation (otherwise known as the Dark Nights of the Soul).

These are periods when all the things one has become used to knowing and working with are withdrawn totally and one is left with only faith to see one through the period.

I can vouch for the fact that it is absolutely horrendous and well named.

Over the next few weeks I endeavored to use other "sites" that I had learnt of in the *FIL* but they were not the same. I had definitely been "removed."

In the past I had constructed, and used successfully, a simple Cabalistic Healing Invocation so, throughout this period I simply made daily use of this and directed its energies to the Earth, the Land and its People.

Meditation
August 10, 1984

Having been very disturbed by the rioting of the striking miners I prepared myself to calm things down through an invocation.

Merlin appeared.

"Continue your absent healing, as you call it, for the Nation. The

"Continue your absent healing, as you call it, for the Nation. The miners' strike is coming to a head. Do nothing. The course is set. No matter what you think; the outcome is in accord with the plan."

Comment

Not exactly a "smacked wrist," but almost. The problem lies in that we only "know" what we are "fed" by the media. Nothing nor nobody can interfere with the Divine Plan—very important.*

Meditation
August 13, 1984

Arriving at where I was supposed to be I saw myself pick up a large sword by the hilt and hold it at arm's length whilst I knelt. A green "haze" materialized upon the blade, which then spread down the blade and all over my complete body.

I tried to get "me" to stand, but could not. Nothing seemed to be happening, so I withdrew.

Comment

Seemed a bit fruitless—filed for possible future reference.

Meditation
August 14, 1984

A re-run of last night.

As "I" knelt, the sword suddenly appeared to "grow" in my hands until I was holding it by the blade, with the hilt uppermost.

The Merlin appeared and stood before "me," took the sword and dubbed "me" upon both shoulders. He assisted me to rise.

"Go. Do our Work."

Comment

Patience is a virtue.

Glastonbury Tor
August 24, 1984

There was "knowing" that I had to go to Glastonbury for some reason, so we went. My wife Val and I traveled without our children.

The previous day, Val had gone shopping by herself and had been moved to buy me a walking staff.

(I later learnt that a staff is symbolic of the initiation of the Grade of Merlin, from Gareth Knight's *Secret Tradition in Arthurian Legend*.)

---

* The national Miners' Strike, as it is simply called, lasted over a year and became a struggle on political and ideological levels that seemed at one time as if it might result in the downfall of the government.

There was a compulsion to approach the Tor properly.

We parked the car at the Chalice Well and walked back to the west of Wearyall Hill.

As we crested the hill I raised my arms in salutation of the East.

We moved on to the Chalice Well. I felt nothing there, except that I was impatient to get on with the climb.

Once again, I felt it was necessary to approach the Tor on the right line. Checking with the compass I found a line due west/east and began the arduous climb along the torside. It was extremely difficult and Val commented that it was almost as if we were being held back—being tested? After this brief conversation it became noticeably easier and we arrived at the top, not the least bit out of breath. We walked straight up to the tower, and the wind was almost overwhelming, hurling in from the east through the tower.

We had arrived far too early, so moved away from the tower, into the leeside of the tor for a bite to eat and a cigarette for myself.

At approximately 12:40 we went back and sat on the ground, against the southern wall of the tower in the brilliant sunshine.

As I closed my eyes I became aware of a green outline triangle that developed into a pyramid. A ray of purple light came down and struck the side of the pyramid, entered and went across the inside, as in a prism, but, instead of exiting on the other side, it was reflected down into the Earth. A number of these rays appeared and did the same thing.

I was reminded of my visit to Stonehenge, some years before, and the feeling that I had had that the Stone Circle was generating power upwards. In at Glastonbury; out at Stonehenge?

The vision dissolved.

I raised my head and became aware of a gold circlet crown above my head. As I looked forward again I saw a pair of hands, possibly my own, placing the crown on an unknown man's head.

I then became aware of warriors, swords, fire and smoke. Not precognitive. I was seeing the essence of the Nation. Britain, the Warrior Nation. This was followed by a definite sense of "something" rising through my spine.

As the Solar Noon came I raised my head to the Sun in glorious salutation.

Comment

This was nowhere near understood and was, simply, marked down as an interesting experience, to be noted and filed.

Glastonbury Abbey
August 25, 1984

Val wanted to visit the Abbey, but I was not particularly interested. Nonetheless, I said a short prayer in St. Patrick's Chapel before we began our tour. I noticed, fairly early on, that there was power in a new wooden cross erected in the grounds.

I was moved to enter the Abbey from the east, over the high altar. I became aware of a sword on my left hip, and a staff in my left hand.

As I turned in the West to salute the high altared East, I spotted the underground Lady Chapel. I descended and walked to the center of this little altar and bowed my head in prayer. A scent of roses wafted over me. There were flowers, but none of them were roses.

Comment

Another interesting experience to be noted and filed.

Meeting
August 24, 1984

Met Derek and Lesley, students with the Servants of the Light School.*

Comment

At last, another cabalist! Someone I could really talk with— wonderful.

Meditation
September 4, 1984

Salutation to the Merlin, Inner Planes, Elemental Kingdoms and the Planetary Being.

Asked the Archmage for confirmation of some incidents during the day. He was tetchy at being asked such mundane, childish questions and told me to get to bed and sleep in order that they may instruct me. Responded that I was without recall of such things. Archmage not amused.

Comment

You see; it's not all sweetness and light.

Meditation
September 16, 1984

Carrying out a new form of daily Working I was in the process of

---

* The Servants of the Light is run by Mike and Dolores Ashcroft-Nowicki, themselves ex-initiates of the *FIL* and very much involved in the Arthurian Traditions.

paying my respects when a knight, riding a white horse, approached. I stopped and bade him wait until I had completed my chivalry. He did so.

In due course I awaited him and he approached.

Taking his lance he dubbed me lightly on each shoulder.

He said, *"You are the one. Care for my country."*

A little stunned, I undertook so to do.

He raised his visor. His horse turned and he showed me the first inch or so of his sword in its scabbard.

As it was extremely late, I commented that I was tired and that if he wished to hold further converse he was welcome to commune whilst I slept. Dropping off to sleep, I found myself in woodlands with the knight. We squatted on the ground and he produced his dagger, digging it into the turf, loosening the soil. He scooped up a handful and placed it in my hand.

I fell asleep.

Comment

I felt I had been talking to King Arthur, but was not sure, nor did I understand what it was all about. File and forget.

Meditation
September 17, 1984

Arthur's disembodied voice asked why I ignored him.

I responded that Arthur had left the Nation and slept, when he returned he would be acknowledged.

He acknowledged that this was well said.

Comment

Don't be browbeaten and dominated into responding to everything that rises. In the initial stages, work with the one who has made the contact. There is a definite feeling that is easily recognizable when one is "passed along."

Winter Solstice
December 19, 1984

At 4 P.M. Derek and I went into the woods.

I opened by making salutation and we waited whilst a roll call was made about the Nation. We were both conscious of the waves of power that pulsated in the gray mist about us. I became aware of faces in the trees. I introduced us to the Elementals and invited them to join with us in our rite.

At 4:30 P.M. I removed my gloves and spun the staff above my head, drawing in the power. I then rotated the staff in front of me like a propeller, and everything began to brighten. I laid the staff across my palms, raising and lowering the staff. Once again, everything began to brighten. At 4:43 P.M. I stepped into the stream, planting the staff on the bank.

I invoked the Spiritual and Elemental forces to combine and awaken.

The Merlin Force awoke. It was done.

I finished at 4:49 P.M. with a closing salutation.

Comment

At this time I had already begun an alliance with the writers of a book on the current upsurge of the energy of the Merlin Force and we were endeavoring to set up a database/information center from those people in the land, and elsewhere, who were finding themselves contacted.

This was my first attempt at being a magician in my own right.

I shall be ever grateful to Derek for his compliance in attending and in giving me the moral support to "have a go." We still chuckle about it even now.

Meditation
March 3, 1985

Whilst carrying out my normal daily Working practice in the silence of my study I heard a noise in the room. Startled, I opened my eyes.

The sword normally hangs, by the claws of its guard, on the picture rail on the eastern wall of the study.

It lifted on one side and fell, to imbed itself in the skirting board, before clattering to the floor.

My skin crawled, hair rose on end, and I yelled for help.

Comment

Frightened the wits out of me.

Inspected the sword and picture rail but could find no physical explanation for its movement. The only conclusion I could come to was that my attention was being drawn to the sword.

Spring Equinox
March 20, 1985

It had been indicated that there were to be six present and each of us was to be allotted a role.

Having been advised some time before that this particular Working was to be carried out, I approached the rite with anything but calm since I had, throughout the "run up" period, been impressed that none of us were to be informed of the nature of the ceremony, nor of the parts to be assumed, nor of the words to be spoken.

I was, almost, as much in the dark as the other members.

Those who joined in the Work that night were my wife Val and four friends, Derek and his wife Lesley, and Mark and his fiancee Barbara.

A number of incidents occurred during the previous weeks to lead me toward the preparation of the area and the articles for the ritual. Val had been present on a couple of occasions when the Merlin had been giving me instructions as to the placement of the six of us.

I left the other five at home and went alone into the woods about 8:40 P.M. to prepare for the Working. The site was a clearing with a small stream meandering from West to East with a small footbridge over it. None of the others knew what I had in my pockets, nor under my coat.

I "sealed" the area and prayed for guidance, lighting the nightlight candle in a small lantern placed in the center of the clearing with a cup of water beside it. The other symbol was duly placed.

I then handed the Work into the hands of the Most High.

Quietly waiting a little way away from the site I heard the others approaching and was aware that Val was placing them in the correct positions, as had been indicated to me.

```
           Barbara                      Lesley
        ============== Bridge ==============
(West) Val                               Myself (East)
           Mark                          Derek
```

Val and Lesley donned their robes; Val in black, Lesley in blue trimmed with silver. I was in amethyst.

I joined them, bade them welcome and thanked them for coming. I began by explaining that each was being asked to assume the role of an archetype. I asked that they try to forget the majority of the myth and legend that had grown about the forces that these persons represented. They were to try to tune in to the essence of the force that they were named after.

Turning to Lesley,

"Lady, we ask you to be the Lady of Avalon. The Seat of the Sacred Mysteries of the Earth Mother, hidden for all time behind the mists; the guardian, and teacher, of the Sacred Wisdom."

Turning to Barbara,

"Lady, we ask you to be Guinevere. Mother of the Nation, royal wife; soothing and supporting the warriors."

To Val,

"Lady, my sister Morgana, Priestess of the Earth Mother and female Merlin. Electing to leave Avalon to travel in the so-called realms of reality; to carry the Wisdom amongst men."

To Mark,

"Sir, we ask you to be Galahad, the questing knight. Forever seeking, searching, but destined, eventually, to find."

To Derek,

"Sir, we ask you to be Arthur, warrior King and Father of the Nation."

"I am to be the Merlin."

There followed a short invocation for the Forces to draw close and attune with us, followed by a pause as the binding took place. Raising my arms I called upon, and welcomed, the Elemental Kingdoms, inviting them to join with us in the celebration of the Rite of Spring.

"With the Sunrise comes the Spring. With the Spring comes birth. With birth comes travail. We must brace ourselves!"

Taking my six-foot staff I began to turn it, as a propeller, to draw the power into a vortex, ready to be used in due course. It was not necessary, so I stopped. Crossing the area I approached Morgana and bade her guard and keep the staff safe, 'ere the Work was done.

Returning to my place I waited a few moments.

"I call for the reinstatement of that which was taken from us and withdrawn beyond our knowledge, laying only in myth and legend."

Stepping very carefully I moved down the bank into the stream. Standing in the water, facing East, I reiterated the call.

"Let that which was removed be returned to us."

As these words were spoken, I plunged my hands into the water and flung the sword aloft. I felt that it would have gone into space had I not held it fast.

"It is returned," I shouted, my heart bursting, *"Excalibur is back amongst us!"*

Leaving the stream, holding the sword in both hands, I approached the Lady of Avalon.

"My Lady, I beg your blessing upon Excalibur."
(She reported later a distinct feeling of being overshadowed at this point.)
"You have my Blessing—the time is now right!"
I moved to Guinevere, asking the same.
"I will give my blessing, and assist in all ways, and do all that I can."
I moved to Morgana with the same request.
"The blessing of the Earth, so mote it be!"
To Arthur, the same.
"My Blessing on Excalibur; may the eternal warrior . . . (words lost) . . . get it right this time."
I moved back to my own station. Throughout this period I had been very conscious of the power, and had a very definite shake in my voice. I moved to the center and, facing South, I raised the sword above my head.
"What was taken away is now returned."
I drove the sword into the Earth and left it there. Raising my arms.
"The Power is now loose in the Land."
Moving back to my place I restated the earlier comments.
"Sunrise brings the Spring. Spring brings birth. Birth brings pain and anguish."
I collected the cup and carried it to the Lady of Avalon.
"From the Isles of Avalon. From the waters about Avalon I give you water."
She drank.
I repeated the same to each of the others and, returning to my station, I did likewise. Finishing with:
"That which came from Avalon is so returned."
The remains in the cup were poured into the stream. I replaced the cup in the center of the area, then moved on to Morgana. Thanking her for the custody of my staff, I reclaimed it and returned to my place.
I raised my arms in salutation, sealing the meeting to a close with the Archangelic Invocation and Qabalistic Cross.
Although it was over, none of the others were ready to move and had to be gentled out of their positions.
The physical artifacts were collected and carried home.

Prologue

Derek later reported that he felt we had loosed a dragon.
Barbara said that she had felt very drawn to the staff and had

wanted to raise it to the skies, hence she had carried it home for me.

Postscript

Back in the woods at 7 P.M. the following morning (Thursday) I picked up the thought, *"Lord, letest thou thy servant depart in peace,"* as if my whole existence had been for the Work that we had carried through the night before.

Post Postscript

Friday I was in the woods at 6 A.M. and what a beautiful, wonderful difference. The area of the bridge was "aware." There is no other way to describe it. The thought arose that in December, Derek and I had "laid" an egg. The other night we had "hatched" it. The power is well and truly loose in the Land—at least in our little bit.

Comment

An evolution from the first attempt at magic, by endeavoring to involve others into a group Working.

I had invited Mark and Barbara along even though they were not involved in the Merlin Group, but they had expressed, and shown, an interest in things occult. They enjoyed the experience but felt it was not their particular path. They are, currently, carrying on the Work in their own way and are making a success of it.

The transcript of this Working was circulated to the forty plus members of the Merlin Group.

Derek's comment was filed and forgotten.

Conversation
April 7, 1985

This conversation was brought about by the unpleasantness generated by the Spring Rite circulated to the Merlin Group to which I had allied myself. The whole was recorded and, subsequently, transcribed. G are my comments, M is the one contacted.

G - What is going on?

M - *We are evolving.*

G - No games. We are fully aware of that.

M - *Ask a damn fool question, you get a damn fool answer.*

G - Are you aware of recent conversations?

M - *I am, but in an indirect fashion. They were not from me. However, the force which I represent to you is so vast that no one part can know what all parts are doing. The Force of the Archmage, that* you call Merlin, Myrddin, whatever, is the force initially, for Britain, and secondly, for the Earth.

The Beings that you care to produce to represent these forces have their limitations.

No one thing can see all things.

The force that I represent to you is the same force that is represented to others. However, each has its own little foible.

The ultimate aim is the same. The ways of getting there are subtly different.

There is no person on Earth who can say they are the Merlin Force. No group of people can say the same thing either. They are all aspects of the same force. Anybody claiming to be the Force, or the Merlin, is to be viewed with a certain amount of circumspection.

Britain itself is Merlin. Britannia is Merlin. Merlin is Britannia. The things of which we speak are sexless, yet sex is there. To say it is Merlin or Britannia doesn't matter. It is the same.

G - Please, get down to the basics of the visit.

M - As you are aware, the Merlin is not very tactful, and can be extremely forthright, blunt and, to use your term, downright bloody rude. However, this forcefulness is necessary. Sometimes that is the only way to get a point across.

The Work that took you six years to do has been done. The FIL, and all that went with it, was designed to enable you to have the confidence to do what was done in the wood. That is it. That is why you were set on that particular path. That is why you moved here and got this house—purely and simply to carry out the Work that was done on the 20th, as you know it.

Whilst the Lady is correct in saying that Excalibur has never been lost, to a degree she is slightly incorrect. It has never been lost, because it was in the lake, and we all knew it was in the lake, and the lake was in Britain. Britain was under the whole of that lake. The psychic lake. Inasmuch as you did what you did, you have released certain elements therefrom.

There are still droplets of water on the sword, and, as long as those droplets of water are there, there will be elements of confusion. The droplets are gently dropping off; evaporating; as gravity takes its toll. It is drying out.

The forces you loosed, it was necessary to loose. The fact that somebody else thinks it is a load of B***s is immaterial. You were moved to do what you did because they wanted it done; not just the

Merlin, but all the other forces, all the archetypes.

It was necessary.

As an example it was the right and left hand that you speak of, not knowing what each is doing. This aspect of the force, through which you have been Working, knew what was going on. Other aspects and forces did not, and were taken by surprise. They knew it would happen, but not when, and they were surprised. Hence the various blunderings that have gone on, and are still going on, and will continue for a little while longer. There is nothing to worry about.

G - Where do we go from here?

M - Initially, you go nowhere. Do you really want to know, long-term?

G - Not particularly.

M - It is a time for rest and reorientation. It is uncertain whether the six will be needed again. Four will, but whether the six? It could be possible, as all things are possible.

As Excalibur dries, other swords are being cleaned. Not sharpened but polished. There is work to be done.

But remember always, the sword that is in its scabbard is doing its work. The sword that is open and unsheathed has failed.

Excalibur is back into the Earth, dry land, and doing its work. Heaven forbid that it should be withdrawn again. It is in the Earth and must remain there.

G - What do we do about the contacts of the other aspects?

M - Think again on what was said. The essence of what was given you. Inasmuch as your work is done, this is true. This is a time for relaxation, this is true. It is a time for preparation for new work, this is true.

It was poorly put across.

As a human you should be treated as you would wish to be treated, and as you would wish to treat others. Bombasts are not helpful. Instead of a week of relaxation, it has been a week fraught. Typical of you, you would not listen when we tried to calm you down.

Enough is enough. It is time for you to leave.

Comment

There was a visualization exercise before and after this conversation, but it is of no consequence to our theme, hence its omission.

It must be borne in mind that there are often things said and done that one would rather not include in a diary. However, the spirit of the Work is Truth. One must be prepared to acknowledge the whole, warts and all.

Meditation
May 13, 1985

Tuning in to the Merlin Force, the call sign immediately developed into the Disney caricature of Merlin. He lowered his right arm and pointed directly at me and told me to go, my Work was done. I would always Work with him, but no more with these people. I remarked about my commitment, but he said this was a moot point.

Comment

I immediately circulated a letter of resignation to all the members of the Merlin group and dispatched all the original documents to the writers. Whilst I was sorry to leave, there was a sense of relief and of fatalism with the move.

Meditation
June 20, 1985

View of being amongst Druid-like men at Stonehenge. Early Stonehenge. Awaiting sunrise.

As the Sun rose a black and white kid was sacrificed.

A large salver was produced and laid upon the King stone. It began to rotate, and then disappeared.

A voice spoke,

"This will be known as the grail. It is hidden where every man can find it. The kid is the last sacrifice to be made. You have been to Glastonbury. They have served their purpose.

*You have **all** that you need, now, within yourself. **All** the power you need is within.*

Comment

Whilst there was no strict announcement that I had been present when the grail had been hidden, there was a sort of inner knowing that I had. In all my Working I had never felt any compulsion, nor interest, in the quest for the Holy Grail. This seemed to explain why.

Grwyne Fawr Reservoir
South Wales
August 13, 1985

(Very dubious about having the two boys with us for a Working—however, situation was such that I could not, nor would not, abandon them. Gerard, 13, Adam, 10.)

Val, North; Adam, South; Gerard, West; Self, East.

Made Salutation and Sealing. Talked through the Temple of

Malkuth, substituting a crystal for the altar. Invoked Earth healing (Middle Pillar of the Tree of Life).

Described rainbows entering through the three doors (Southeast, East and Southwest), and impinging on myself. Directed the rainbows onto the crystal. Invoked the power to keep running from the Cosmos into the Earth. Deep and health giving.

Buried our small crystal, commenting that here was a crystal in the Hollow Hills.*

Sealing and salutation.

Adam's Comments

Crystal was like a skull (see Gareth Knight's European map in *Secret Tradition*).

No rainbows, but bars of light. Blue light was entering Dad's head; white light was entering Dad's back; red light was entering Dad's legs. All three were joining up inside Dad, and leaving Dad's tummy to go to the crystal.

Saw bands of angels between each of us, completing the circle. As we finished, the crystal spun slowly in to the Earth.

Gerard's Comments

Felt pressure on my shoulders, forcing me to kneel.

Rainbows went through Dad to the crystal. They spiraled about the crystal.

As we finished, I saw an old, gray bearded man, wearing a blue/purple robe.

Val's Comments

Very clinical visualization. Aware of dark figure at my shoulder.

Own Comments

Aware of very little, save golden light all about me.

Did notice that the echo from the surrounding hills had ceased when the Working started, and resumed afterwards.

Comment

This Work was undertaken whilst we were on holiday in South Wales utilizing our Caravanette and local campsites. The actual site was on the reservoir lake side and involved a tricky and arduous walk to the remote spot. I didn't know where we were to actually Work, it wasn't until we turned a small headland and I saw it that I knew we had arrived at the correct place.

---

* Without giving away anyone else's magical secrets I can say that there have been several other unconnected groups and individuals who have likewise buried crystals at certain spots, during Workings of their own. It is a lovely thought that Man is at last beginning to put something back into the Earth after doing no more than rob and abuse it for millenia past.

Meditation
August 14, 1985

Visualized the Temple of Malkuth with the rainbows entering the lowered crystal. The power is running well. Saw the "seeded" crystal overlay the visualized crystal. It was turning slowly, as if burrowing deeper into the Earth.

Was reminded of the *Star Wars* film. The torpedoes going into a funnel to reach the heart of the Death Star. Our Work had been similar, but to heal, not destroy.

Visualized the "Y" Call sign, but it immediately changed to Merlin with a rainbow between his raised hands. An intense feeling of happiness radiated from him and myriad stars danced in the rainbow. At his behest the stars leapt and cascaded over me.

I broke off, somewhat overcome.

Comment

I find the latter part of this type of exhibition very embarrassing and never really understood.

Meditation
September 12, 1985

Rising Sun at Stonehenge. Imagined power flowing into me with the rays of light.

Rode the ascending vortex into nearby space. Viewed "this Sceptred Isle." Discharged various colored rays into Britain.

Comment

Felt distinctly uncomfortable in "lower regions," also very warm, beads of perspiration and itching. Broke off due to doubt and uncertainty.

Autumn Equinox
September 12, 1985

Departed from home, alone at 9:30 P.M.

Journey through woods uncertain. The lantern threw very little navigable light and care had to be taken not to destroy night vision.

No problems, in the main, with woodland creatures. Only startled once when a bird challenged, loudly, and flew off.

Located the site without real difficulty.

Implements placed in the center at 9:50 P.M.

Prayed quietly and stated reasons for presence and intentions.

10 P.M. — Salutation.

Opened, using the Pentagram Ritual, drawing with the staff. Faced each Archangel as invocation made. Placed the symbols at the cardinal points.

The sword felt strong and powerful, bedding in well and true.

The lantern a little awkward, due to a tree slightly blocking the true position. The cup disappeared from view during the invocation, as did the rock.

Quartz crystal used as center.

Saluted the Elemental Sovereigns, inviting them to assist.

The invocation for Earth healing went well, until I found I was making the final call through. For some reason I was doing it in triads, with a pause between each.

Invocation for crystal charging and the amplification of the healing powers.

Communed with Merlin.

Thanked those present, withdrew the symbols and sealed.

Final salutation at 10:25 P.M.

Postescript

The following morning, in the half state betwixt waking and sleeping, I was shown a picture of myself, in the glade, in my robes, surrounded by the Faeries/Elementals. All about thigh high. The Kings on their respective thrones.*

Only a very brief glimpse.

Comments

Initially, I had felt very insecure being totally physically alone, but this had soon passed. Had felt comfortably warm throughout, but, on arriving home, had discovered my shirt was sodden.

Whilst nothing "seen," had felt confident that I was not alone.

The rock had had a subtle "light" about it throughout the ritual, making it reasonably easy to see in the dim light of the lantern.

Woods
September 22, 1985

Having been shown a site for a future Working in the wood, Val and I visited it. We found that a small tree had been uprooted and collapsed. This worried me and we speculated as to the possible reason. Was I possibly damaging the wood with my Workings? Or clearing dead wood? Discovered that two of the standing trees were

---

* A reference to the Elemental Kings of Air, Fire, Water and Earth, found seated in the East, South, West and North respectively.

Faeries and Elementals

due north-south, seven paces apart. The fallen tree had made possible a circle of seven paces in diameter.

The fallen tree was dragged away.

Later

Our two dogs, Kiri and Zeeta, are released for a run when we go to
the woods and are quite good at returning when called. However, they
decided they didn't want to come home.

After some time, at 2:05 P.M., I sat on a tree stump and "spoke" to
the Elementals/Faeries, asking them to arrange the return of the dogs.

Telepathically I was told to have a cigarette, then the dogs would
be back. I responded that I didn't want a cigarette.

They responded with "10 minutes." I questioned as to why 10
minutes. The reply was that they had to let everyone know. Whereupon a rook, or some such, began to call. Zeeta returned at 2:13 P.M.
Kiri was back at 2:15 P.M.

I gave my thanks.

Comment

No matter what Work is carried out on behalf of the Inner Planes,
one must *always* acknowledge the Elemental Kingdoms and gain
their acceptance. They are aware of what is going on, and *must* be
involved.

Here we have two instances, on totally different levels, of their aid
in the overall Work. The preparation of the site for a Working, which I,
as yet, did not know about. An indication that they were prepared to
assist us.

Home Working
November 7, 1985

Placed candle and incense burner (Excalibur incense) in the
South.

Whilst waiting for 8:50 P.M. I was musing upon the finding of my
active defense. Going over the invocation, in my mind, the small candle flame burst into bright light.

Made salutation to the Bringers of Light, Life and Love (the Inner
Plane Adepti) and the Archmage.

Cabalistic Cross.

Opening, using the Lesser Pentagram Ritual.

Saluted the Elemental Kings, each in turn.

Requested all present assist me.

Cabalistic Healing Invocation for the Earth. (Felt very powerful.)

Crystal Song - World ⎫ The Crystal disappeared
                Nation ⎬ in the
                People ⎭ power
                All   pulse.

Repeated the Cabalistic Healing invocation for the Earth. (Very much aware of the power pulse.)

Gave thanks.

Communed with Merlin.

Cabalistic Cross.

Close and Seal.

Salutation - the candle flame shrank, barely shedding light, as before I started.

Postscript

Comfortably warm throughout. Very much aware of the "chill" when I finished.

Comment

Felt very stimulated by this Working.

PHASE II

Meditation
December 5, 1985

During the Healing Invocation I became aware of a female head. At the finish of the invocation it came again, but, this time, devolved into a complete figure, although the face was unseen.

In her hands she held a goblet which she offered to me. Instead of my reaching out for it, it grew until I actually became the goblet.

I politely asked who she was. She gave her name as "N," the Lady of Avalon/Lake.

During the final sealing I was very much aware of Merlin on my left and "N" on my right.

Comment

The Presentation of the goblet (Grail) is symbolic of the Initiation of the Grade of Guinevere. See Gareth Knight's *The Secret Tradition in Arthurian Legend*.

The name that she gave is very obscure, and for some time I didn't know of it. However, in due course, I stumbled across it as an alternative name for the Lady.*

Winter Solstice
December 19, 1985

With Derek, West; Lesley, South; Val, North; Self, East.
Small nightlight lantern lit in center of circle.
Cabalistic Cross.
Energize.
Salutations.
Opening.
Elementals.

I moved to the North of the lantern, facing North. Derek moved to the Southwest, and Lesley moved to the Southeast.
Healing invocation to the Earth.
Crystal song for the World, Nation, People, All.
Returned to our places.
Invocation for the Earth to be at rest for the Winter.
Built a dome of light and put it around the wood, excluding all that should not be there, and allowing in all that should be there.
Invited any of the others to speak: no takers.
Cabalistic Cross.
Closed, and Sealed.
Salutations.

Lesley Report

Before starting, a vision of a fetus in an embryonic sac.
During Earth-rest invocation for the Land to be healed the words, *"It can not be healed for some time, or ever, due to religious blood being spilt thereon."*
Vision of a multi-pommeled sword stabbing into someone.
A short vision of a tower, with a top like a knight's tent. On the top part of the tower there were round beacons of light raying out. The upper tower was turning slowly. The lights were duplicated on the lower portion, but were stationary.

Val Report

During the crystal song the crystal seemed to jump in my hands a couple of times.
Quite often I felt I was in the Earth. I felt that, if I looked up, the Earth would be over my head.

---

* This was *not* Nimue. Geoff has deliberately refrained from giving it for practical reasons that will become apparent later.

Own Report

During the pause for the building of the dome the flame in the lantern flickered, relit, then went out completely.

Derek Report

On entry noticed a change of wood feeling to the West. Felt we were being watched by someone in the West. Felt it was a physical projection. Somewhat smoky grey, cloaked figure—Sandeman Port advert. Felt a steady rise of power. Most noticeable when returning to the cardinal points.

Caught visions of others with us. In the East, there was a black female, in mourning dress, yet not sad. In the Southeast a man, white bearded, very Saturnian (old and grey). In the Southwest a man, auburn beard, very Jupiterian (fluctuated between mid-grey and mid-blue). Both the latter stayed until the sealing, then dissipated.

Comment

Derek's description of the cloaked figure will, no doubt, remind many of the figure of Dion Fortune, as she liked to dress. Whether she was actually watching or not is not for us to say; however it would be nice to think that she had taken an interest in what we were about.*

Woods
December 22, 1985

Entering the wood alone I became aware of a satyr-like figure dozing. He rose up and accompanied me around the woods, not speaking.

Holding my crystal in my left hand and my staff in my right, we toured all the places we had used for various Workings. We paused for a few minutes at each. Felt very much like the Tarot Emperor.

At the last site:

Archangel Invocation.

Healing Invocation for the Earth (very gently, in order not to disturb the sleepers).

Crystal song for the World; Nation; People; All.

Sealed and strengthened the dome.

Comment

There was, very much, the feeling of completion.

The job was done!—whatever it was. Subsequent visits were to be used, simply, to strengthen the dome.

---

* There are in fact many parallels between the work that Geoff was doing then, and that of Dion Fortune's group during the War. See *Priestess* for a summary of this, the full account being contained in her weekly *Letters*, as held in the British Library.

Woods
January 5, 1986

Going for a Sunday morning walk I was shown the final site to be used for the last Working in the wood—the Rite of Spring.

Arriving at a previous site came over very dizzy—an attack of vertigo? Input or attack? Decided the former, so sat and let it happen.

Comment

Even if one believes in the ability of one to attack another, the fact that I was in the domed wood precluded any such occurrence.

PHASE III

Meditation
January 6, 1986

Called on "N," she appeared.

Her hands held a goblet. The base was a pair of gold Atlases, back to back, supporting a bowl of pure, clear, crystal. It was full of clear water.

I put my hands about it also and we poured the water on to the ground at our feet. Immediately it was empty we righted it, whereupon it was full again.

I took my hands away.

She continued to pour, and it kept filling.

In due course, she stopped pouring.

However, she began to swirl the goblet and water centrifuged out, all over. I was a bit alarmed at first, but this passed, and we laughed.

Next, she was holding a crystal ball, playing with it. At first I could see nothing, then I became aware of vortices of light and color.

Suddenly, I was confronted by an immense, marvelous, fire-breathing dragon, with a rich, deep, dark red skin and brilliant green eyes.

Despite his appearance I felt he was a friend.

Reflected in his eyes I could see "N" holding a grounded sword in both hands. She was with us.

A knight appeared at his side, holding a lance. They stood together, "shoulder to shoulder." Comrades. I felt I might be the knight, but am uncertain.

Comment

The dragon really made me jump.

Thoughts of knights versus dragons in mortal combat flashed before my mind.

What the H*** was going on? Me fight a dragon? A test of some kind?

Then the recollection that "N" had been presented and was unperturbed calmed me down.

I would have to wait and see.

Meditation
January 13, 1986

Merlin's symbol devolved into "N's," which in turn became the stripes on the dragon's head.

Flame roared forth, and he circled me in Fire—*"Protection."*

Exultation poured through me.

Comment

Patience is certainly a virtue.

Meditation
January 14, 1986

The dragon appeared.

Eyes dulled, as he was at rest. The former brightness of eye purely for impact on the initial contact. No flames.

I queried a name, and was given one.

The words rose, *"My friend, you and I have far to travel together."*

During the Closing the words arose, *"Dragonrider of Earth."*

Comment

Oh yeah? I have read Anne McCaffrey's wonderful dragon books and could understand the commitment of such a statement, and was prepared to accept such, but found it very difficult to understand what was going on.*

Meditation
January 15, 1986

The dragon was asleep, with Merlin and "N" on either side of him.

---

* This is where the amateur psychologists will prick up their little ears. But in fact Geoff is following in a long line of magicians who have used contemporary fiction to make valid (and very real) inner contacts. Seymour did it via *The Centaur*; CCT via *Puck of Pook's Hill*. Others, I know, have had extraordinary results via Tolkien and Ursula le Guin. Many of the best examples of modern "fantasy"—in both literature and film—are really direct responses to very persistent inner realities.

Dragon at the Stones

"It's not yet time."

Withdrew.

Comment

A real exercise of patience was being called for here.

Over the next few days I tried just to be near him, sometimes with success, sometimes without.

Meditation
January 21, 1986

Allowed to walk around the sleeping dragon in order to get his measure.

I was shown a diagram of a saddle and its fastenings, and where and how I was to ride.

Comment

They really got me going now. If there is one thing I am absolutely terrified of, it's heights.

Me fly? They have to be joking.

Meditation
January 23, 1986

The four of us (Merlin, "N" and the dragon) were together, the dragon still asleep.

I questioned, "Of what use will the dragon and I be together? You have said I am to be a Dragonrider of Earth. What will it accomplish?"

"There is much ground to cover and work to do."

"Work I cannot do equally here?"

A moot point, but it will be better. You will be able to accomplish more. You will see the effects of your work and actions."

A vision arose of a great golden cauldron, turning slowly, deep in a mighty fire. It rocked occasionally.

Comment

It is standard magical practice that one remains where one is and carries out one's Work from there. The necessity to hurtle about over the land is alien to magicians.

Meditation
January 25, 1986

The dragon sleeping.

Over him a golden dragon, rampant, wings spread and beating the air. It appeared to be impatient, ready for the takeoff. It settled to wait.

The thought arose *"They await him to lead them."*

A view over a recumbant bomb aimer, through the nose cone glass of a bomber nearing its target.

Merlin's purple mist became evident.

Comment

I had a lot of problems with mind wanderings, not a particularly good Working on my part. File and await confirmation.

Meditation
January 27, 1986

I asked if the dragon was the Pendragon?

"No, he is the son of Pendragon. When you go to Wales, your lives will start together. Man and dragon, the ultimate fighting machine. Forget Pegasus, he's but a steed." Brief vision of myself dragon-back.

"Impression March. Life after Wales. Invincible. Total weapon."

Comment

Very disturbed by these words—not at all happy. Even dug out the *Oxford English Dictionary* just to make sure I had understood the words properly.

Dragons may be forces/what have you, but I'm currently a living mortal with work to do.

Total weapon? As an "old soldier" I know that a weapon is a last resort instrument, and things are supposed to be pretty bad before one resorts to their use.

Meditation
January 28, 1986

Vision of Merlin and "N" riding with me. Flights of dragons followed us.

"Is he really Invincible?"

"As a dragon, yes."

"Are there other dragonriders?"

"A few. Each rider leads a flight. However, Pendragon will lead all the flights."

Comment

Where are they? Have not met any of them.*

---

* Nor have I, but they will be around. No magic is exclusive to the magus. There are always others who tread similar paths, and awaken similar forces.

Meditation
January 30, 1086

With Pendragon.

"I look forward to our times together."

"Perhaps you would not be so keen if you knew what we must do."

"?"

"I cannot tell you. It is forbidden. I do not know."

Comment

A supreme example of the doubletalk one occasionally gets. What is forbidden?

Meditation
February 1, 1986

"He is in his deepest sleep. Wait."

I extended my arms and "linked" with Merlin and "N." Our arms rose and we stood YYY.

Comment

More patience.

Meditation
February 2, 1986

Informed of the essence of the "Marriage Ceremony" between myself and Pendragon (PD).

Val reported that I will, in due course, need a tree, not in our wood, and that another tree will point the way.

I spoke with the Lord and Guardian of the Wood, requesting that only Merlin, "N" and those that bear allegiance to the Lord and Guardian of the Wood be allowed access to PD.

Comment

This was starting to get a bit heavy. Marriage? More patience. Val's report filed for future reference.

We had discovered that the wood was the kindergarten of the dragon and, as such, needed all the protection we could muster, not only from external influences, but also from himself.

Woods Meditation
February 9, 1986

Found myself calling on the Lords and Guardians of Avalon.

Closing down to the physical environment I was washed in Netzach green.

I became aware of the purple eyes of a dragon looking at me. Subtly aware of Merlin close by.

"Others have been responsible for protecting these islands from the dangers without. You are to go onto the offensive against the darkness within. The dark is rising.

You need to develop your clairvoyance. You have it. You must gain confidence in its usage. Petty clairvoyance will be your key to platforms."

Became aware of a hawk settling on my arm. It would be my constant companion, and PD would stand with me.

"You are to go into battle against bigotry and intolerance. You are to "take on" the archbishops of England and Rome.

You are to take the new job in London. This will give you the access to various places.

Your sword is in your hand. PD stands with you in support. The hawk rides your arm.

Your life is forfeit. You will pay with your life.

All the help you will ever need is with you, albeit there are the formalities to go through for the completion of the rites. Necessary, yet unnecessary.

The plot was shown. Insemination at Glastonbury. Laying and hatching the egg. Its subsequent guardianship in the womb of the wood. PD is released in five weeks' time.

The Cabalah has served its purpose, let it go.

Return to the church. Get on the platform.*

Val Report

Geoff looked very white when he had finished.

My own feelings had been to get as far away from him as possible whilst he was Working, and to get off of the ground, hence I had climbed into at tree.

Church Service

Message through a local medium.

"When building, ideas and plans change. The foundation remains

---

* This is a reference to the local Spiritualist Church which Geoff and his wife occasionally attend, and exercise their clairvoyance. W. E. Butler once did similar. Many so-called Adepts are very much against this for a variety of reasons—only some of them genuine. The plain truth is that many so-called Adepts just aren't good enough, psychically, to risk going anywhere near such a set of complete strangers and bring through messages from the Otherworld with adequate accuracy.

the same. Your ideas are changing.

"There is the pink of peace, and the yellow of the mind freeing itself."

Comment

When I had been initiated within the *FIL* I had been assisted throughout the rite by a very dear lady, Debbie, with whom I am still in contact. Interestingly, in later conversation, it transpired that we had both left the *FIL* at about the same time. Debbie has been involved with setting up an organization known as "Merlin's Enclosure" which, as I understand it, is a continuation of the occult activities undertaken during WWII when a "psychic shield" (to use a term) was built about Britain to keep out the threatened invasion.

Very unsure about the use of clairvoyance. I am quite happy talking about things that I know, but infiltrating into other people's private lives I find disconcerting. However, the church's mandate is to prove survival of the individual beyond death, and in order to gain the platform and the right to speak requires the ability to give the messages. I would have to wait and see.

Less than happy at the injunction to "take on" the Establishment. However, bigotry and intolerance are the greatest causes of unrest in mankind. Working toward man's acceptance of man cannot be a bad thing.

In the firm that I work for, a new office is opening in Hatton Garden and I had been offered the possibility of transferring but was uncertain about it.

Life forfeit? As a devout coward I find this rather disturbing, to say the least.

No more use of the Cabalah? What method was to be used to make contact, and use, the forces to which I had been aligned?

Not a very happy fellow, I can assure you.

Woods Meditation
February 16, 1986

The "Marriage" is to be between equals. Neither superior to the other. Comrades, partners.

Comment

File for future reference.

Incidental Realization

Singing to diamonds is the same as communing with crystal.

Commune with diamonds in Hatton Garden and most of the diamonds in Britain resonate to the vibrations.*

Comment

An advancement of crystal singing and healing, basically, from the Earth to the People.

Church Service

Message from local medium.

"You are going to be involved in something different. Something you hadn't thought about.

You have traveled many pathways and come up against blank walls.

You are going to travel. I don't know if it's both of you, they're not saying. It's just for you. You're going to be away for a short while. It will be difficult.

All that you have learnt on your pathways will stand you in good stead. Although this is new, it will all tie in.

You've been slapped down quite a few times, but you needed it.

There is a lot of buttercup yellow about you. Sunshine yellow. It's alive, not dead."

Comment

Seems logical and to tie in with what is going on.

Church Circle
February 17, 1986

Seven others present in the circle.

Psychic clairvoyance for six—well received.

Comment

Merlin was right.

Meditation
February 19, 1986

"You live in a dark age. People fear for their lives and property. It is the time for the return of knights and an age of chivalry. The Pendragon must return to lead man into the golden Age of Aquarius.

"You must write about this."

Comment

Confusion! When, where, to whom?

---

* A reference to where he worked at that time. Hatton Garden is the center of the diamond trade in Britain.

Is this book what was meant?

Meditation
February 20, 1986

Vision of a diamond ring with a "Y" on either side.

Comment

To be obtained?

Meditation
February 21, 1986

Questioned the necessity of the ring. Vision of a gold ankh in answer.

Comment

The symbol of life.

Woods Meditation
February 23, 1986

"Knowledge of PD is abroad. Many are curious. They seek to see him."

Enjoined the Guardian that only I, Merlin and "N" and those who bear true allegiance to the Lord and Guardian of the Wood are to be allowed access to PD.

"Llyn Cwellyn is PD 'Coronation'."

Comment

Like any parent I was trying to be cautious about who PD got entangled with as a "child."

Woods Meditation
March 2, 1986

Whilst carrying out the normal Working had a vision of being dragonback with the Lords and Guardians of Avalon, who are the dragonriders, watching myself Working.

During the crystal song, was aware that the dragonriders were singing with me, aided by the dragons.

During the commune I questioned that I hadn't seen PD and also asked that Val be allowed access since she will be involved with PD. Reasoned that she had met Merlin and "N," briefly.

"He has been taken away for training. He is with the other dragons, but he will be back for the 20th. It's only 18 days.

Comment

They were keeping better track of the time than I was.

I had to keep checking the diary to verify the count that was being given.

Val Report

Vision of Geoff, crucified, riding a whirlpool down into the hidden depths.

I was not allowed to follow.

Comment

Charming! Lovely lady, Val is always full of good cheerful news.*

Church

Settling into the congregation, approached by the president of the church and asked if I would take the stand for the clairvoyance. Agreed. Very conscious of warmth throughout the work. Gave seven messages. Very hesitant and slow.

Comment

Needs more development and practice. Very restless and dissatisfied afterwards.

Woods Meditation
March 9, 1986

The "Spell of Making," from the film *Excalibur*, is a call for the dragon.

Vision of a very vivid Netzach green with Merlin's "Y" in vivid purple.

There were a number of "Y's" moving about.

Comment

Felt it was very powerful.

Val Report

Vision of Geoff hanging. Very clear. No staff. Hands limply at his sides. This vision arose many times between the other visions. There was a feeling of inevitability.

Vision of something unseen rushing down a tunnel (as in film *Raiders of the Lost Ark*).

Vision of one of the stones carved into faces on Easter Island, which changed into an angelic figure, complete with wings and halo.

Comment

Humph!

---

* Despite what it might seem, Geoff is in fact a Christian.

Dedication
March 10, 1986

The usual Opening and Salutations.

Invoking the Lords of Light and Darkness to acknowledge the Ring.

Dedicated the Ring to the Light, in accord with Divine Law.

Invoked the cardinal points to see and acknowledge the Ring.

Similarly the Elemental Kings and the Lord and Guardian of the Woods.

I claimed the right to wear the Ring and put it on.

Invoked Merlin to acknowledge this as the Ring he instructed me to obtain.

Invoked "N" and PD to acknowledge the Ring.

Invoked the East, from whence comes the Light, that I wore the Ring by right.

Invoked the South, from whence comes the greatest Light, the same.

Invoked the West, to whence the Light goes, the same.

Invoked the North, whereon most Light falls, the same.

Invoked PD that I was a Lord and Master, yet a Servant of the Light.

I was the Dragonrider.

(The candle flamed brighter.)

Sat quietly for a short while, letting the power simply flow.

A feeling of well-being pervaded.

Closed as normal.

Comment

Felt absolutely great whilst all this was going on.

However, when I sat back and read what I had written I began to doubt my sanity. Lord of Light? Megalomaniac, more like.

Even now, at the time of writing, this bothers me, even though I have learnt that many magicians find themselves making grandiose statements, which will/can only be verified in the due passage of time. Filed for future reference.*

---

* He is perfectly right. Every magician goes through a phase of megalomania. Considering the energies involved, it would be surprising if they did not. Really it is a feeling that is common to every creative person in the throes of his craft, a feeling that they and they alone stand briefly, with potency, at the center of the universe, affecting all things. And perhaps they do—for a time. The only danger in megalomania, or any mystical experience, is if the person in question gets "stuck" within his rapture and tries to cling, refusing to let it go.

Meditation
March 12, 1986

Acknowledged Merlin's request that I transfer my job to the London office, and undertook to go. However, felt somewhat let down by the proposed salary. Was reminded to have faith.

Asked to be reassured during the evening. Also asked for the hawk on my arm, the Lady at my side, and PD behind me.

Comment
Personal paranoia creeping in.

Church Fledgelings Evening
March 12, 1986

Requested to be tail end Charlie. Went up as number 11. Eight short, sharp messages.

Comment
Felt better, although there is still room for improvement.

Meditation
March 13, 1986

Unable to visualize. Body felt very warm. Legs ice cold. Very lightheaded and dizzy. Worried I may be incontinent or sick. Asked Val to join me—no let up. Decided to ride it.

Comment
Just did not know what was going on, but felt the need to stick with it.

Val Report
Geoff did not speak in English. Not sure what he said. I simply sensed around, but found nothing.

Comment
??????

Meditation
March 15, 1986

The vertigo had begun to build again, but dissipated.

View of a vast, high roofed hall. Bustling with many people. It was something to do with the coronation.

Many nationalities and creeds. Recognized Amerinds, Buddhist and some others. Many others I did not know.

I watched from the "dragon shelf" (?). Very conscious of the

Dragon Call.

Vision of King Arthur. Excalibur grounded between his feet. Pommel held lightly in his hands.

"You are the Merlin. Serve me well."

He came very close, smiling.

Short vision of Britain, with Excalibur embedded in the country.

Comment

More megalomania?

Woods Meditation
March 16, 1986

Bathed in golden green.

Val Report

Vision of a pendulum, bob to the left.

"Soon it will start its return swing."

Vision of a man, unrecognized, on fire.

Vision of the same tunnel, as before, but flaming.

Vision of flames rising toward a spinning, cut, diamond.

"Fire Diamond."

Lots of lights reflected from the diamond facets.

Church Meditation
March 16, 1986

Vision of power pulsating from a central point, like ripples.

A comet passed, very thin tail streaming behind it.

Unusual 'cos the tails are on the opposite side of the comet from the Sun.

Power center not the Sun? Something greater, outside the solar system? The unmanifest? (no stars) The edge of Kether?

Cuts to deep space (stars). A fleet of giant spacecraft coming in from deep space. Help (?) is on its way.

"?"

"You/Man cannot do it alone. Man is his own worst enemy."

Figurative aid.

Puppeteer lowering many puppets on to the stage. All on one boom, but each had its own string.

Comment

A reminder that we are not alone.

Beyond our conception lie greater forces that are on hand when properly contacted.

Reassurance that help would come.

Church Circle
March 17, 1986

Clairvoyance

The triangles interlacing (Star of David). Vortices binding the triangles together. The whole devolved into a gyroscope.

"These are the gyros of the world. Little groups, like this, coming together."

Message

"Leave the past. Go forward on the new path."

Message

"Big, strong, all-powerful man. You and he will be so close you will be one. You have a lot of real philosophy to give."

(Inference of platform work?)

"I bow to you. Chinese guide as well. You hold God in the highest esteem—it's wonderful."

Message

Described Merlin in silhouette in full robes.

(Mistook him for a samurai.)

Arms raised. An owl with me.

Comment

Margaretta felt the power of the ring. She asked to hold it, but I refused.

Fairly straightforward messages. However, I was extremely surprised that Merlin allowed himself to be seen in a Spiritualist environment.

Bath
March 20, 1986

"Hello, little brother. We await you."

"Hello, big brother."

"I have been trained to carry out your commands, or requests, but not blindly, with discretion."

"Thanks to . . ."

"There is no need for thanks to any. You have earned the rights."

Comment
Felt very secure for the coming evening Working.

Vernal Equinox
March 20, 1986

Val, South; Derek, West; Lesley, North; Self, East.
Salutation.
Opening.
Elementals.
Val to Southeast; Derek to Southwest; Self to North of center facing North; Lesley held crystal.
Crystal song—World; Nation; People; All.
Diamond song—People; All.
Returned to positions.
I knelt in submission. Stood and called the dragon. Introduction and presentation of Pendragon's son.
Invitation to others to speak—none.
Gave thanks to all.
Freed the woods.
Bread and wine—fifth wafer and libation to the unseen.
Salutations.
Close.

Val Report
Vision of chalice.
Usual tunnel, but light shining through the walls.
Fairy sitting in a tree. The area was calm and pleasant. Very floaty and spacious—unreal.

Derek Report
At start, an impression of large ring of eyes watching—the members of the wood. A sense of emptiness.
After the Dragon Call, the vision of an old man sweeping a hall, after everyone had left.
On speaking of Abram (bread and wine) a circle of fire ringed Geoff.
There was no wood participation, although there was plenty of elemental activity.
Became aware of a soldier in a barred helmet (roundhead style), and wearing a very dark blue cloak. He was talking to someone,

unseen, to his left. The name of "Montveil," or similar, was given, and Sedgemore. Do not understand the correlation. They stood atop a steep hill.*

Lesley Report

Between each of us was a soldier with a spear, leather skirt, bareheaded; possibly Romans (?).

On the crystal song, a massive, big crystal dropped into the ground.

I shifted levels. There were a lot of iridescent, misty, hooded, people; unaware of what was going on—puzzled. Shifted back.

Many Golem-type faces watching from the trees (see film *The Lord of the Ring*).

Many elemental children started coming forward as we finished. Woods felt unreal.

Geoff Report

I am uncertain of the factuality of the ceremony. I have little or no recollection of much of it.

Apart from a flash of brilliance on taking up the bread and wine, I saw, felt and heard nothing.

I do not even recall what I said.

Promptings from the others produced:

On presentation of PD—Pendragon is free. Let the Age of Chivalry return. The battle is set.†

Freeing the wood—thanked the Elementals etc. Spring due in the morn, let all activity recommence. Let the warriors be raised. Time for rest.

Comment

Derek noted that the fresh wind dropped at the start of the ceremony, and returned at its completion.

As we walked home, Val drew our attention to the North, from whence a mist had formed and was following us through the wood (see film *Excalibur*).

I felt very dispirited and depressed—a non-event as far as I was concerned.

---

* Sedgemoor was the site of the last battle on English soil, because CCT and FPD had a vision of this place too, in a "far memory" that I deemed too dull to be included in *Dancers to the Gods*.

† Again this was something that actively concerned Dion Fortune in the mid 40s. She foresaw the return of the Chivalric Code in the New Age. This, she insisted, had nothing to do with pacifism, but with Might for Right.

Reminded of the earlier comment *"Necessary, yet unnecessary."*
I felt very drained.

Taking the dogs for a walk in the woods the following morning, I found there was "no one" there. The magic had gone. It is but a wood again.

My Work here had truly finished.

Currently, very hesitant about Llyn Cwellyn.

Meditation
March 21, 1986

"Merlin, I feel very dispirited."

"Cast your mind back to the bridge working."

"I had the power in my voice then—I knew."

"How come you don't remember the words? We spoke through you. You will get your reward."

"? I don't . . . "

"You are now free to move. We will handle things our way."

Mind wandering—so cut off.

Comment

Not every Working can be a "good" one, there must be a poor one, now and again, to make the others more appreciated.

In essence I had been rehearsing this ceremony for many weeks and, technically, PD could have been freed on any of them.

Conversation

Speaking to a work colleague who is a member of the Sealed Knot (an organization that re-enacts historical battles) produced the following information.

"Mon Vieux" (My regent) was used for Monmouth.

The cloak's significance not immediately apparent, but would investigate.

Sedgemoor is noted for flatness.

Investigation

Jeffrey, Duke of Monmouth, was the bastard son of Charles II. Fell out of favor with James on his accession to the throne. Defeated at Sedgemoor and subsequently beheaded.

Meditation
March 25, 1986

Vision arose of hands lowering a gold circlet crown on to the light brown hair of a young man. Possibly my own hands—not 100 per cent certain.

Dark knight holding Excalibur. His armor changed to gold. He turned and walked away. I fell into step behind him and the thought arose that that was where I should be.

Comment

Felt comfortable.

Church Platform
March 30, 1986, Easter Sunday

Clairvoyance

A Chalice appeared before me in a beautiful, white metal, possibly silver. Very ornate and heavy looking. A hand appeared to hold it, offering it to me, and the vision extended to show the bearer. Neck length, brown hair. Bearded. White burnous. Made no claims as to his identity.

I took a sip of the wine (not broadcast to the congregation).

The scene cut to a vision of a huge golden cross, towering over the barren Earth. Merlin's Light appeared at the center, which devolved into brilliance. The Light flared outward, covering the Earth.

Prompted to say that it was the Christ Light that was free in the world, if people would only reach out for it.

That seemed, to me, to be the Message of Easter.

Broadcast five individual messages.

Comment

Was not allowed to give any messages until that vision had been broadcast.

Conversation

John and Margaretta thanked me for our meeting, and allowing them to meet Merlin.

Thought

History of the Kings of Britain, which first chronicled the exploits of Arthur, was written by Geoffrey of Monmouth in the 12th century, predecessor of the Rebel?

Meditation
March 30, 1986

Gave thanks for the clairvoyance.

Vision of myself in full robes, with crystal pendant.

"This is how you should, and must, be."

"In the physical?"

"Sometimes. We will tell you when."

"What about PD?"

Vision arose of dragon smoke pluming down on either side of me. Devolved into many smoke streams.

Vision arose of a new crystal pendant.

"Oh, c'mon! I haven't paid for the ring yet."

"No rush."

Comment

Found this very unsettling. Whilst I am extremely content and comfortable in my robes, the idea of being in them when I'm out and about feels a bit peculiar.

Conversation
March 31, 1986

A friend commented that she had wondered if people were smoking in the church last night because of the smoke that was curling about the congregation.

Comment

Dragon breath.

Instructions
April 2, 1986

Merlin arrived ten minutes after meditation finished.

He informed me that setting "Wards," etc. totally unnecessary.

A real magician doesn't need them. I am a real magician, therefore, cut it out. It's inhibiting and slows things down.

He pointed out that my platform work was done without it.

Comment

I don't feel too happy about it, must needs dwell on it.

Woods
April 6, 1986

First return since March 21.

Saluted the Lord and Guardian of the Wood. Not aware of him.

Toured all the sites, checking they were all completely closed down.

Found all in order.

Became aware that there is no longer any need, for me, for "magical" places. The whole of the realm is magical for me. I can work anywhere and everywhere in Britain.

Comment

Llyn Cwellyn is a special occasion, requiring working, and using, Snowdon,* the highest peak in the realm.

Meditation
April 9, 1986

Lengthy nothing, then M's Y developed into a raptor flying just ahead of me. Became aware of flying. Soared with the music (tape of Grail music, purchased at Glastonbury, playing), following the bird.

---

* Snowdon was, to the druids and those before them, the Home of the Gods. When the Romans came they retreated there, and beyond to Anglesey, where they were eventually destroyed.

Became aware of PD's neck between my legs.

A green dragon, flaming, crossed our path.

We soared on, even doing a roll.

Suddenly I was being shown an old, slim book to read. I couldn't make out the writing properly, but there were diagrams. Currently unidentified.

Next a group of men were offering me tattered parchments to have or to see. I felt very stern. They were somewhat frightened. They left the documents on a table and departed hurriedly.

Next, looking upwards an obstruction was passing away and I became aware of a brilliant, golden light source.

Next, I was looking up a gun barrel into the sky, at the blue heavens. The barrel seemed to track and then I could see into the depths of space.

Comment

Enjoyed the flight.

Rest of it not understood, filed for future reference.

Church Circle
April 14, 1986

Mini address on love and what it means.

Accepting people for what they are, rather than any emotional entanglement etc.

Laying down one's life for a friend meaning more than simply dying, but, also, undertaking commitments and responsibilities on behalf of others.

Comment

Self-evident.

Discussion
April 14, 1986

Lengthy conversation with Margaretta and John. Tried to give them the general gist of the Work I am trying to do.

They know who I am involved with, having met him.

Found myself inviting them to join the Quest.

Initially, they have accepted.

Comment

Was a trifle surprised at myself!

They have no knowledge about the so-called occult, even though they are involved with Spiritualism.

Church Message
April 20, 1986

"Unbend a little more in your Work.

"The others need it for their progression.

"There is an Indian. Jeweled turban. You will see the jewel in due course, and probably the eyes.

"Spend time sketching."

Comment

I have extreme difficulty drawing a straight line, so this was not really understood. I'll give it a try.

Realized later that I could manage to sketch the dragon stones* and thereby aid the visualization by Margaretta and John.

Delirium
April 22, 1986

Rushed into hospital with renal colic—*"Forget Merlin, concentrate on PD."*

PHASE IV

Woods
April 27, 1986

Short, recuperative, walk.

Working is to be August 10 with the new group. The music needs editing and rearranging.

1. *Clarion call for the Forces.*
2. *The Forces' arrival.*
3. *Address by the Forces of Britain.*
4. *Acknowledgement by the Forces.*
5. *The Forces' departure.*

Comment

Arriving home I dug into our music collection and utilizing the record of the *Excalibur* score, opted for the following pieces of music to cover the criteria stipulated.

1. "Siegfried's Funeral March" from *Gotterdammerung*, Act III.
2. "O Fortuna" from *Carmina Burana* (Fortuna Imperatrix Mundi).

---

* This is the Stone Circle described in the Practical Section, shaped like a horseshoe with a pool at the open end.

3. Prelude to Act I *Parsifal*.
4. Reprise "O Fortuna."
5. "Ride of the Valkyries" (Prelude to Act III *Die Valkure*).
Taped the above and copied for John and Margaretta.

Announcement
April 29, 1986

Set tape running.

Visualized the call going out over the Earth to the Otz Chiim, and into the depths of space.

A few tummy quivers as the vortices of power passed close by.

I was broadcasting the call from the Pendragon to meet on August 10.

Returning to Earth for "O Fortuna," I found myself in the horseshoe. Pendragon was beside me, his head bent down, allowing me to put my arms around his muzzle—very touching.

I fell asleep.

Comment

The Otz Chiim is the Hebrew name for the cabalistic Tree of Life.

Very uncertain as to what I was doing, and felt some satisfaction at having made a start—at this stage I do not know what the real objective is.

Conversation
April 30, 1986

Discovered and informed Derek that Sedgemoor is beside the Vale of Avalon in Somerset, and that the Battle of Sedgemoor was deemed to be the last battle fought on English soil.

Multi-Broadcast*
May 2, 1986

John, Margaretta, Val and I.

Visualization of the horseshoe stones, and I made the Dragon Call.

Mist formed between the arch and circled the stones.

Requested the group to concentrate on the Earth Elemental King

---

* **Broadcast** heading indicates that I was either Working alone or with Val. **Multi-Broadcast** heading indicates that at least one other member of the group was present and participating in the preliminary Work.

and broadcast the Pendragon's call.

Set the tape playing.

I went to the other Kings, introducing the group, and broadcasting the call.

I broadcast to the Otz Chiim and then went into space, broadcasting the call.

Vortices of Force spiraled and played and rejoiced about me.

Returned to the horseshoe. I talked through the Sunrise.

Vision of a lady's neck with a diamond or crystal necklace in the Sun.

Thanked all.

Margaretta Report

Pressure on head, requested it leave, gradually clearing.

Quite happy with the king.

Vision of the Pendragon.

Saw the "little people."

Felt the heat of the Sun, still warm afterwards.

Merlin appeared and bustled up to my side, thumbing through a book. He suddenly had glasses on.

John Report

Lower legs cold.

Smelt, tasted and felt the droplets of water in the mist.

All visions to my right.

No problems with the King, who appeared as a pillar of black in the blackness of the night.

A sword arose, which was ejected as per instructions.

Summoned all elements and creatures to come.

Felt quite at ease and at peace.

With dawn the pillar turned into a cone, like a Witch's hat. Female with silver hair.

Then as narrated.

Val Report

Couldn't hold the visualization.

Nothing on the King.

Pendragon appeared, playing peek-a-boo about the stones.

With the rays, columns of troops marching—ejected and lost everything.

Comment

King Arthur then appeared, holding a very large Excalibur. He swung it about and laughed, saying *"We'll get 'em!"*

I asked each of the others, individually, to hold their hands out, palm upwards. As they did so, they reported "something" across their palms.

Arthur had laid the sword across their hands.

They were bound to the Quest.

Arthur saluted and left.

A power then built up which I was unable to comprehend.

Val named it the "Banner Bearer," a white banner with a golden Dragon.

Margaretta saw the dragon and a gold circlet crown.

Val said the bearer was spreading the word.

Reading
May 4, 1986

Rudyard Kipling's *Puck of Pook's Hill*, discovered concept of "seizin." The giving of a turf symbolic of handing over the title of land (See Phase 1, September 16, 1984 (???)).

Broadcast
May 5, 1986

Dragon call. Elementals. Introduction of group.

Otz Chiim. As the call rose, the paths lit up.

On leaving the Earth, I looked back and was aware of Val standing in the stones, glowing faintly.

Planetary call—commencing with the Sun and Moon.

Cosmos—Broadcast into the depths of space; nothing seen.

Standing on Earth again, as the Sun arose, became aware of Val and I, side by side, Pendragon at rest, between us. Val and I each had a hand on his neck. We were merely watching the Sunrise together.

Comment

Val had slept throughout.

During the "Fortuna" reprise the power hit my stomach again. It built and built.

During the "Valkyries," cosmic power arrowed into the ring and arced out of the facets, not just over the country, but over the whole world.

Still the gut power sensation continued. Even the dogs were unsettled by the surge. Most unusual, they normally sleep.

Broadcast
May 8, 1986

As before, in essence, but, during the broadcast to the Otz Chiim: *"By what authority?"* I showed the ring and told from whence it came.

On returning to the stones I was very much aware of PD, although not seen.

Comment

One must always be prepared to be challenged and to justify the actions they are undertaking.

Meditation
May 16, 1986

Stood in the stones, on the altar lay a sword.

I drew mine and laid it on the other. They melded.

For some reason I then snapped my sword's blade. Hardly had the parts fallen than I looked down and the blade was whole again. The actions were repeated a number of times, yet, each time, the blade was immediately whole again.

Comment

The Sword cannot be broken!

Woods Meditation
May 18, 1986

We will need seven for the Working on the 10th—one each for the four elementals, the Otz Chiim, the universe, and the cosmos.

Comment

Speculation, on my part, as to the identity of the seventh person. *"Wait and See."*

Church
May 18, 1986

Medium failed to attend, so I was called.

Clairvoyance: eight messages, three held, five confirmed.*

---

* In Spiritualist circles if the message is not immediately understood then the speaker asks the recipient to "Hold" it until such a time as it may become clearer. Often it does.

Broadcast
May 20, 1986

As before, however, beginning to fit with the music.

Visualization strengthening.

Showed each of those called where the Meet is to be.

No problems with the power surge.

Initially I was stood to the left of PD watching the sunrise. Suddenly I was astride, still watching the sunrise.

Then I saw myself aloft on PD. He (we) were rolling and looping.

On occasions, my sword was in my hand, waving it in the sunlight. A shield on my left arm, emblazoned with the red dragon.

"We will ever fly in the sunlight."

We landed and I dismounted.

King Arthur stood before me. He offered his sword, and I went down on one knee and kissed the point. He smiled and I stood. He put his arm about my shoulders and we walked a little way with him talking to me. No knowledge of what was said.

Comment

The seventh person—for the Planets—is to be an astrologer.

Multi-Broadcast
May 23, 1986

As before, but asked the group to concentrate on Water. Went through the normal routine.

Own Report

Whilst waiting to start was aware of a knight upon his restless horse on the altar.

Otz Chiim felt good, and visualization good.

Felt elated with the music whilst in space. As the music lowered I returned to the Stones.

As the Sun rose, I reclined in my chair and became aware that I was stood on the altar, with a woman to my left. Between us and the eastern horizon were a multitude of people, their arms raised. They were singing "O Fortuna."

I could not zero in on the sunrise.

"The sunrise is not for you."

The Stones glowed with brilliance and throbbed, then pulsated with rainbow colors.

Val Report

Saw water as a crystal.

Sunlight developed into a shield, with a cross upon it. In the center was a crystal, from which a ball of light came and I caught it in my right hand.

Multi-colored dragon started smoking as the candle "cracked" in the room.

There were knights roaming the Stones.

The Stones were alive with force.

John Report

Poseidon with trident.

Very much aware of a knight in the mist. Upon asking him to wait, he challenged by saluting with his lance.

Constant broadcast.

With "O Fortuna," the Earth Goddess came to my right, which pleased me, and then the mist came back in.

The knight approached, I smelt the horse sweat, and I went pillion around the circle. His shield bore a doubleheaded eagle, which I queried. Symbol of the fish eagle, which I tied in with water.

Just before the end I fell off the horse and it took flight.

Margaretta Report

Water, a crystal chandelier.

Water very calm and clear. Stones changed color, mostly purple and blue. There was light shining on them and they were glittering.

As the Sun rose I walked across the beautiful green grass, all was at peace.

I had a strong feeling there was someone at my left in the room (unknown).

I was in the middle of a lotus, trying to get up to the light.

Very difficult to get back.

Lovely calm, no problems at all.

Comment

King Arthur then appeared and raised his goblet in salutation. *"The Work goes well!"*

He spoke of our having the right to do this Work, as against being chosen. Four simple, small minds cannot comprehend the result of the actions we take. Four minds will effect millions.

I was reminded of the Lady laid over the map of Europe (see Gareth Knight's *Secret Tradition in Arthurian Legend*). Britain is the Brain.

Also reminded of the nail for the horseshoe, for want of which, etc. etc., the war was lost. No matter how small a part, it is significant and necessary.

Margaretta reported a banner completely encircling the room.

Arthur then told us to close down, wished us Godspeed, drained his goblet, banged it on the table, turned it upside down and left.

Broadcast
May 26, 1986

Merlin and PD at the Stones. Broadcast as before.

During the Cosmos there was only blackness, apart from a single, blue spiral of Force passing.

Merlin's Sword broke through, but was rejected.

Returned to the Stones. Recalled that the sunrise is not for me, so ignored it.

Broadcast
May 29, 1986

As before, but some mind wandering, which I fought off.

Returning to the Stones, aware of my robes fluttering in the wind of my passage.

PD was there and he flamed as I approached.

On landing I was aware of Merlin and "N." I fussed PD for a moment.

Merlin and "N" indicated that I should stand on the altar, which I did.

From there I leapt onto PD's back. I discovered I was wearing some greyish chainmail, with a hint of armor. Shield on my left arm. I flourished my sword over my head.

PD leapt skywards and we completed a couple of circuits before landing.

I apologized to PD about my mind wandering.

"Fear not little brother, you do the Work well."

For some time we stood (I still astride) listening to the music.

With the finale we took off for a couple more circuits, PD flamed with the crescendos.

We landed.

There was a brief glimpse of King Arthur and it ended.

Comment

The Forces acknowledge our humanity and our fallibility.

Broadcast
June 1, 1986

Joined by John.

I gave the Dragon Call.

Otz Chiim particularly strong.

Cosmos gave views of nebula, comets and space crystals.

Returning to the Dragon Stones PD joined me.

I was standing on the altar stone to bring me on a level with PD.

With "O Fortuna," I mounted PD. We took off with the music and circled about. We landed and I climbed down onto the altar.

Merlin and "N" approached, bearing between them Merlin's Sword. They laid it in my hands. There seemed to be the shadow of another sword across it.

"It is not your sword, nor never will be. You are but the Guardian."

I remounted PD to discover there are loops in the saddle to hold this sword. I placed it in them.

We took off and did a few more circuits before finishing.

Val Report

Waves, which developed into seahorses, which developed into unicorns.

Geoff, as Merlin, was stood on the cliffs, arms raised. The waves were pounding the rocks. It alternated between Geoff trying to calm the waves and also stirring them up.

At the start of the music I was stood watching the Stones. Out of the altar stone came a beam of gold light. As the source of this light rose to the surface of the altar, the beam changed into a hemisphere of golden light.

In "O Fortuna," I was looking at a set of islands. On each island groups of stone castles arose. On the biggest island was the biggest castle. I then saw a procession, on horseback, going up to the biggest castle. Leading figure had dark blue cloak, covering his horse's flanks. Ermine edged all around. Open crown. Retinue all had cloaks, single colors, but every color shown.

Finished with spinning crystal, scattering light.

John Report

Started with Stones. Front of Stones black, but rest white.

Found myself in a vortex which spun out of the circle. Didn't want that. The Stone became all caught up and fell apart in the vortex.

Changed to conscious effort to rebuild the stones.

Broadcast to Earth and Water.

With "O Fortuna" it was still difficult to hold.

Mist formed and came in like the tide.

Asked for help from PD. Horse's eye was all I got.

Comment

I felt more than a little humble at the presentation of Merlin's Sword and do not really understand its significance yet.

Val's comment about me being the Merlin caused a little alarm; however, the symbolism of the calming and stirring the waves would be logical. Water is the symbolic representation of the emotions. Those who one day read this diary may find their emotions stirred or calmed.

John had had a very bad day and was tired.

He did not recognize the "dragon smoke" that is shown in the form of mist.

With regard to the Horse's Eye he was shown, Christine Hartley's book *The Western Mystery Tradition* explains that the symbolism of a horse is a derivative of the unicorn, which, in turn, is a derivative of the dragon.

Broadcast
June 7, 1986

Sue, an astrologer, came as an observer.

Tree good, definite sense of flash rising.

Throughout "O Fortuna," I was astride PD, having been given the Sword again by King Arthur.

We circumnavigated world, like a ball of wool. I was bearing the Sword to the world.

Very much aware of skin warmth throughout.

Sue Report

There was a large hawk about, and a lot of red.

A sword.

With "Valkyries," horsemen riding through a ravine, wearing different colored robes.

Grail came from the east.

Val Report
On left, "something."
Bright golden light most of the time.
Dark crystal for the water.
Comment
An astrologer had appeared to answer the need.

Sue had not been informed of the Work prior to starting, but had simply sat as an observer throughout and had simply "picked up" what was about the room.

Broadcast
June 10, 1986

Visualization poor, but message broadcast was very strong.

Back at the Stones, my robe came off and I was in armor. I bestrode PD and simply held the Sword; pommel of Sword resting in a suitable knotch in the saddle pommel.

PD occasionally flapped his wings. *"This is how we will be throughout the actual meeting."*
Comment
Aware of the power pulse in my tummy.

Multi-Broadcast
June 13, 1986

Prior to start, PD was in center, King Arthur to east of altar, Merlin to his right, "N" to Arthur's left.

I stood on the altar, facing PD, stroking his forehead. I was in robes.

The Stones were circled by knights, no lances, but swords resting on shoulders.

Broadcast, as before, except that I carried the Sword throughout.

I mounted PD, having stripped off my robes. I raised the Sword; Arthur and the knights responded. Arthur leading, "N" to the right of PD's head and Merlin to the left.

We set off around the outside of the Stones, but inside the circle of knights. Merlin's Sword resting on the pommel of the saddle. The knights lowered their swords in salutation as we circled. We completed the circle and returned to our places. Swords were raised again, then I put Merlin's Sword away.

I dismounted onto the altar.

I went down on one knee to Arthur, and PD lowered his head to the stone. Arthur smiled.

PD and I honored "N" (very aware of her crystal necklace), then Merlin.

Merlin handed me a golden arrow.

"For the benefit of Britain and humanity as a whole, and to the Glory of God. Travel swiftly."

Val Report

Stood at the altar, wearing chiffon, blowing in the breeze.

With "O Fortuna," I became a comet in space.

Margaretta Report

Nothing—just flying, telling the birds and the fairies what was going to happen.

Feeling of great rejoicing.

I saw the crown and a knight raring to go.

John Report

Very much aware of tingling of arms during first part. Touching fingers was like an electric shock sensation.

Usual routine and broadcast.

Air was a cloud, as in Ace of Cups. (Rider-Waite Tarot Pack.)

"O Fortuna;" usual knight turned up on a horse. I questioned his name. He immediately changed into a cloaked figure with short, goat-like horns. He was there to be whatever I wanted him to be, without name. He changed back.

I went pillion and rode around the circle with him, as I'd done before. We stopped before each of the images and we both paid our respects.

Outside the circle countless lights and houses. I asked Why? *"The Work has to be done!"*

Comment

The arrow not recognized.

Margaretta had been sad, initially, that "nothing" had appeared to symbolize the air, not recognizing that the birds etc., were of the air.

Broadcast
June 16, 1986

(Started work in London.)

Sat alone. As before, however I vocalized the calls; felt a bit better.

Waves of heat washed over me and the ring pulsated occasionally.

Played the tape right through.

During *Parsifal*, became aware of the royal standard blowing at the lance head.

Only dimly aware of King Arthur, Merlin, "N" and PD.

Comment

The power was very strong, as I became aware on finishing.

Solstice
June 21, 1986

5:30 A.M. Hadleigh Castle. Val and I.

Overcast sky, high winds.

Standing on the eastern high ground, just outside the castle, became aware of my stick thrumming with the wind. *"The Light is there, even though you cannot see it."* The gesture has been made.

As we were leaving we met up with a local holistic group of dancers.

They insisted we join them.

Back to the hollow on the east of the castle.

A simple little dance, hands crossed and linked. They were singing the tune. Into the center, dip dip, out, dip dip, right, dip dip, and repeats. (I meet you, I give you room, I move on.)

Comment

Gestures are important, signifying a willingness to assist in any way possible.

It is also important to acknowledge that there are ways in the Work other than the one you are Working. There must be a willingness to participate in the Work in any situation that arises. "Magic" has many vibrations, each necessary to the overall Work.

Broadcast
June 22, 1986

I sat alone.

Dragon Stones, King Arthur, "N," and Merlin.

Called the Kings, the Otz Chiim, the Universe, announcing myself as PD's envoy.

The invitation given, stated that another would come to collect them.

Moving to the Cosmos, announced myself, uttered the invitation, and said that I was the envoy who would collect them on the day.

"Do you bear the seal?" asked an unknown voice.

Spreading my arms in the Y, "I am the seal."

"Do you know the dangers you are in?"

"My life is forfeit to the PD I serve."

"Well said."

Returning to the Stones I was met by PD, who flamed.

I removed my robes, mounted PD and drew the Sword, honoring the three.

We took off. Looking down I saw the knights encircle the Stones, and Arthur mounted the altar. They all drew their swords and saluted.

Dragons flew in from the horizons. Some ridden. Swords flashed and flame seared the sky. They landed and took up formation about the knights.

The many robed horsemen appeared on the horizons and galloped up to join the outer ring of the dragons.

PD and I slowly circled down and landed in the center.

PD reared, and I held the Sword aloft. Swords and flame flashed.

"To the glory of Britain. To the glory of God." reverberated across the land.

Finished with a sense of elation.

"We've got it."

Comment

Had felt very powerful throughout.

Broadcast
June 25, 1986

As before.

Returning to the Stones and mounting PD I drew the Sword.

Circling above the Stones I was aware of the blade shining dully in front of me and I seemed to feel it, physically, against my nose and forehead.

King Arthur, Merlin and "N" were standing in line in the East watching.

There were brief flashes of representatives of the riders, knights and dragons present.

We landed and I dismounted.

I went to Arthur and we clasped hands, as in arm wrestling, and he drew me over with the others.

There was a very brief glimpse of Herne.

An illumined curtain rail appeared upon which a very thin gauze curtain was drawn between us and PD, who was talking with those present.

I missed PD and longed to be with him, but Arthur kept me by his side. We stood and waited until the end of the *Parsifal*.

With the "O Fortuna Reprise" the curtains swung away and I became aware of the owl and saw him for the first time. I also saw the reaper—signifying, I felt, change.

As it drew to a close a golden light appeared from the sky, down which came the circlet crown, which I reached out and caught, placing it on Arthur's head. He would be restored as a result of our actions.

Val Report

Started with Stones, but changed to a dry wall church. Some windows stained glass, others broken.

Arthur and a woman (Guinevere?).

Then I was leading a horse.

In space yet again.

Comment

Very pleased that things were building well.

The longing to be with PD had been very intense, however, there were things afoot that did not involve me.

Broadcast
June 28, 1986

As before.

Visualization weak, but broadcast strong.

In Cosmos was questioned who else was going.

Listed those who were invited.

Whereupon various types of powers appeared to begin the journey toward Earth.

Back at the Stones I mounted PD and drew the Sword, which is the herald for the concourse.

Riders, dragons and knights arrived.

Vision of my furnished cave (?).

An unidentified, bearded man appeared.

Fell asleep.

Comment

The apparent start of movement toward the Dragon Stones I find quite intriguing. It took me but a few seconds to get out to them, so to speak, yet here they were, weeks away from the event, beginning to move in for it.

Broadcast
July 1, 1986

As before. Visualization good and broadcast strong.

Back at the Stones I mounted PD and drew the sword.

Riders, dragons and knights circled in.

PD reared, I held the Sword aloft.

We took off, circled a couple of times, then landed and faced the trio.

King Arthur mounted the altar stone and drew Excalibur, raising it aloft.

Merlin raised his staff in his left hand and "N" raised her cup in her right hand.

PD reared again.

All drew swords and flourished them in the sky.

Stayed like that for some time, then withdrew.

Val Report

Darkness lifting around the Stones, hundreds of horsemen, King Arthur, Gawain and Percival prominent.

Aware of a lady riding (as in "Excalibur"—to a wedding).

With the change of music, hundreds of Pegasusi flying to the music, coming from the sunrise, all ridden.

Later, Neptune and Seahorses, huge waves crashing down on a piece of land.

Then on top of a hill looking over the woodland. Along one of the trails a procession which was a funeral procession. Horsemen, walkers, carriages, the body was crossways across the carriage. As I was zooming in to look at the body was disturbed by outside forces (dog barks). Hundreds of people following the carriage. Many colored robes and fur cloaks among the people.

Suddenly I was standing, holding out my hands.

Was told: *"If you want Air, you could hold a cyclone in your hands. If you want Water, you could hold water. If you want Earth, it is yours. If you want Fire, you could flame. You can also show Excalibur, but it is to no purpose. Not yet!"*

Aware of other people around me, robed and people of power,

highly placed. *"One day it will be your turn to display, to let the forces through, or hold them out."*

Comment

There is a quiet satisfaction in knowing that the Work will continue, even after one has left this "mortal coil."

Multi-Broadcast
July 4, 1986

As before, plus introducing Derek to the Otz Chiim as PD's envoy.

I moved into space to make the broadcast and a suggestion came that Sue should sit at the black pillar, with myself at the apex of the triangle.

Returning to the Stones, I hovered and could see the South brilliant with flames.

Landed and bowed to Arthur, Liege Lord and King.

I disrobed and mounted PD. Drew the Sword and flourished it. PD intimated that we must remain and not fly.

Aware of hordes approaching and circling the Stones; not just knights etc., but commoners as well.

Viewing the circle I saw animals, birds, fishes and salamanders inside the circling humanity.

Had been very much aware of the power pulse and tummy shakes during the Opening.

Val Report

The Stones in the darkened sky but viewed from all sides.

The Sun rose, the invitation issued. The answer was forked lightning.

I was aware of ice, huge clusters of ice pushed out of place to form peaks and pillars.

Then I was in outer space, but I was a huge figure. Although I could see myself I could also see the stars through me. The Earth was a speck of dust at my feet. I was so powerful.

Then I was in a valley with steep pointed spires all around me. In the valley were Merlins. They could fly, although they only had arms. When they spread them, a wing, like a bat's, was unfolded.

The ice melted and there were people living in a fruitful land.

The feeling was it all didn't matter, I could do more on my own.

Margaretta Report

First a ring of daisies in this room. Fresh flowers.

Golden crown as usual.

Felt I was getting smaller.

The PD came as a force. Heard the roar of fire and then great pleasure.

The knight was toasting everyone—going to a party.

Then saw initial "M," with glasses taken off. The "4" after.

Peace and quiet. Waiting for something to happen.

Stood under the Stones. The Sun rose on a new day—all was well.

John Report

Temperature change (cold).

Straight away a pillar of fire. Asked to wait 'til a broadcast was made to others. Got to it and fire changed into a "coped" person.

Black cope with gold flames (also a Negro). Then back to the pillar of fire.

Strongest one to date.

Temperature change (hot).

Many, many knights on horses. All going same way, down valley. I joined them as an equal. Riding own horse, not, as previously, behind the knight.

Much cheering. A joyous event. Everyone going "To August."

Lesley Report

Stone circle, a grey foreboding color. Surrounding color the same. Seems uninviting, further into the music, a thunderstorm.

Second music. A man gazing at me. Blonde hair, with crown, with chain of office about his neck. Just under shoulder length hair and holding staff, or sword, in his right hand.

Someone, or thing, is trying to kill the dragon.

Ring of fire around the outside of the stone circle.

Derek Report

No Stones.

Whole picture was blotted out by the tree hanging like a huge jewel in the sky. First in white, then found myself looking upwards with arms outstretched. Malkuth came in in full autumn colors, followed by the emerald and orange of Netzach and Hod. Then the indigo purple of Yesod. Golden yellow of Tiphareth. No colors for Geburah and Chesed, just misty figures. Daath was like an endless hole in the sky.

Found myself on my knees and a pure golden light began to fill it.

I knew that we could no further 'til August 10.

I turned to come back.

As I passed Geburah and Chesed, from Chesed came King Arthur, from Geburah came Sir Lancelot.

Looking back, Daath had become the Grail Castle.

As I passed Tipharth, Merlin came forth.

Carrying on down from Netzach "Excalibur," from Hod a "scabbard." From Yesod, Morgana. From Malkuth, the Round Table.

Then the Stones came into view.

Music change. During second piece of music, all the soldiers that have ever died started to climb out of their graves. All colors, creeds, shapes and sizes. By the end of this piece they all stood around the Stones.

Thoughts, "The triangular crystal of Atlantis begins to rise. Are we ready? Who will line up on which side?

Comment

I don't really know why I should have been so surprised when all the many types of people and creatures should have turned up, but I was. Applying logic to the idea shows that they are as much a part of the nation as any other. In fact, it could be argued, that they are the nation, rather than the hierarchy. Having invited the Elementals to assist it is, therefore, only natural that their representatives should be present.

Val's feelings are interesting. She is no magician, nor does she make any claims in that direction. However, she aids whenever she can, but admits that she is not particularly interested in the Work at present. She is a Spiritualist, developing mediumship and following her own path. It should be noted, however, that during this period her work in a Spiritualist circle came to a complete halt—she was totally unreceptive to the vibrations generally associated with such circles, hence she was unable to contact those she normally works with.

Margaretta is a very good Spiritualist medium who has undergone traumatic, physical hardship and had been at a total loss as to where to turn before our chance meeting.

John is, basically, another Spiritualist, who used to be a deacon in the establishment church. We all tend to receive the symbols that we, individually, understand. He found this very significant.

Lesley started in the Work as a Spiritualist, before moving on to initial training as a Cabalist. However, she has moved on to the world of aromatherapy, essential oils, Tarot and healing.

Derek is a trained Cabalist who runs an organization, in his spare time, known as the ROTA Foundation, for courses in the Cabalah.

Broadcast
July 7, 1986

Saluted Merlin, "N" and King Arthur.

Gave the Dragon Call. *"No need to call. I'm coming."* PD arrived.

Usual routine, but identified the envoys to each element/area.

In space a cosmic cloud appeared and swirled about me. I uttered the invitation.

"There are dangers!" was the response.

"I know."

"Yet you call?"

"I dare, on behalf of PD."

"We shall come!"

As I looked I saw a narrow strip of white light leading back, through space, to Earth.

Returned to the Stones. Mounted PD and drew the Sword, lofting it. PD turned that all might see.

Hordes of people circled the Stones, and more were coming.

I broadcast that it wasn't until August 10, but still they came and appeared to simply stand and wait.

At the end I dismounted and began caressing PD.

He nuzzled me, then pushed gently.

"It's time to go."

Val Report

Stones and sunrise.

Leprechaun holding the Earth in his hand.

Comment

Yet another challenge.

Broadcast
July 10, 1986

Simple acknowlegement to all the forces.

Went into the Cosmos and broadcast.

Very little seen, but a lot of "surface skin" power felt in hands and legs.

Back at the Stones mounted and held the sword aloft with PD rampant.

Creatures surrounded the Stones, in their due places.

Outside them the waiting multitude sat or stood quietly and watched.

Outside them the knights and riders paused in their repast and turned at their tables to watch.

I, eventually, dismounted and knelt to King Arthur.

I was aware of hands giving me water in a glass goblet and I was drinking. Looking up, I saw it was a smiling Arthur.

Looking into the sky I became aware of the bluish aura of a cross. As it drew nearer there was the concept of a crucifix, whereon a figure was trying to come down off of it. It could not, because it was attached and was constantly being pulled back onto the cross. I felt sorrow for him.

Val Report

The Stones in a darkened sky.

When it lightened a dragon was dancing amongst the Stones. He was on his hind legs, twirling about, but very, very happy and contented.

I then saw the scene come to life. Rivers, fields, trees, flowers, butterflies and birds. I felt very uplifted, very pleased, as if I had really accomplished something good.

Comment

It has long been a contention of mine that the concept of the crucified Christ has been overplayed. To my mind He lived to prove to the rest of us that there was something beyond the state known as death. However, the mass, mental imagery of the centuries has refused to allow Him to be taken from the cross and placed in the sepulchre, from where He *proved* His teaching. From the psychological point of view, a cross on an altar holds more emotive sway than, for instance, a circle.

Val's feelings of satisfaction were, very much, a morale booster.

Broadcast
July 13, 1986

Announced myself to the elementals, Otz Chiim and Solar System. Stated that others would be envoys on the 10th.

I lifted off and found I carried the Sword.

Arriving in deep Space I lofted the Sword, announced myself and stated my business.

"We are aware of your summons." pulsed into my mind.

"It is a request."

"That whichs stands with you makes it a summons."

"From me it is a request."

"That is as may be."

The Sword came down and closed the top of the Y formed by my upraised arms. My left hand then slid along the blade to the hilt. I held the Sword aloft in both hands, then brought the blade down in an arc to "rest," grounded between my feet.

As the music drew to a close I turned for Earth.

I had not been aware of movement up to this point, however it became apparent that I had "circled." Moving back I was aware of the Forces closing in with me, toward the Earth.

"It is not yet." I said.

"We come to see exactly where you go."

They accompanied me 'til the Stones were in sight.

"We go now. We shall come."

(Landing was interrupted by Adam's return from church, but no problem. Picked up where I'd left off without trouble.)

I mounted PD and flourished the Sword. The multitude rose to their feet.

"The invitation has gone out to the Elementals, the Inner Planes, the Universe and the Cosmos. The forces of light and darkness. All will be here on the 10th." I stated.

A mighty cheer went up from the horde.

I "sheathed" the sword and dismounted onto the altar.

Went down on one knee to King Arthur, whilst PD lowered his head.

I rose and, passing Arthur, went a couple of paces, passing Merlin and "N," then turned to face Arthur's back.

PD turned away from us, toward the West.

Val Report

Darkened sky, lightened to reveal the Stones.

Then it was sunset, with King Arthur's boat sailing out into the Sun.

Thought of the Earth, saw the leprechaun playing a penny whistle, out came the fairies, gnomes, elves, all the little people.

Then I was above the Earth and it was changing. Where it had been land, it was now sea, and vice versa. There was no violent disturbance, i.e. earthquakes, tidal waves. The water just covered some land and uncovered other land. The easiest way to describe it is as if watching a cloud pass over. One minute sunshine, the next dull.

Was very aware of different Beings and Force gathering around.

Saw Arthur's boat again, but it was more of a feeling of "The King is dead; long live the King!"

Did not feel disturbed by the change in the Earth. It seemed natural and right.

Comment

My own morale booster!

Aquarians the world over will happily spend hours telling anyone who will listen of the changes that are coming to the Earth with the birth of Aquarius.

Broadcast
July 16, 1986

Visualization poor, but broadcast strong.

No evidence of the Force's presence, although I know they are there.

Back at the Stones bowed to the court and mounted PD.

He turned and faced the west. Drawing and lofting the Sword, PD reared.

As I had mounted, so the riders and knights also mounted.

I remained holding the Sword aloft throughout. I spoke to the assembled multitude of lords, ladies, gentlemen and creatures of the Earth. I stated, in effect, that I was looking for Earth healing in its broadest aspect.

At the end I didn't want to leave. PD gave me a nudge with his head and told me to go.

Val Report

Stones in a darkened sky, shooting star, comet blazing from the right side through the center pillars to burst in a very bright light over the altar stone.

Very much aware of mounted people all around, not just knights and warriors, but girls as well.

Following some sort of path, which was lined, either side, by knights. All had their shields turned toward me, or, rather, the one I followed. As we passed they fell in behind. The path stretched way away into the distance. Someone on a silver horse, solid silver metal, but rider was of gunmetal, riding over the Earth. As he passed he left a trail of light. His hand was cupped toward the Earth. Power was being drawn upwards through the palm and the rider was transmuting it into the trail of light.

Comment
With approximately a month to go things were beginning to build up. I was getting very attached to the Stones.

Val's report another morale booster for us both.

Broadcast
July 19, 1986

Once again visualization not too good, however kept broadcasting strongly. Otz Chiim was in gold. Very aware of power about. In Cosmos nothing seen.

Returning to the Stones honored King Arthur, Merlin and "N."

Mounted PD and drew Sword.

Broadcast to all assembled.

A knight came up at the gallop with a banner. At first I thought it was blue over white over red, but the lower third was a golden orange (?).

Became very much aware of swords held as an archway for me to travel through—only I was alone, no "bride" or such, and it was a going in, rather than as a leaving. Persisted.

Withdrew at end.

Am in need of a break.

Val Report
Started at the Stones.

Thought of the Earth and it changed from shades of grey to all bright colors as if it was coming alive.

There was a rider on horseback, but he was riding in the sky, the only recognition point was his helmet, bronze with a peak and a black horsehair tail, from the top of his helmet, which streamed out behind him.

Found myself in space looking down at the Earth. Said I didn't want to be in space, but was told I had to watch the aura of the Earth which was blue edged in gold.

I was then flying along a river with very rocky sides, fjord style, but couldn't say where or why.

Very conscious of golden light getting stronger.

Didn't want to leave, but found myself back in the room.

Felt I had left something undone and not being allowed to finish something.

An awful lot of power about.

Comment

Beginning to feel that I was really needing a break/rest.

The banner and archway filed for future reference, as are Val's comments.

Broadcast
July 22, 1986

Broadcast as before.

Returning to the Stones I mounted and drew the Sword.

A veritable forest of swords rose in response. Everybody, including women, had obtained one. I lowered the Sword to the pommel as before and we simply stood throughout the music.

Very conscious of the power about my arms and legs.

We have arrived at the time to simply wait, two more calls, for the day.

Val Report

Large black horse. All black, harness, rider wearing cloak and hood. Horse rearing above the Earth, the rider holding what appeared to be a sickle, scythe, but the word that came to mind was flail. He was whipping the Earth. A time of darkness, but after the whipping, a new Earth, new life.

Comments

Patience, again.

The darkness giving way to the light.

Broadcast
July 25, 1986

Introduction and Salutation.

During the Call to the Otz Chiim, Kether exploded like a brilliant firework in the Sky and tendrils rayed out.

There had been a glimpse of the sword as I traveled out to the Cosmos. During the call to the Cosmos became very much aware of my Indian guide.

Caught a glimpse of his purple turban and the golden brilliance of the jewel. His eyes also shone. He became indistinct but a blue skinned woman with dark hair, wearing a metal band about her forehead, appeared and kissed his cheek. She had a very beautiful smile.

Returning to the Stones only dimly aware of them all gathered.

Astride PD after the initial salutory flourish of the Sword I simply sat holding the Sword on the saddle pommel.

Two thirds of the way through "O Fortuna" there was a definite, material, flash of white brilliance across the darkness of my eyes.

Sixteen days to go. One more visit with the complete team in three days' time. Thereafter we would be back on the 10th.

Very annoyed with the dog's scratching throughout.

Val Report

Very aware of the power all around, pulsating, even to flashes of Light.

A flaming sword, blade upwards, hung revolving, in the Sky. A knight, I feel King Arthur, came through the darkness.

Very strong feeling of crowds gathering to wait. Although some know not what for, but just know they had to be there.

John Report

(Absent on holiday.) Feeling cold at first, ended very warm.

Welcome to all. Spread the news as required.

AIR. The figure of Victory on a pillar high up in the clouds, with a light behind her head. Surrounded by clouds. Clouds then covered her. Message to Air. Felt I wished to be as one with the Air.

Change of music: With many others near destination by a cliff edge. A town nearby. Knights on horses. Felt self flying with others. Above town saw sea below, bays, cliffs. Saw again the figure of Victory, this time much nearer. The words, "Victory, victory" being repeated many times.

Feeling of joy. End of tape. Returned.

Margaretta Report

(Absent on Holiday.)

WATER. First saw Neptune. Gave message.

Changed to scene of a big hall, crowded with people listening to music. The conductor, stopping the performance, spoke to the people telling them, if they understood, the power of healing. From the people came a great power.

Then I saw the sea and rowing boats on the shore. Wherever it was, the power was being directed to this island.

Then the dragon appeared flying.

Then the coronation—then the Letter "F."

Music changed, knight arrived with others all lined up to begin a salute to the coming event.

Then sunrise. All was peace.

Geoff and crew in their room, but with us sitting with them.

Comment

With the Otz Chiim Kether is the point of ultimate manifest God-head, a point unattainable to living persons. There was the feeling that something we were doing would penetrate that highest of levels and cause an influx of God-power elsewhere.

I do not, knowingly, look to my guides for assistance in the Work, being orientated toward the archetypes. Should guides wish to join in, they are welcome.

The kiss not understood!

We seem to attract physical manifestations during Work, although they are not sought—this may be a problem with correctly "earthing" the current. Something to be worked upon.

Earth Spirit Festival
July 27, 1986

Purchased the amethyst crystal to complete the robing, as per instructions.

The Meet
July 28, 1986

Leaving Work at 5:35 P.M. the words *"Go for it."* hammered into my mind, repeatedly.

Arriving home Val accepted it with equanimity.

I prepared the room.

Derek and Lesley arrived and were not unduly perturbed, Derek having sensed it might be tonight.

The other three arrived.

Sue robed in black with red cord. Derek robed in light grey. Self robed in usual amethyst.

Positions:

Val (North—Earth)

Sue (Black Pillar)

Self   Margaretta (West-Water)   Candle   John (East-Air)   Mirror

Derek (Silver Pillar)

Les (South—Fire)

Since there was no physical ritual involved, until the end, there was no movement to be made; purely a mental ritual.

I simply told them that this was deemed to be the 10th of August and that the Work was to be carried out now.

Throughout the Working we listened to the music and I found myself introducing each action for visualization.

On completion I gave bread and wine to all, not forgetting the unseen there present.

John Report

Heavy. Pushed into chair. Hot.

Welcome to all.

Victory Lady, clouds around her, close to me.

Felt grey figure between Margaretta and Val.

A marriage, the bride gets the crown.

Hole in the Stone's ground

What did I expect it was? Done; loosed?

Drifted away on horseback.

Saw the sword symbol arise from many buildings in the land.

Felt sad. Why?

One knight, only, returned to Stones. Got off horse, held it for me to mount. Did so.

Lonely again?

The shield symbol being held up for all to see.

I knew it was finished.

I knelt as a page among knights.

Finished. Thanks. Peace.

Lesley Report

Numb feeling on right side of head over eye, sharp pain in right side.

Djinn in red, flowing robes. Bright red. Spectacular. Carrying tall white staff, with white ball on top, in right hand. Seemed to glide, not walk.

At the end a crown, extremely ornate, covered in all manner of precious stones and pearls in platinum.

Then, in its place came a plain yellow gold crown.

There could possibly be a natural disaster involving all four elements. Could be involved with a lot of water?

Wizard involved at the start conducting all around him and in the skies. Omadon?

Margaretta Report

Calling all forces.

The sea roaring away, as if everywhere was frightened.

Then came the knights on horses, circled.

Then excitement mounted, PD spoke to all.

After all the excitement, great calmness.

As people and forces go away the knights turned and rode off.

Val Report

Called the Earth forces, leprechaun, elves, gnomes and all life of Earth, Air and Water. Anything that had need to set foot on Earth for any reason.

Saw what appeared to be a pair of eyes, bright, many faceted.

Could not visualize due to the music until Valkyries leaving.

Sue Report

Gold (?) Band around the middle four—spinning at start (thought there was not supposed to be any Warding?).

Fireworks—weapons—many people. Plumes. War elephants on my side of room. Five. Red.

I think I may have been given a scale—well, something that looked like a flat, greenish-brown piece of tortoiseshell.

Faces, swords, lights, dancing, flying, fun, laughter.

Difficult to say, because, last time, I was an outsider—this time I joined in.

Lots of spinning—strange objects spinning through the air.

Initially I found it difficult to get airborne—I felt very heavy and earthed. Could this have been my seating position? Felt I was being pulled down constantly—I had to fight to stay aloft.

Yes, there was some interference, not dreadful, but a bit of a nuisance.

Thunder.

Derek Initial Report

"You have just Worked the Second Coming." Unable to tell any more at this point.

Own Report

Having sent the others to collect their forces I went straight to the Cosmos. Calling, calling.

What I took to be a star came and took station beside me, and stayed with me.

I returned to the Stones and watched the gathering. Vision not too good.

Astride PD I held the Sword in its accustomed place.

During PD address saw a giant diamond spinning, slowly, reflecting light, shafts of light, everywhere. Encased in the diamond was the Sword that I held, and still held.

This all changed and I saw what I took to be ladder rungs ascending and descending. They were every color conceivable. The perspective changed and I found that they were, in fact, a huge rainbow over us all.

During the response swords flashed on high, but all pointing in one direction. Being slightly disorientated it took me a while to realize they were all saluting King Arthur.

The departure was amazing. A golden pillar of light leapt skywards and tore through the darkness. Vortices of Force spiraling away into the darkness.

People running, jumping, laughing and disappearing from view.

It was finished.

Comment

A dream (July 30, 1986): I had organized a coach outing to somewhere.

On arrival the group of us descended into a cellar where we found gold coins. We took the gold, placed it over fire and made it into a block, which was poured into a box shaped like a Roses Chocolate Box.

This box was placed in straps for carrying, although it was too heavy to do so.

Next I was in the left hand filter lane approaching a set of traffic lights, coming from the east. I was dragging the little box along, on my hands and knees.

A policeman approached and asked if it was millions of pounds. I replied it was gold.

Next thing, he and I were in the police station, and there was a great deal of merriment in the air.

Derek Supplementary Report

As with other times building up to the day, I was not particularly well able to picture the Stones right at the beginning.

That opening scene always left me with a blankness; never could find it. However, when we started, as per usual, the Tree of Life came in straight away.

My task was to go up the Tree, which I had done before in relation to this ritual.

However, I had found, prior to this day, I had never been able to jump Daath. The Abyss had always been exactly that, an abyss. So I started with some trepidation, wondering whether or not it was going to be jumpable, and what aspect They would show me if I landed, successfully, on the other side.

Left Malkuth, taking the Center Pillar as my method of exit and return.

Yesod came up violet, no problems.

Found no colors to the Paths at all, it was just the Spheres that were illuminating.

Carried on up the Tree, with emerald coming in strongly from the right, flame orange from the left, with a color burst between Yesod and Tiphareth, a mixing of green and orange.

Gently assimilated and overcome by the golden glow of Tiphareth.

At this point I was beginning to wonder whether I shouldn't be looking at king scale colors, rather than queen scale, but, nevertheless, carried on.

Blue coming in from the right, deep red coming in from the left, forming a sort of purple haze which dissipated to the ice blue that I have come to know belongs to Daath.

Up to this stage, slow and even, no problems.

Found myself surrounded by the ice blue void which I associate with Daath.

The abyss loomed before me, a black void.

Pushed on, finding no restriction this time.

Seemed to be in blackness for some moments, expecting a change, not knowing what change to expect, but expecting something. The change, however, was subtle to begin with, remarkably subtle, because the blackness still persisted. It just, slowly but surely, became interlaced with bright shining stars and planets.

I found myself in space.

Felt, as I sometimes do in these situations, that there was a need to change perspective, a need to focus the situation; that I was too far away from where I was supposed to be, or too close to it.

Decided it was the latter. I panned the vision out and was struck by what was before me.

There, huge, the most huge thing I could ever imagine ever seeing in my life was . . . the term came to mind, a huge spaceship, to be replaced by another term, a huge bird.

I cannot say definitively whether it was either. It really seemed to be a mixture of both.

The body I find difficult to recall, because it was the thing that least struck me.

Its tail was huge and fanned out on the horizontal plane behind it.

Coming from the body were two huge wings, which curled underneath and met wingtip to wingtip, forming the shape of a rectangle, only with curved corners.

It had a huge long neck, which seemed to stretch on forever. At its end was a head, very reminiscent of a swan's head.

The gigantic size of it was demonstrated by the fact that it was holding something, within the encompassing space between the body and its wings as they curled underneath—I don't know whether it was the solar system, a galaxy, a universe, maybe even the Cosmos.

There was nothing else around it. All the stars, all the lights, were encompassed in that wing-wrapped space.

The tail, on later reflection, was very reminiscent of the tail pattern of that place in South America (Nazca) where there is a bird drawn on the ground and a lot of people have supposed it might have been a runway with the wide feathers panning out behind in a horizontal plane.

I was a bit bemused at this stage. I wasn't too sure what I was supposed to do with this.

Anyway, I registered the music changing to start the return, and I turned to come back and found it was not easy. In fact, I had difficulty, for a few moments, forcing a reversal of the procedure.

I seemed to be stuck where I was. I didn't know what I was meant to do, nor what was going to happen. I knew that I was meant to bring something back with me, but what I was supposed to bring out of the scene I had observed I don't know.

I turned and, anyway, succeeded in removing the scene from my mind, and, to do this, I had to reverse the procedure and go back into the stars, which afterwards of course was logical, but wasn't the first thing that came to mind at the time.

Back in the stars then the darkness, and just when I was beginning to wonder what was going to happen, the pale ice blue of Daath began to creep in from the edges of my vision and I was soon bathed in it.

I was not aware of bringing anything back with me. I was prepared to accept that it was not tangible, whatever it was.

I came back down through the Spheres and, as on other times, the same configuration of the same people and the same objects, coming forth and presenting themselves as I journeyed.

I ended up back in Malkuth, slightly behind schedule, but I seem to remember there was a breathing space for us to think. I was still unaware of bringing anything back.

In fact, the only thing I brought back was an understanding, I think, probably, because the next thing I saw was the dragon standing on the altar, ready to address the multitude.

The multitude really was a multitude, very much a cross section of Life, I felt. Perhaps more warriors and soldiers than normal proportions would expect; then that might have only been my bent, my way of looking at it.

The Pendragon caught my eye, purely and simply, because it was a ten, twelve, fifteen foot version of exactly what I had seen in space.

It was a baby plane/bird, as the case may be.

I wondered, I must admit, how it was going to address this multitude and, in actual fact, it addressed it in a very peculiar way.

There was a huge flash of brilliant white light and the dragon literally exploded into millions and millions of tiny little shining stars, which cascaded up into a huge fountain and fell in all directions upon those that were watching: the multitude.

Some it fell upon, and some it didn't.

Then an interesting thing happened.

Those that were touched by one of the small stars that was once the dragon stood there held in a trance with a gaze of ecstasy on their face; whereas those that weren't slunk off, like dark shadows in the night.

I thought I would try and see if I could get a look at some of those sneaking off, but that opportunity was closed to me and I was not able to do so.

What did I expect from it, or what did I not expect from it? I don't know.

Derek Comment

The end of a cycle certainly, but, of course, the beginning of another.

Of course, remembering that I have been in this since the beginning it came to fruition in the only way it could.

The dragon? Sue was of the opinion that the dragon was purely an Earth Force or Power that had been awoken. I'm not so sure. Yes, there is that element in it, of course, there has to be.

There is very much an inner and outer concept at work here, because the dragon exists within each and everyone of us, but, on the other hand, there is much, much more at stake.

As we approach Aquarius, I think perhaps it is time for each one of us to take the time and the trouble to look at what is in the water bowl that we, as the water carriers, carry around with us.

To me it was the symbol, perhaps, of the start of a New Age. The symbol of the expression of the Aquarian Cosmic Master, as and when he chooses to appear.*

I feel the symbology of the fact was in the way the dragon exploded, touching each person, because, of course, with the end of the explosion there was no dragon, yet a part of him is resident in everybody that it touched.

Yet it was a finality, in a way. One was either touched or not. I feel that is the way the Aquarian message will come through; it either touches you or it doesn't. There isn't going to be an on-drawn, on-running concept as there was with Pisces.

One is either open to the statement of Aquarius or one is not.

---

* This is the only place where I would differ. I don't think that we will, on this earth, experience a single Cosmic Master for the onset of the Aquarian Age. I believe that the Spirit of the Age will make itself felt within many people, spreading throughout the world and down the generations. This is how I choose to interpret Derek's vision of the exploding and cascading Dragon—a Second Coming of myriad proportions, under the tone and influence of Gawaine/Lancelot. This was the essence of my earlier book *Gate of Moon*. On the other hand, I wouldn't mind being wrong. I prefer the single Coming, even if it doesn't match my vision. (A.R.)

The symbology of the starship or bird, as it was, is not something I was working on at the time, nor is it something with which I am particularly acquainted. It is not one of the symbols which is in my working format.

Any bird symbol that is within my working format is the hawk, with which I work quite well, more often than not.

This was definitely not a hawk; if I had to attach it to an earthly bird I think I would call it a huge, gigantic swan.

Attack.
August 4, 1986

10:15 A.M. Val dropped me at the foot of Foel Rudd and I started up the path from Planwydd, through Bwlch Y Moch and followed the boundary fence to a tree point.

Turned north to climb, following sheep paths. Climbing from one to another. Found myself in a slate shale face, trying to climb in loose slate. Realized it was extremely dangerous, so worked my way off southwards.

Found another track leading back to the proper west northwest footpath. The thought arose, *"Not for me the direct ascent; ever the lightning flash."*

Arriving at a flat space/hollow at 11:49 A.M., with a large, flat, cuboid rock on the edge of a precipitous drop.

A commanding view of the westerly valley.

By compass, I discovered that I was in a position exactly due west of Snowdon's west face. On the face, glittering in the sunlight were large waterfalls combining to make a Y.

Having rested, at 12:30 P.M. I began to prepare myself.

At 12:42 P.M. I was ready and moved to the Stone.

At 12:45 P.M. I invoked the Most High and introduced myself by name. There came a distinct impression of entities laughing at me. I added that I was PD's rider, whereupon the laughter broke off abruptly.

Having paid my respects to all I informed them that I was on PD's business.

I gave the Dragon Call.

I called on all the Forces of Ynys Wrytten and Avalon to rise and assemble in the western valley.

(At this point a lot of red and green swam before my eyes.)

Called on King Arthur, Merlin and "N" to ride.

Called on all to ride to cleanse and heal, not to kill and hack. Ride to drive out the darkness.

Across the ridge, across the valley, up the slopes, over the water, and up the face of Snowdon, from thence out over the land.

At 1:00 P.M. I released them.

"Ride, ride," I roared. Over and over. I didn't see them go. It was almost as if they were there one second and gone the next. Faster than light.

Still I called. I fell to my knees, sobbing, "Ride, ride," overcome with emotion.

I paused, the sound of a passing jet roared across the sky, filling my heart with joy.

I sat back and took the bread, broke, ate and gave to the unseen.

I suddenly saw that I had neglected the crystal, buried in the turf. I arose and drove it into the Earth with my staff, claiming a crystal in the Holy Hills.

I took the wine, drank and gave to the unseen.

I gave thanks to those still present, sang crystal and finished at 1:15.

I moved away to my bundle to eat and write this report.

Comment

I descended the mountain. Pausing at a stile I looked back up the slope, and saw five large black birds wheeling in the sky above the site. I took them to be ravens. I walked the four miles back to the campsite.

The following day felt very tired and lackluster.

Discussion
August 10, 1986

With Val, Derek, Les and Sue.

Having reported on the activities in Wales, handed over to Sue. She had discovered that the astrological significances of doing the Working on the 28th rather than the 10th were important.

Didn't understand a lot of what she said but, in general, the effect of doing it on the 28th was extremely important. The 28th was benefic, rather than malefic on the 10th.

We must wait and see.

In general discussion, the acceptance has come that the later date was set in order to obviate the build-up of nerves. It happened all too quickly for anyone to get over worried.

Epilogue

The Work is done.

Pendragon is loose over Britain, and his influence is being felt in the land. Over the following months the media have come up with a lot of stories of dirty deeds coming to light.

One little story caught my eye. A reverend gentleman in Yorkshire has formed a "Polite Society," inviting people who join to return to the ways of chivalry and courtesy.

Over the following months things have been very quiet on the Arthurian front. I still make contact daily, but, up until the time of writing, there is no news of any further Workings.

When the time is right, we will start again.

Merlin

You may recall that in the diary when I was being "expelled" from the *FIL* I was being passed on to Merlin, who was my first contact with the Arthuriad.

At that time I was in a complete panic, not realizing what was going on. It took more than a little time to settle into the new Work.

The question arises, who/what is the Merlin?

In an endeavor to answer these simple questions I must ask you to come with me, back in the mists of time, to the Island of Ruta, the capital and central pivot of the island lands of Atlantis.

Atlantis derived its power from the transmutation of sunlight and Earth energies through a mighty crystal, which was housed in the major Sun temple, on a plateau atop the mountain in the center of Ruta.

The priests and priestesses tended the temple and its crystal with the utmost devotion and reverence. There were no human sacrifices to Sun gods etc., just an all-pervading joy in service to the one God, who is all Gods.

Depending on the aptitude of the members of the priesthood they were allocated a particular "vibration" to mediate on behalf of the land and its people.

Some were, therefore, mediators to the Moon, the Sea, the Earth, the Sun, etc.

Atlantis had reached the height of its power and influence; it could evolve no further.

Elements of the priesthood were, therefore, "moved" to endeavor to reorientate the crystal power to other means. It is unclear and unnecessary to know what this aim was.

Suffice it to say that they were allowed to attempt it.

Other members of the priesthood were fully aware that the end of Atlantis was due.

In an attempt to retain the essential elements of their way of life, these priests and priestesses arranged a colonization program for expansion.

Volunteers were called for an expedition to colonize the Western lands and they set forth, taking with them, naturally, representatives of the priesthood to care for the explorers, to be their High Priest and

High Priestess, and to carry the knowledge with them in order that it should survive.

Time passed and the Atlanteans lost interest and contact was broken with the settlers.

A further expedition was then mounted, but this time to head toward the East, the West having been considered a failure.

The migration repeated itself inasmuch as the priesthood traveled again, for the same reasons.

This journey was even longer than the previous one and contact was lost almost immediately.

Time was running out.

A third and final migration was hurriedly gathered together and they were bundled aboard a single ship. On board were a Priest of the Moon and a Sea Priestess. They were to be the colony's High Priest and High Priestess.

There was no decision made as to where they were to go; there just wasn't time.

Three days out, looking astern, the migrants saw a cloud of blackness on the far horizon.

There was no time to grieve. Crew and passengers leapt to their feet and frantically prepared the ship to ride out the coming tidal wave.

And come it did, with a vengeance.

For days the ship was flung from billow to billow, often in dire straits, never far from totally floundering. Any pretense at following any specific course had been blown to the winds.

As with all things, it eventually came to an end and the sea calmed.

Battered and bruised the migrants began to take stock of their surroundings.

To starboard there were inhospitable cliffs, pounded by the ocean rollers, without, it appeared, any suitable landing area.

It was decided to keep heading, generally, toward the north, following the coastline until they should chance upon a suitable landing point.

Two days later, in deep water off the coastline, they became aware of the fact that they were in real trouble with a lack of drinking water and, cliffs or not, they would have to make a landing.

Fortune smiled on them and a small beach, with scalable cliffs, hove into view.

Thankfully, they landed in what was to be their new homeland.

After many attempts they finally managed to get everyone up onto the clifftop, where they discovered that there was an indigenous population of a semi-nomadic people.

They were received courteously and, before long, were accepted into the tribe. A relationship developed, each learning from the other, as their tenets were found to be compatible.

The Atlanteans learnt that there were many of these tribes scattered throughout the land, but each tribe was bound by treaty to a specified area of the country and they remained therein.

After a few weeks of traveling and resting the tribe came to a region of small islands in a vast lakeland area.

The Atlantean contingent, feeling somewhat homesick, decided to start their colony in these islands, and the tribe moved on, leaving the Atlanteans to sort themselves out.

The Atlanteans settled quickly and soon became a sizable community. Word of their settlement soon spread throughout the land.

Tribal elders from the semi-nomadic peoples expressed the desire to meet and talk with the newcomers and the word was passed back to the community.

Here was a new concept for the Atlantean priest and priestess, so far they had always remained in their temple and those who sought them knew where to find them. But, these were new conditions in a new environment and required adaptations to be made.

After lengthy considerations it was decided that the High Priestess would remain in the community, whilst the High Priest was given a roving commission to travel the land, meeting the tribal elders, teaching and learning, but to return to the community for each winter period.

The High Priest was also encouraged to seek out prospective candidates for the future priests and priestesses, and to send them back to the islands for training.

The system worked well for a number of years. The community settled into a routine and the knowledge spread throughout the land. Candidates duly arrived for training and ordination into the priesthood.

In the fullness of time, the original High Priest and High Priestess died and were replaced by suitable successors, and the wheel continued to turn with the passing of time, and a new High Priest and a new High Priestess were chosen from the priesthood as required.

Early one spring, word was received in the community of the arrival of a new group of people on the land's shore.

The High Priest was dispatched, forthwith, to meet and greet these newcomers and to invite them back to the community if they so wished to come.

Come they did, were made welcome and were soon accepted into the priesthood. The tenets were extremely compatible and blended well.

Over the next few hundred years things continued pleasantly, but evolution required movement.

Schisms erupted, basic tenets were "adjusted" to meet the changing face of life and the ways of men; they lost the original theme.

One broke away from the other, setting up a separate establishment in close proximity to the first.

The first battle for the hearts and minds of the populace was launched. It was a long and, sorry to say, bloody exchange, which produced nothing.

A halt was called, finally, because a war-like invader was crossing the eastern sea, bent on rapine, pillaging and looting. Previously, invaders had landed and settled into the land without, comparatively, undue problem; allowing the religions to flourish as they would. A truce was called between the religious factions in order to meet this foe with a common front.

A search was instigated throughout the land for a common war leader to lead the armies against the invader. One was found, a tribal chieftain known as Uther.

The High Priests of both factions joined his cabinet of ministers in order to aid the war effort.

A High Priestess was quickly trained to undertake the roving commission of the High Priest, since he now had other duties, and was dispatched into the land.

In order to differentiate between them, the two sects chose names to identify their leaders.

One called himself the Archbishop, the other called himself the Merlin.

The roving High Priestess chose to call herself Morgana (from the Sea—harking back to the original Sea Priestess).

The static High Priestess adopted the title, Lady of the Lakes.

The rest of the story lies, hidden, in the Legends of the Arthuriad (King Arthur and the knights of the Round Table).

With the coming of peace to Britain the religious factions prepared to battle for their individual existences, but the Merlin refused to allow any further hostilities and disbanded his priesthood, offering them the opportunity to join the new church or of returning to their homes.

It is unclear how the Lady of the Lakes took this, but legend has it that she wove a mist to conceal her island home in Avalon, down in the Summer County, and that maidens, still drawn to the Old Ways, may find their way there.

The legend tells us that there was a final battle and that King Arthur was mortally wounded. He dispatched one of the surviving knights of the Round Table to return the sword Excalibur to the Lady of the Lakes. (There is a lot of controversy over the exact identification of this knight, but it is not essential to our present tale.)

The legend continues that Arthur was taken by royal barge, accompanied by three ladies, across the sea to Ynys Wryten (the Isle of Glass) to be healed of his wounds and to await his country's call.

The Merlin himself disappeared into obscurity once his task was done, and he took himself off to a cave where he sealed himself away and slept until the day he was needed again—when England stood in Peril, just as she did in the early 1940s.

An old school friend of mine, Terry (we do have friends who are not in the Work), very kindly furnished the following information.

In 1936 a gentleman by the name of Mitchell, an aircraft designer, was commissioned by the then Ministry of Aviation (or Air) to design an aircraft around a prototype engine that had been designed and built by a Mr. Rolls and a Mr. Royce.

Suffice it to say, he did so, and produced the Spitfire, and Hurricane fighters.

(Interestingly, let us have a look at the name "Spitfire": A machine (beast?) that flies through the air, "sleeps" on the ground and unleashes flame against its enemies. Are we defining a plane or a dragon?)

In September, 1940 came the Battle of Britain. These little aircraft and their pilots battled their way to supremacy of the skies over England averting the threatened invasion by the Third Reich.

The name given to the engines? Merlin.

As well as being used in these fighters, the engines were also used in Lancasters, Mosquitoes, and Halifaxes.

Additionally, Britain negotiated with the United States of America for Mustangs under lease/lend. On arrival the aircraft's Packard engines were inspected, overhauled and modified by the Merlin engineers.

It could be argued, philosophically, therefore, that Merlin awoke and came to Britain's aid in her darkest hour, in fulfillment of the legend/prophecy.

Additionally, the various aircraft propelled by the Merlin engines became the modern weapons, the swords wielded by the modern Knights. The spirit of Excalibur, driven by the Merlin energy, carried the pilot/knights, with the spirit of King Arthur and the Round Table Knights in their blood, in the final defense of the land.

(By and by, when these engines had been modified and boosted as far as possible, a new engine was produced and fitted to, amongst others, the Seafire, for use by the Royal Navy. This engine was called the Gryphon—a mythological beast on the lines of a dragon. It could be argued that the Dragon took over from Merlin, in this context.)

These lines have indicated the Merlin of the past, his origins and his intentions.

But what of Merlin today?

He appears to a large number of people in different guises. I wish it to be strictly understood that I lay no claims to being the *only* one to have contact with him, nor do I lay any claim to being the Merlin of Britain today.

There are a vast number of people, not only in England I would add, who have made this contact. Friends in the United States have also made the contact as a result of their visits to England and Wales; admittedly they are Anglophiles.

As far as I am aware, and he has never given any indication to the contrary, he very, very rarely appears in the Spiritualist environment. He has once muttered something about not being dead. On only two occasions that I know of has he done so: once to John and Margaretta, and the second time to a platform medium when I took a Sunday evening break from pounding the keyboard with these words to accompany my long-suffering wife to church. All three, initially, described him as a Chinaman, full of philosophy and wisdom.

There is a particular, symbolic picture that he presents to me clairvoyantly. There is a "feeling" that accompanies this vision that "tells" me it is not my mind-generated anthropomorphism.

It is very difficult to explain; it is a *knowing*.

There can be, under these circumstances, absolutely no question that it is him.

Yes, I admit that on many occasions when I request his presence I am only aware of my own impression of him, but, on the important occasions, when he feels it is necessary, he makes damn sure there can be no question of it.

He is there.

As you may have noticed in the diary, the representations and impressions vary, from time to time.

He has appeared as the Disney version (see *Sword in the Stone*), as the Boorman portrayal (see *Excalibur*) and, quite often, simply as a vortex of Force, or a patch of color (amethyst).

The "uncertainty" of *how* he will appear adds a little zest to the contact when it is made. One seems to expect one thing, and something the complete opposite turns up.

His self-portrayal in human form is in the guise of a monkish style habit, with hood, drawstring at the waist, but with long flowing "wings" from his ankles to wrists, so that when he raises his arms the movement is emphasized by the sweep of the cloth.

He, quite often, but not always, carries a staff, almost as tall as himself. I have never truly discovered of what wood it is made. It is totally plain, without any embellishment whatsoever.

Naturally, he is bearded, but the eyes defy description—I leave that to you to find out for yourself. They are rather wonderful.

In essence, he is the wisdom of time and energy that is England and Wales.

Although there is the legend of "sleeping" during the past 1500 years, it has been a "sleeping" whilst watching. He is more than fully aware of what has gone on during this time and has kept an interest in all things dealing with the evolution of these islands.

There is a distinct and very severe streak of sternness. He can be extremely caustic, if not downright b****y rude, even though he can laugh and display a bright, merry sense of humor.

Unfortunately, this does not happen very often. He is a stern taskmaster, who drives hard, not because he wants to but because he *has* to.

He is constantly impressing on me that time is short (for what I am not sure) and that we must buckle down to the job in hand.

He maintains that we need all the hands we can muster, but, above all, they must be willing hands, without coercion, not just here in England and Wales, but also the other lands need Workers for their own archetypes.

It is the worldwide situation that needs rectification and restoring to balance which can only be resolved through people, ordinary people, being prepared to act as catalysts.

Finding

The Path

Part III

Personal Alchemy

Introduction

The Magical Currents worked within the Golden Dawn are still there, as potent as they ever were. They always have been and always will be. But the methods of working them both, and looking at them, must necessarily alter.

There are several techniques that we can use which will trigger off a certain resonance within ourselves. This in itself is akin to what Dion described as "the call of Isis," vibrating on the inner planes, drawing like-souled individuals into the personal orbit, linking him with the Current.

Any individual can and eventually must create his own techniques. He need pay no fees for mystic wisdoms, submit himself to no occult initiations, or bow down to any portenteous dogma spooned out on a monthly basis.*

To an extent, *any* self-devised technique will create the upwelling of magical energy that will attract the otherworld contacts like moths to the flame. Or, if we look at it another way, will bring the Secret Chiefs surging out of our own depths, toward the light of our own new dawn.

But far more important than the techniques we will shortly look at is attitude—especially an attitude that was first put forward within the oath of the Adeptus Exemptus as taken within the **GD**. The oath itself was probably created by Felkin during one of his more expansive days, but it is a supremely important one nonetheless, and which contains the keys of all magic. It is to the effect that everyone must learn to look at every event, every happening and circumstance as a secret dealing between himself, and the spirit of the Gods which move him.

This is not a matter of swearing by bell, book, and candle—and then forgetting about it. It is a matter of *living* it. In effect, this turns the whole of one's life into a very potent "Pathworking," as they call it. We

---

* Few modern lodges in England obsess themselves with the old Masonic/*GD* type grades. The best magical groups are formed by individuals, admitting friends or fellow-enthusiasts only, with no intention of throwing their little lodges open to the public, or turning themselves into empire-building Ipsissimii.

deliberately choose to act as if our lives could be seen in terms of some great and unfolding mystery. Nor is it a matter of bringing powerful intellectual weapons to bear, analyzing each incident in the light of current psychological formulae from whatever school. Rather should we sit down before magic like a little child: with awe and wonder, and the simplicity that we all tend to lose in growing old.

Slowly—and sometimes not so slowly—things will happen. Synchronistic events will become commonplace; far memories will spring up with varying degrees of intensity and accuracy; a life of augury and omen will become possible when one learns to interpret the signs effectively.

This in itself is not a substitute for High Magic. Nevertheless, the practice of High Magic without this attitude will mean that the energies will fail to earth themselves properly, or work out in effective ways. On the other hand this *can* provide a valid byway in its own right for those who are not attracted to the path of ritual and group ceremony, and who would rather enter the emerald mysteries of the Green Ray by more individual routes.

But when this little byway becomes the *sole* path, the person who treads it will quickly discover that it is not an easy, lazy means of avoiding the rigors and hardships always encountered in more formal, structured systems: in its own way it will throw up quite as many tests and obstacles.

The moral being that there is no easy or soft path within the realm of magic; never has been and never will be.

Whether one links with the Magical Current of the *FIL*, the Stella Matutina, or the loyalist Temples of the Golden Dawn (or something completely different again) cannot really be predicted. It is a matter for the individual to make sense of as he wills.

I believe, for example, that in the absorption of typing up the magical diaries of Charles Seymour and Christine Campbell Thomson, I touched upon the egregore of the *SM*, which in itself overlapped with the work being done between the wars in the Fraternity of the Inner Light. I also believe that the ideas about this tribal system of magic were stimulated in some sense by an inner contact with Dion Fortune, who seems to me to be most surely a member of my own inner tribe—whether I like her or not.

The Magical Current and the tribe are largely synonymous, as I understand them—even given that these, especially the former, are terms of convenience. Using the oath as described earlier, I have tried to make sense of it all to my own satisfaction. It would be blissful if the student could rip it all to shreds and substitute ideas of his own, to *his* own satisfaction.

We must backtrack within the text now and look at something that was discussed earlier. In fact, we need to find ourselves a Name, in order to begin creating ourselves anew. The Name should neither be mundane, nor relate to any specific character from myth or legend. Perhaps, like the Adepti of the Golden Dawn, we might choose one from a book of mottoes—though it need not be one appertaining to our own family.

The Magical Name often has, in a sense, a life of its own. The initiate (and thus the beginner) will often find that it will come to him apparently of its own accord, and seem so supremely appropriate that he will have no hesitation in using it. My own Name appeared when I happened to open the back of an old dictionary and came across some foreign phrases and sayings. The Name in question, in Greek, seemed to leap from the page, causing the crude predecessor that I had been using for convenience's sake to drop out of my mind entirely.

We can add weight to the Name by any number of simple ritual acts:

Write it on a slip of paper, take it to some meaningful Holy Place (meaningful and holy to you, that is), and if possible push it into the ground.

Write it on a slip of paper and burn it, scattering the ashes, and visualizing the Name spreading its resonance throughout the Otherworld as the smoke thins in the air.

In some country place, or even in the garden, scoop a small hole below a favorite tree or bush, and whisper the Name into it, "burying" it again afterwards.

Plant the Name, with due ceremony, along with some long-standing shrub.

These are all simple and obvious devices, easily and infinitely varied, but which nevertheless can have a great impact when it comes to imbuing the new Name with a sense of its potential.

Never tell anyone your true Magical Name. If you ever join a group which uses the system, devise an Outer Name—an alternative Magical Name that others can know and use, but keep the Inner Name sacred.

The Body of Light

Reversing the usual procedure of the mundane world, we have to think of a new body to match the Name. This is the Body of Light, as it is rather pleasingly called.

Build a mental image of yourself as you would want it to be. Make it larger or smaller, dark or fair—the sort of physique and presence you would have had if you could have chosen.

Then clothe it in the sort of way that would feel appropriate for the work in hand, preferably in the essentially timeless classical or Egyptian garb. Keep it simple, and bright. If the visualization and the need compels, you can always make it more exotic in the later stages.

The next stage is to weld the Name and the Body together. Once again the procedure is simple, but must be done over a period of time.

Sit or lie down in some appropriate place, where you are not likely to be disturbed. Visualize the Body of Light standing in front of you; then, imagine that your consciousness is *within* that image, that you *are* the Body of Light, and able to see the room from its perspective.

Although this is one of the techniques which leads to astral projection we need not worry ourselves about achieving this particular feat. Time and space being relative, there is little need to travel by this magical means, for we can just easily *bring the places to us*. And indeed, the magi of today are far less prone to simple astral projections than the more lurid commentators would have us believe.

With a sense of your consciousness planted within the Body of Light, then, looking down upon your physical self, begin to intone your Name, using it as a sort of mantra, visualizing its vibrations like a heartbeat, energizing the Body and making its colors brighter, its image so much more strong.

Sometimes on these occasions there really will be a strong transferral of consciousness and the initiate will to all intents and purposes be experiencing full astral projection—but this is by no means essential or indeed common. In fact, the first experiences of this technique are likely to be confused, dull, and a bit dispiriting when nothing cosmic happens. Often, the initiate will fall asleep. On the other hand, if he persists easily and gracefully and with determination, in a surprisingly short space of time he will come to realize that there is now something positive and potent within his psyche that did not exist before. The Body of Light will form with remarkable ease; the Name will imbue him with a definite sense of energy. He will become aware that he now has a vehicle that will help him enter the Other-world, and bring portions of its wonders back with him.

Contacting the Chiefs

At this point, as most people do, we might make some tentative efforts toward making contact with those tribal leaders known as the Secret Chiefs. It would be very unusual if the initiate made a conscious inner contact during these early stages, but human nature being what it is the newcomer will always skip ahead to this apparently more dramatic point.

We must choose our own Chiefs, understanding as we do so that they have already chosen us. We must choose them knowing that they are part of ourselves—but not in the crude psychological sense that they are merely dramatized projections that exist solely within our own individual consciousness. If the tribe is a living corporate whole, then we exist on equal terms around the circle, but in different realms. Contacting the Chiefs is nothing to do with worshipping them, or making a cult out of them, because if we do that we are really worshipping ourselves, with all the attendant problems that would cause.

Choose one of the Chiefs, then. It can be one of those used by Dion, or it can be the trinity of Kha'm-uast, Cleomenes III and Lord Eldon as envisaged by Seymour. It can be someone quite different indeed, if none of these appeal. If any historical character has ever made any impact upon you by virtue of his or her wisdom, courage, or grace, then use their image and act "as if." It is exceedingly unlikely that anything will come through in these early stages, but the value of this exercise is not in mediating the thoughts and impulses of discarnate entities, but in exercising the mind in these directions. There is nothing inherently dangerous about this: orthodox Christians do it every time they go to church and pray. Nor is there anything particularly wonderful: you are doing no more than seeking to exercise your birthright, and become part of your inward tribe.

So, the step to be taken now is to visualize two pillars. The right hand pillar should be white, and the left hand pillar black. They should be slightly taller than yourself. They can be in any style that your imagination can support.

Merlin

Using your Body of Light, stand before these astral columns and look into the darkness beyond.

If you have determined to make contact with, say, Merlin, then picture him as you see fit, building his image as strongly as you can until he stands before you at the other side of the pillars—almost like a reflection.

If you are able to hold the image with any degree of strength then the next stage is to "talk" to Merlin. This should be in simple, straight-forward language. You are not making the plea of some wretched soul toward some unearthly and terrible power, begging for favors and promising things in return. You are not demanding psi powers and domination over others—or any nonsense like that. You are a "free born man" doing no more than saying something like: "I would like to learn from you: I am willing to listen."

That said or similar, just hold the image as long as you can and give it a chance to reply. It probably won't. Although in a few cases, as happened with Dion and the Master Rakoczi, a conscious response might well occur. This might take the form of actual words, or ideas; it is more likely that the image that you had been holding with some effort will suddenly become vivified, intense, and apparently in no further need of your mental support.

This is a signal that the form you have provided to make the contact has become "filled" with the essence that has decided to respond.

The figure of Merlin was suggested for this exercise because after all he has a unique status in the magical world and the minds of men. Morever he is not plagued with the sort of problems that are attached to the likes of Lord E., Carstairs, and the rest. In his remarkable book *The Prophetic Vision of Merlin*, R. J. Stewart comments:

> In one sense we all inherit (Merlin's) influence through time; in historical and cultural patterns epitomized by the models of Arthur's court which he helped to create, in ethical terms by his refusal to be a sacrifice to dark powers, and in magical terms through the specifically western . . . meta-psychology associated with his name. It is this last area in which his direct heirs and pupils are found, for those who apply to this system of defining and altering consciousness are literally under the tutelage of Merlin. Other figures stand out in the inner vision as heirs and teachers, but Merlin stands at the head of the fountain, and awaits our questioning awareness.*

* *The Prophetic Vision of Merlin*, R. J. Stewart, R.K.P. Ltd. London 1986

So like those people once did in Carnegie Dickson's room in upper Harley Street, we might do worse than take out the two pillars which symbolize the gate to the Otherworld, and set our conscious-ness toward the archmage awaiting in the darkness beyond.

This is not to say that we must think our task achieved in the unlikely event of making an instant contact with the entity who had once given Arthur the sword Excalibur, and taught him the secrets of real kingship. Bearing in mind that we must hold all things lightly, there is the story of Jung and Elijah to be considered.

> One of his first attempts to talk to such figures was with an old man and a girl who surprised him by telling him that they were Elijah and Salome. Jung thought it the strangest combination, but Elijah assured him that they had belonged together through all eternity. Later he found other examples of such couples in many myths: Klingsor and Kundry, Lao-tzu and the dancing girl, the Gnostic tradition of Simon Magus, who was always with a young girl he had picked up in a brothel who was said to be a reincarna-tion of Helen of Troy, and many others. Elijah and Salome were accompanied by a large black snake that took a great fancy to Jung. Elijah seemed to Jung the most reasonable and intelligent of the three. This trio was with him for some time and gradually the figure of Philomen developed from Elijah.

Philomen was a kind of sub-angelic non-historical entity which comprised all the qualities of the preceding figures, and who became a very effective inner teacher for Jung, although he would not have looked at that being in quite the same way we have looked at the Chiefs. But the real significance of the tale is that Jung did not get "stuck" upon the image of Elijah, as magicians and more ordinary mediums become fixed upon the identities of their inner contacts. That wise old man would have let Lord E., for example, work himself out within his unconscious, and allow for the opportunity of change. Likewise, he did not believe the LaoTzu and the dancing girl were later incarnations of Elijah and Salome—but he made use of the suggestiveness.

So whoever or whatever appears beyond the gate, understand that while you might make use of their form, you must never try and hold it. Let them come and let them go. They cannot hurt you, any-more than you can hurt yourself by pulling faces in the mirror. They are parts of you. Ask them what they have to teach you.

So . . . the pillars are the prerequisite, fashioned according to the nation, artistic style, race, or religious system to which you feel most drawn. They define the boundary between this world and the Otherworld. And in time, with practice, you will be able to build your own temple in much the same way.

Imagine this to be situated *within* the brain, below and to the rear, joining the cerebrum and cerebellum, linking the right and left halves. Picture it as being here, rather than at the front of the forehead where most visualization feels as if it occurs.

The actual structure of the temple can begin with no more than a simple cubic-shaped room. Traditionally the floor is seen as covered with black and white tiles, with a double-cubed altar in the center. If your imagination can support it, try and use the pattern of the red dragon that writhed across the floors of the Golden Dawn's vaults.

What is important is to have some sense of the quarters. Decide that the direction you enter the temple is from the East. You can use your now-familiar pillars again here, built into the wall, or you can build up an appropriate and entirely magical gate, or door.

In these early stages you should keep all the walls blank, except for that in the North. It is here, in the quarter of night, that you might care to set the symbols of whichever Order or system of magic you would wish to contact: the Rose upon the Cross, the serpent-mounted Kronos column from Atlantis, the Eye in the Triangle, the Star within the Crescent, or a variety of Egyptian god-symbols. Individual research and/or intuition will provide the right ones. Set them into this northern wall like images in stained glass and hold them there as you go about your other Work. As with the entities whose images you have built beyond the pillars there will come a time when they will take on a unique intensity, or change into something very specific of their own accord. It is a sign, in fact, that your inward call is being answered.

As before, however, the real task is to build your temple as *you* wish it, use it as *you* deem fit. If nothing else you will be creating a place of peace and sanctuary that will always be open to you within this rather troubled world. Start with nothingness and silence, and as the years go by you will realize that these are the most powerful and magical qualities of all.

T hus far we have made some considerable strides toward picking up the essence of magic, and learned to do it for ourselves, by ourselves. If the initiate, while practicing the techniques already described, also goes about his daily life looking at it in terms of the aforementioned oath, then he will begin to find himself linking with something very subtle, very old, and very real. The so-called synchronistic events will start to become commonplace, indicating that inward energies are being used; people of like spirit will be drawn into his orbit; the knowledge needed for the next stages will appear from the most unlikely sources.

There was an exercise given in my book *Gate of Moon* which is largely a summation of this, but using the mythos of the Round Table in lieu of the tribe. Actually, this image of the Round Table, where every man is equal even with the king, and where they are all part of one corporate whole and nothing without each other, is perhaps the best concrete image of the tribal concept to work upon.

> Picture yourself entering a medieval hall which contains the Round Table. Twelve of the thirteen seats are filled. The last one, the Seige Perilous, is yours to claim by right. See yourself in a simple white tunic, feel yourself to be the best knight in the world, the culmination of our ancient heritage and yet the precursor of a new order. You know that when you take your proper place that a lost piece shall be found and the circle will come alive. The other knights look at you expectantly and in some awe. After a moment of great deliberation as to the significance of the act you finally take your place at the table. Arthur, on the other side, smiles at you and nods. You nod back for this is your liege, and you have no inflated conceits. Now the Company is made whole, now the ancient torn web is rebuilt, yet you know that without the others you are nothing. The Company joins hands. The table is suddenly seen to be made not of wood but of light. It becomes a disk whirling at enormous speed, deosil. You can hear the rhythmic humming it makes as *awen, awen, awen* . . . Become aware of the center—of an invisible yet strongly felt axis. Watch the center split open to form a hole. See the hole expand. You and the Company are now looking into the hole as it widens almost to the table's rim, so that only a thin ring of light surrounds the darkness of interstellar space. Now you can express one wish into that night but it must be as a single word. You can cry out for light, love, learning, health, unity or whatever concept is most important to you. Express this Word powerfully and imagine it traveling through the infinite depths of space. The darkness now becomes radiant, lit by stars, planets, whole galaxies which gleam like jewels on velvet, and which are the atoms of your own bones. The hole begins to close again. The surface of the Table is once more unbroken. The whole scene fades and you slowly come back to the present . . .

One of the techniques used within one modern occult school is to build up this great circle and then see who or what appears directly opposite, this being the magician's counterpart upon the inner planes, and a direct guide for the work ahead.

While in his essay concluding this book, Colonel Seymour gives some fairly explicit directions as to how each person can make direct mind-to-mind contact with Kha'm-uast, and Ne Nefer Ka Ptah—two of the greatest magicians from Ancient Egypt. This may or may not work, for it all depends upon the Magical Current and the tribe. The effort alone will ensure that one day the right contacts and linkage will make themselves felt, and by that time the initiate will *know* it, even if nothing visual appears to his psychic senses: He will feel it in the gut.*

Of course he will make mistakes, and make a fool of himself on more than one occasion—usually through an excess of enthusiasm. But that, too, is part of the way, part of the "secret dealing" between himself and his Gods.

S o far the initiate has taken a rather passive stance. He has taken his place between the pillars and waited for his contacts from the Otherworld to appear before him.

It is possible now to extend the magical practice in the form of journeys, both actual and visualized.

The latter is what is now known as Pathworking, and has risen to an unusual degree of prominence in the world of modern magic. Perhaps it is something to do with the extent that today's generations are influenced by visual stimuli in the form of television, and cinema. It was a major part of the Golden Dawn's system too, in which one person would narrate a journey and the rest of the group would attempt to join in. Anyone who has taken part in any effective Pathworking will testify as to the high degree of agreement achieved within the visions of an experienced group. Again, the reality of the landscapes is not the important thing, for the images themselves awaken the sort of feelings that real and impressive natural features would have within the soul; more, because these are inner landscapes charged with the energies of Myth, the impact can be far deeper than the non-participant might imagine.

---

* One of the wisest and nicest magicians I know cannot *see* a thing, but in other ways he is just as aware as anyone, and more than most.

An example:

Imagine yourself in your Body of Light, at twilight, facing into a deep and narrow valley, the long pale hills at either side stretching away before you, joining in the distance at a thick triangle of woods. The sky is silvery-violet, there is a crescent moon and star rising above the valley's end, above the trees. The evening is warm and thrums with life; you are keyed into a peculiar expectancy, with the sense that you are returning to a place that you have known for many aeons . . .

The end of the valley is immediately before you. The trees fan away up the slope. The moon and stars are only just visible above the tops, turning them into silver and black shapes amid the gathering darkness.

Ahead of you, just visible, is a narrow path between the first two trees. It is a straight path and a short one. You follow it. It brings you into a small glade where you feel safer and more complete than you have ever done.

There is a deep, dark pool in the glade with a standing stone at the far side. This stone is your exact height, and carved with strange symbols. You walk around the pool and touch the stone and feel an electric thrill. Clearly, it is alive and sentient, and contains the knowledge that you know to be locked within your genes, if you could but tap it. The water of the pool laps against it. Its darkness acts as a mirror. Determined to learn what you can about your own occult roots, you kneel down at the edge of the pool and stare into it, willing the images to arise . . .

Such is the basis of a crude but very effective piece of solo pathworking, and one which is based upon some obvious feminine symbolism. To get the best out of it, go through the stages of the journey very casually with your conscious mind at first, making sure that the symbolism is clear, and then begin the journey toward this Great Mother with deliberate magical intent. You will find that the images will spring into being more easily if you keep up an internal running commentary, rather than if you just let the mind drift along. Thus, with your inner voice, begin: "I am standing at the mouth of a valley. It is twilight. The sky is . . . The hills at either side are . . . Ahead of me . . . " And so on. It is an individual thing, of course, and no virtue should be made of any poetic evocation along the way. If images do arise within the pool—and they nearly always do—don't be startled, and don't stop to analyze them. Just observe, remember, and keep up the commentary. A lot of it may well be no more than flotsam and jetsam thrown out by a busy mind, but in due course images akin to "far memories" will arise and which may very well be that. This, in a sense, is the Pool of your Ancestors, the watering place of your tribe. This glade can in turn become your own magical temple. It is your place, use it how you will, and adapt it as you see fit. Keep quiet about it, and keep it holy to yourself alone.

The other journey is an actual one. It depends upon each person's assessment of those places upon this Earth that are, to him, "special," and where he feels that he most surely belongs. It is nothing to do with identifiable centers that have long architectural and religious associations. It can be a place in the backwoods where a sense of peace and rightness has been felt. It can be a corner of a busy square in a large city. One old Adept told me that the most vital power center he had ever felt was, to his immense surprise, just outside Charing Cross railway station in the heart of London.

Ideally each initiate should try to identify a high place, a valley, a stream, a moor, and a lake or pond where he feels most at home with the elemental forces. It does not matter in the slightest that these places are entirely undistinguished in the eyes of others. If there are any ancient remains there, so much the better, for if nothing else they act as confirmation of both antiquity and singularity. This is not an essential criterion, however, for in the New World the initiate finds himself akin to those magi from pre-history, scouring the land for those sites which would one day be graced by the megaliths, tapping the forces within like the needles of an acupuncturist.

If such physical journeys are impractical then the initiate can, in his Body of Light, bring those places to himself. In this wise the time-lost temples of Egypt, Greece, Rome, Babylon and ancient Britain are forever open, forever potent. It is simply a matter of building them up in the imagination, getting a real sense and feel as to their inner nature, and waiting for the energies within those primordial altars to begin to thrum. The magicians of the Golden Dawn did so not so very long ago, and there is no reason why those mystic portals should not admit us still today.

And although I am not personally interested in Atlantis despite some clear images of that place over the years, several modern magicians are convinced as to its effectiveness as a source. It is so obviously the homeland to so many of the Adepti that it would be worthwhile to build up the images of its various temples and see what comes through.*

---

* See *The Sea Priestess*, Dion Fortune, for vivid descriptions of that continent and its temples. This is the best novel on magic ever written.

A parallel technique to all this, and one which ties in with the oath, involves research into one's own family background. It is more than just finding out the names of one's forebears: it involves research into *where* they lived and *when*, linking their existence with local myths and legends, with family traditions, and trying to create a reasonably elegant narrative. Of course the researcher will not lose track of reality during all this, acting at all times under the Ignatian formula (see page 292 of *Children of the Great Mother* in Part IV).

In the fullness of time the initiate will come to make a very powerful link with the land itself. He will come to feel himself as involved in a symbiotic relationship with that part of the Earth he regards as most surely his home. In different and non-intellectual ways the land will come to talk to him, and teach him things.

Once, my wife and I rented an old gardener's cottage from one of the local gentry, a lovely and kind man who exemplified the best of a bygone age, and who had been born and raised in the valley wherein we all lived. Devoted to the land, passionate in his quiet way, it was no surprise that at the moment of his death the springs under his house dried up—for the first time in recorded history. He was part of the valley, and the valley was a part of him; and when he died, that was the way the valley showed its grief.

And there was Old Griff, who once lived on a mountain in the heart of Wales, and who had a reputation of being a wonderworker among the locals in the pre-television era. Every day he went up the mountain to tend his sheep, and commune in his quiet way with the spirit of the mountain. After a bad fall, when the doctor told him that he must never climb the summit again Old Griff replied: "Then it is time for me to die."

And he did.

This sort of mutual response is the necessary end result of the oath, which in some rare folk is more of a genetic bond than a conscious act. D. H. Lawrence, no small nature mystic himself, gave one of the best descriptions of this process in the final paragraphs of his final book *Apocalypse*.

> For man, the vast marvel is to be alive. For man, as for flower and beast and bird, the supreme triumph is to be most vividly, most perfectly alive. Whatever the unborn and dead may know, they cannot know the beauty, the marvel of being alive in the flesh. The dead may look after the afterwards. But the magnificent here and now of life in the flesh is ours, and ours alone, and ours

only for a time. We ought to dance with rapture that we should be alive and in the flesh, and part of the living, incarnate cosmos. I am part of the sun as my eye is part of me. That I am part of the earth my feet know perfectly, and my blood is part of the sea. My soul knows that I am part of the human race, my soul is an organic part of the great human soul, as my spirit is part of my nation. In my own very self, I am part of my family. There is nothing of me that is alone and absolute except my mind, and we shall find that the mind has no existence by itself, it is only the glitter of the sun on the surface of the waters.

So that my individualism is really an illusion. I am a part of the great whole, and I can never escape. But I *can* deny my connections, break them, and become a fragment. Then I am wretched.

What we want is to destroy our false, inorganic connections, especially those related to money, and re-establish the living organic connections, with the cosmos, the sun and earth, with mankind and nation and family. Start with the sun, and the rest will slowly, slowly happen.

All of which is really an extension of the old initiatic cry "There is no part of me that is not a part of the Gods!" To which might be added: "Nor is there any part of the Gods which is not also a part of the land."

Yet as with all things concerning the Earth Mother or the Great Mother this is by no means a path of sweetness and light, and simpering magi walking hand in hand into some ineffably benign sunset. No spiritual path is ever like that. If one is to become a whole person then the darkness and the hardship has to be confronted too, and the initiate will find himself tested in those very areas of his personality he would hope to specialize. As Dion Fortune pointed out during her own moments of despair, Isis as the All-Mother has black and white sides, and it is the former that must be thoroughly dealt with before the *real* power can come through.

In other terms this is also Morgan le Fay versus Guinevere, the latter name meaning "White Shadow," and who in the original tales was far far more than an empty adultress.

All of which must bring us back by slow, inevitable stages to Merlin himself—that archmagician who stands on the cusp of the aeons and who overshadows all those more localized, more specialized figures of Michael Scot, Lailoken, Herne, Thomas of Ercildoune, Gwyn ap Nudd—or whoever. These all blend into a single whole, like drops of liquid in a chalice. So if we are still in doubt as to how we might travel that savage and beautiful landscape beyond the pillars we have created, then we might do worse than begin with him.

The techniques given herein are simple, crude, but very effective, and capable of infinite extension. They will help to make the final link between yourself and Merlin—or whomever might choose you. All the mythological imagery needed can be found in any public library. If the would-be magus has neither the wit, imagination, energy nor willingness to do research of his own, and create his own techniques, he will not get very far in magic. Anyway, the real magicians do not practice magic, they live it. It is all to be found within the head, the heart, the gut, and the good earth.

There are several books which *can* be recommended, although these are not in any way essential.

Ellic Howes' *Magicians of the Golden Dawn* is the most meticulous and thoroughly researched history of the Order, although this is best balanced by Francis King's *Ritual Magic*, which has a greater understanding of the principles behind magic.

For those of an intellectual "Hermetic" bent there is *Magical Ritual Methods* by William G. Gray. Covering the same topic, but rather more accessible, is *The Ritual Magic Workbook*, by Dolores Ashcroft-Nowicki.

The latter is also the editor of *The Forgotten Mage*, which is a compilation of Colonel Seymour's essays, some of which rank amongst the best ever written.

Two of the most important and innovative books of recent years are *The Underworld Initiation* and *The Prophetic Vision of Merlin* by R. J. Stewart. Be assured that these will become classics.

And finally, not wishing to lose an opportunity to promote my own work I would suggest that those readers who are interested in more detailed and broader analyses of the present themes should read *Priestess*, the full biography of Dion Fortune; *Dancers to the Gods*, which contains the magical diaries of Seymour and Hartley during their halcyon years in the *F.I.L.* and *Gate of Moon*, which suggest a variation on the Qabalah using images from the Celtic and Arthurian traditions. To an extent this book has been intended as a distillation of all three.

In the following pages Geoff suggests techniques of his own enabling you to make contact with the Elemental Forces and the Archmage of the land. Choose which you prefer, and start your own magical journey. And luck and love to you all . . .

Visualization Exercises

GENERAL

The Objectives of these Exercises are to:

1. Create a start and finish point for your Workings.
2. Introduce you to those, without whose aid there can be no Work; neither on yourself, your environment nor anything else.
3. Train the mind to follow a set course, without deviation, or wandering.
4. Put you in contact with the archetypal mage of your land.

HINTS

In order to obtain the best results from these exercises it is recommended that you get into a comfortable position, but *not* lying down (this could easily lead to your falling asleep) and try to ensure that you will not be disturbed. Telephone off the hook? Animals put out of the room? No visitors, etc., expected? Electrical appliances switched off? You don't want a meal to spoil in the oven while you are "out."

Complete the exercises every day for five consecutive days, then take two days off. For example, five minutes a day for five days will bring far superior results in comparison with 25 minutes once a week. There are six exercises and each should be dealt with one at a time, not moving from the first to the second until complete mastery is gained over the first. In the second exercise there is an important realization that must be fully appreciated before you should proceed to the third exercise.

In order to obviate any confusion it is important that you fully understand what is meant by a *realization*. It is natural to understand a thing intellectually. It is equally natural to understand a thing through the emotions. The tricky part is understanding through both the intellect and the emotions. To be blunt, it becomes a sort of "gut" reaction. The concept strikes both the heart and the mind; a sort of "flash of inspiration," but on both levels.

This restriction is imposed by those whom you are endeavoring to contact, and is repeated in all the subsequent exercises.

Many schools maintain that you should sit at a specific time of the day each day. However, I feel that, under the present pressures and stresses of life in general, this is no longer totally practicable. Make sure you do it at the most convenient time for you on a particular day.

This can often involve an element of forward planning. If you are going out for a meal, or to a dance, theater, whatever, do it *before* you go since you may not be in a fit state on your return. Alcohol and/or a heavy meal tends to remove the essential mind control you need for these exercises.

Those of you that are already clairvoyant in any degree will find that "visions" will rise as per normal—however, they must be *rejected totally*.

This is not the purpose of these Exercises; they are all about *control*. A spontaneous vision is uncontrolled and uncontrollable. Get rid of it.

For those of you who work clairvoyantly, you will find that your clairvoyance will cease, temporarily, during this phase of training. Don't be alarmed. It is a natural part of your evolution. It can be likened to working, constantly, on the second floor of a building when it is decided that you are to change jobs. The new job is on another floor and you must move, via the elevator, to another floor. This is the time of being in the elevator, moving between floors, out of contact with what you have known and not yet in contact with the floor where you will work in the future.

I assure you that you will move to far, far greater things and that the loss you will experience, no doubt a trifle traumatic, will be well worth it. Be warned that once you start this Work there will be a quickening of your life in general. Lots of little irritations will arise that must be resolved, their lessons learned, and new understandings of life experienced. It is not, as many have claimed in the past, the "other side" testing you, trying to deflect you from this path. It is a clearing of the base metal of the essential you, a tempering of the blade to make it strong and usable, a clearing of aspects of your life that must be cleansed before you can Work. Face up to them, learn from them, and emulate the pheonix.

Make sure that the environment where you are going to carry out these exercises is at a comfortable temperature and that you are not sitting in a draft. There is absolutely no need to be uncomfortable, nor to practice any of the mystical postures, breathing exercises, etc. These can tend to lead to too much concentration being paid to maintaining such.

Some may find that the lighting of an incense is beneficial, but it is not essential. I would suggest something light and delicate, such as a gentle sandalwood, if you feel it is really necessary. At certain points in the exercises you are requested to pay your respects to someone. Do whatever you feel is correct.

Some visualize themselves going down on one knee, bowing the head. Others bow, while others simply do not. To reiterate, do whatever you feel the occasion warrants.

Those that you meet will be described, as tradition demands, in a masculine form. However, they are neither male nor female, but androgynous, being both. They are always referred to as kings, simply because they rule kingdoms. It must be emphasized that there is no such thing as sex, in the way we know it, in these other realms.

In preparation for carrying out the exercises, do whatever you feel will be conducive to attaining a relaxed state of mind and body. Try releasing those tight constrictions in your clothing, and be comfortable. A short prayer for the dedication of your work to your conception of Almighty God is always beneficial, and a closing prayer of thanks in such a case is, if nothing more, polite. Above all, *take your time*; there is no need to rush. Softly, softly . . .

Magical Name

AIM

To create an identity whereby you may exist in the other worlds in your Body of Light (see *Definitions & Explanations*).

INTRODUCTION

Myth, legend and tradition tells us that to know the name of somebody gives one an element of control over that person. Whether this is strictly true or not is debatable; however, for the time being, act as if it is so. Tell no one on the physical what your Magical Name is.

There is a lot of thought required in determining what exactly you wish to be known by to those on the other levels.

This Name should be a marked indication of your aspiration in regard to the Work, and, equally, how you intend to carry thorugh the Work.

Having decided on your Magical Name there is then a requirement to be, to use a term, Baptized. To undergo the Baptism of the Magical Name, I suggest that you adopt the following visualization exercise for the initial naming.

PRACTICAL

You are standing/sitting in your room, wearing your Body of Light. A ball of brilliant, colorless light appears about six feet in front of you and slightly above head height. You acknowledge its presence, whereupon, in response, a gentle beam of light comes from the ball and, expanding, bathes you in its light.

You call softly but penetratingly along the beam of light the Magical Name that you wish to be known by. As the Name is accepted, a short needle-like ray of golden light is emitted from the ball and impinges on your forehead in a gesture of acceptance. The ball withdraws the beam of light, disappears and you disperse your Body of Light, returning to the physical World.

POSTESCRIPT

A simple exercise such as this makes you ready to carry on the Work that we have started. Do not feel that once you have named yourself you are stuck with it. As you evolve, so should your aspirations increase/evolve as well. Having formally introduced yourself in your first Magical Name it is relatively easy to then approach the other levels in that Name and politely request that you should henceforth be known as your new Magical Name.

Exercise One

AIM

The aim of this exercise is an awareness of the totality of life; not just of yourself, but also that of the land, and the great omnific deity we refer to as simply, God: the One who caused us all, who created all things and remains with us and sustains us through "setting the Sun and the stars in the sky to light our life."

PRACTICAL

You stand on a broad plain of rolling grassy hills at that moment of the night that immediately precedes the Dawn. The Moon has set and, above your head, the stars glisten in the dark heavens. A chill breeze blows, gently, against your face and your loose clothing rustles against your body.

As your eyes adjust to the encircling gloom you become aware of a horseshoe of six megalithic stones in front of and about you. The

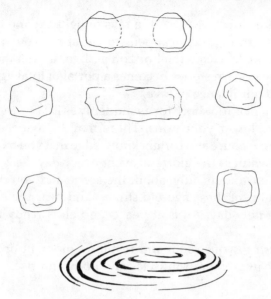

View of Horseshoe-shaped Area of Stones and Water

center pair immediately in front of you has a capstone bridging them. Between you and the centered, capped stones lies another stone on its side, serving as an altar. Behind you, closing the "mouth" of the horseshoe is a pool of water (see diagram).

There is an air of expectancy pervading the whole scene, an utter stillness, a waiting. Dimly, through the capped stones you become aware of a strip of cold light edging the distant horizon. Slowly it expands across the eastern edge of the landscape.

In the grass about the stones you begin to hear the rustle of small creatures and insects as they stir from their slumbers and start their quest for food and sustenance.

The Dawn Light grows and the breeze blows chill against you. Between the capped stones a sliver of the Sun peeps over the edge of the world and a brilliant golden ray of light flashes across the land, through the stones, and surrounds you. This ray, strong as it is, neither blinds nor hurts the eyes. You raise your arms until you stand like the letter "Y," in salutation and welcome to the warmth and love that rides that ray of light.

The breeze drops and disappears completely. The warmth penetrates your body and mind, driving the chill out, setting your blood racing with the heat.

As the Sun slowly rises, so the rays of light expand and course across the land, through the capped stones, about you and through you. The Sun finally clears the horizon and, for a brief moment, the archway of the eastern stones becomes a portal of total light, blazing with the golden brilliance of love.

The moment is too short, for as suddenly as it came the ray disappears and you lower your arms. There may be a sense of regret, however, there is a sure and certain knowledge that you have the right to return and witness the glorious event every day.

Your gaze wanders, idly, about the scene and you drink in the solitary splendor of these age-old stones, and hear the call of birds heralding the new day. All is at peace, and all is ready to face this day.

You return to your room and rest for a moment or two. Then, slowly, you reawaken your muscles and body and rise.

POST EXERCISE

Before proceeding with your life, it is important to make a report, note, or diary entry of your feelings etc., that were experienced during the exercise.

It should be made *immediately* after you have finished the exercise, while things are still fresh in the mind. Be *honest* with yourself—they are for your reading, nobody else. It is equally important to record a "nil report"; "nothing felt," etc. These reports are just as much a part of your evolution as the time you reach the stars. Do not be put off by long periods of nothing; it happens sometimes. Having written your report, have a cup of tea, coffee or milk and a biscuit, as having a snack and a drink helps you to return to this world.

Exercise Two

AIM

The aim of this exercise is to gain acceptance from the first of the four elemental kings and to pay your respects to him.

The first is the element of air.

PRACTICAL

(Complete Exercise One up to the point where the portal of total light has gone and your arms are lowered.)

You pause for a moment, gazing into the archway, directing your wish for an audience with the King of the Air. Start forward, passing to the north of the altar stone and move to the center of the archway, where you pause. During this moment, mentally announce your Magical Name and request permission to pass through. Permission is granted and you confidently step forward.

As you exit the archway, the scene of the rolling hills disappears and you find yourself at the beginning of a tunnel of light grey luminescence. The walls and floor seem to flow with movement, however this is merely an illusion and, beneath your questing feet, you feel the solidity of a sure path.

The tunnel rises very, very gently and you ascend without effort. It is a short tunnel and soon it opens into the large form of a cavern in the sky. The floor of the cavern appears to be of clouds which rise up the walls. The roof is of the most beautiful azure blue of high summer. There is an airy, spacious feeling to the whole of the cavern.

Down either side of the cavern, but leaving a clear, straight path for yourself, stand ethereal figures of every shade of yellow: the Sylphs. They are the people of the kingdom of the Air.

You move confidently forward toward a high throne on a low dais at the far end of the cavern. Some of the Sylphs eye you warily, others ignore you. There is a slight air of tension, a waiting.

Having passed down the path you come to the clearing before the dais and stop. You pay your respects to the throne, stating your Magical Name.

Your eyes focus on the throne, which appears to be made of a single, solid cloud and the figure seated thereon. It is a man, clothed in various shades of yellow robes, but the shadings blend subtly into one another. On his head there is a cap vaguely reminiscent of a bird's head, with the bill upon his forehead, stopping short of his eyebrows. Atop this cap is a crown, apparently made of cloud, but solid and real, glistening in the sky light. From his shoulders and arms depends a cape, symbolizing the wings of a bird. Light, tawny eyes regard you steadily from either side of a hawk nose over tight, thin lips.

His Majesty, Paraldar, King of the Air and Ruler of the Skies, acknowledges your respects with a nod of the head and the slight wave of a hand. The realization comes that *here* is the seat of wisdom in the world; true wisdom, not that which passes for such in the world of men. He recognizes your adjustment and the face relaxes into a slight smile.

Into your mind comes a gentle whisper, "Welcome to the Kingdom of Air. What do you seek?" You give thanks for his welcome and state your reason for entering his kingdom.

He responds suitably to your reason and rises to his feet.

The audience is over. You pay your respects and he departs, leaving you to return to the stones.

You turn to leave down the path and the Sylphs acknowledge your departure. Their king has accepted you, therefore so do they.

It is but a short journey back down the tunnel and you stand between the archway stones in the sunlight. Passing to the south of the altar stone you return to your original position and pause. Next, return to your room and rest for a moment. Slowly, reawaken your muscles and body and rise.

POST EXERCISE

Write up your report *immediately*. Write down *exactly* what your request was, and *exactly* what His Majesty's response was. Write down your understanding of the realization received. A drink and a snack will bring you back to normal.

Exercise Three

AIM

The aim of this exercise is to gain acceptance fromthe second of the four elemental kings and to pay your respects to him.

The second is the element of Fire.

PRACTICAL

(Complete Exercise One up to the point where the portal of total light has gone and your arms are lowered.)

You pause for a moment, turn to your right and look between the two stones, gazing into the gap between them and direct your wish for an audience with the King of Fire. Start forward and move to the center of the two stones, where you pause. During this moment, you mentally announce your Magical Name and request permission to pass through. Permission is granted and you confidently step forward.

Exiting the stones you come to a tunnel of flame and fire. Apparently it is all ablaze, but there is no heat or burning to bother you. It is another illusion.

Once again your questing feet find firm footings and you step forward in confidence along the short, level tunnel toward the cavern of Fire. In size and shape this cavern is very similar to the cave of the Air, except that the floor and walls are colored in liquid fire and the roof is a very light, bright, grey rolling billow of smoke.

The ethereal figures in attendance are every shade of red. They are the Salamanders, the people of Fire. Once again, as you proceed down the central path the Salamanders take little or no notice of you. Where you are seen, there is wariness.

You stop in the clearing before the throne and pay your respects to the throne and state your Magical Name. Your eyes focus on the throne, which appears to be made of a single, solid flame, and the figure seated thereon. It is a man clothed in various shades of red robes, but the shadings blend subtly into one another. Atop his head is a crown apparently made of flame, but solid and real, flashing in the firelight. Light pink eyes regard you steadily from either side of a slender nose, over tight thin lips.

His Majesty, Djinn, King of Fire and Ruler of the Flames, acknowledges your respects with a nod of the head and the slight wave of a hand. The realization comes that *here* is the seat of love and energy in the world; true love, not that which passes, emotively, for such in the world of men. He recognizes your adjustment and the face relaxes into a slight smile.

Into your mind comes a crackling whisper, "Welcome to the Kingdom of Fire. What do you seek?" You give thanks for his welcome and state your reason for entering his kingdom.

He responds suitably to your reason and rises to his feet. The audience is over. You pay your respects and he departs, leaving you to return to the stones. You turn to leave down the path and the Salamanders acknowledge your departure. Their king has accepted you, therefore so do they.

It is but a short journey back down the tunnel and you stand between the two stones in the sunlight. You return to your original position and pause. Next, return to your room and rest for a moment. Slowly reawaken your muscles and body and rise.

POST EXERCISE

Write up your report *immediately*. Write down *exactly* what your request was, and *exactly* what His Majesty's response was. Write down your understanding of the realization received. A drink and a snack will bring you back to normal.

Exercise Four

AIM

The aim of this exercise is to gain acceptance from the third of the four elemental kings and to pay your respects to him.

The third is the element of Water.

PRACTICAL

(Complete Exercise One up to the point where the portal of total light has gone and your arms are lowered.)

You pause for a moment. Turning to your right you turn about and look out over the pool of water, directing your wish for an audience with the King of Water. Start forward and move to the water's edge where you pause. During this moment you mentally announce your Magical Name and request permission to enter. Permission is granted and you confidently step forward, into a tunnel that has opened in the waters, leading gently down into the depths of the water.

Once again your questing feet find firm footings and you step forward in confidence along the tunnel toward the cavern of water. In size and shape this cavern is very similar to the other caves. The floor is the color of the deep, dark blue of the ocean and the walls are colored in light blue. The roof is a very light bright blue/grey with shifting sparkles of light, as of sunlight on the surface.

The ethereal figures in attendance are every shade of blue. They are the Undines, the people of Water. Once again as you proceed down the central path the Undines take little or no notice of you. Where you are seen, there is wariness.

You stop in the clearing before the throne and pay your respects to the throne and state your Magical Name. Your eyes focus on the throne, which appears to be made of a single, billowing wave, and the figure seated thereon. It is a man, clothed in various shades of blue robes, but the shadings blend subtly into one another. Atop his head is a crown, apparently made of spume, but solid and real, flashing in the reflected sunlight. Light, piercing blue eyes regard you steadily from either side of an aquiline nose, over tight, thin lips.

His Majesty, Neksa, King of Water and Ruler of the Waves acknowledges your respects with a nod of the head and the slight wave of a hand. The realization comes that *here* is the seat of power in the world; true power, not that which passes for such in the world of men. He recognizes your adjustment and the face relaxes into a slight smile.

Into your mind comes a bubbling whisper, "Welcome to the Kingdom of Water. What do you seek?" You give thanks for his welcome and state your reason for entering his kingdom.

He responds suitably to your reason and rises to his feet. The audience is over. You pay your respects and he departs, leaving you to return to the stones. You turn to leave down the path and the Undines acknowledge your departure. Their king has accepted you, therefore so do they.

It is but a short journey back up the tunnel and you stand at the edge of the pool in the sunlight. You return to your original position and pause. Next, return to your room and rest for a moment. Slowly reawaken your muscles and body and rise.

POST EXERCISE
Write up your report *immediately*. Write down *exactly* what your request was, and *exactly* what His Majesty's response was. Write down your understanding of the realization received. A drink and a snack will bring you back to normal.

Exercise Five

AIM
The aim of this exercise is to gain acceptance from the fourth of the four elemental kings and to pay your respects to him.

The fourth is the element of Earth.

PRACTICAL
(Complete Exercise One up to the point where the portal of total light has gone and your arms are lowered.)

You pause for a moment. Turning to your right you turn and look between the two northern stones, directing your wish for an audience with the King of Earth. Start forward and move to the stones, where you pause. During this moment you mentally announce your Magical Name and request permission to enter. Permission is granted and you confidently step forward between the stones. A tunnel has opened in the ground, leading gently down into the depths of the Earth. Once again your questing feet find firm footings and you step forward in confidence along the tunnel toward the cavern of Earth. In size and shape this cavern is very similar to the other caves. The floor, walls and the roof are all the colors of granite, marble, coal, gold, silver, etc., sparkling with an inner light that illuminates the cavern.

The ethereal figures in attendance are every shade of black and the darker greens. They are the Gnomes, the people of Earth. Once again, as you proceed down the central path the Gnomes take little or no notice of you. Where you are seen, there is wariness.

You stop in the clearing before the throne and pay your respects to the throne and state your Magical Name. Your eyes focus on the throne, which appears to be made of a single multicolored rock, and the figure seated thereon. It is a man, clothed in various shades of black and dark green robes, but the shadings blend subtly into one another. Atop his head is a crown, apparently made of crystal flashing in the reflected sunlight. Dark, piercing black eyes regard you steadily from either side of a Roman nose, over tight, thin lips.

His Majesty, Ghobb, King of Earth and Ruler of the Land, acknowledges your respects with a nod of the head and the slight wave of a hand. The realization comes that *here* is the seat of meditation and transmutation in the world: transmutation and meditation of all the wisdom, love/energy and power directed here from the other kingdoms. He recognizes your adjustment and the face relaxes into a slight smile.

Into your mind comes a grating whisper, "Welcome to the Kingdom of the Earth. What do you seek?" You give thanks for his welcome and state your reason for entering his kingdom.

He responds suitably to your reason and rises to his feet. The audience is over. You pay your respects and he departs, leaving you to return to the stones. You turn to leave down the path and the Gnomes acknowledge your departure. Their king has accepted you, therefore so do they.

It is but a short journey back up the tunnel and you stand between the two stones in the sunlight. You return to your original position and pause. Next, return to your room and rest for a moment. Slowly reawaken your muscles and body and rise.

POST EXERCISE

Write up your report *immediately*. Write down *exactly* what your request was, and *exactly* what His Majesty's response was. Write down your understanding of the realization received. A drink and a snack will bring you back to normal.

Exercise Six

INTRODUCTION

Having gained the acceptance of the Elemental Kings you are now in a position to start the *most important* part of the exercises: *Contacting the archetypal mage of your land.*

I am not in any position to describe *who* you will meet, as I do not know in which country you reside as you read this. This is a very important qualification. No matter *where* you were born; no matter *where* you were brought up; no matter *where* you long to be; it is *where you are living now that counts.*

I can only give an indication of whom I met. I am English, living in England, therefore I met the archetypal mage of England and Wales, renowned throughout the world as Merlin.

For other countries you must look in the myths and legends of the land for the wise man/woman who has guided the heroes and heroines of the land down through the ages; the influence without office. There you will find the one you seek.

Do not be put off by slanderous misconceptions that have been woven about the figure, but seek the purity of their endeavor in working for the long-term good of the land.

To readers in the American continents it has been strongly impressed on me to suggest to you to look toward the essential spirit of the nation, that of the American Indian Great Spirit, Mãsaw (pronounced Mar-sow). This is just a suggestion, not a directive.

AIM

To contact the archetypal mage of the land, to gain his or her acceptance, and to offer your dedication to their service and the service of your the and its people (irrespective of color, class or creed).

PRACTICAL

You stand on a broad plain of rolling grassy hills at that moment of the night that immediately precedes the dawn. The Moon has set and, above your head, the stars glisten in the dark heavens. A chill breeze blows gently against your face and your loose clothing rustles against your body.

As your eyes adjust to the encircling gloom you become aware of a horseshoe of six megalithic stones in front of and about you. The center pair, immediately in front of you, have a capstone bridging them. Between you and the center capped stones lies another stone on its side, forming an altar. Behind you, closing the "mouth" of the horseshoe, is a pool of water.

There is an air of expectancy pervading the whole scene, an utter stillness, a waiting. You move forward, passing to the north of the altar stone, to the archway stones and pause, facing through the stones. You call your Magical Name.

You pay your respects to Paraldar, King of the Air, and while in that attitude, you invite him to attend the stones. A misty form swirls in the bottom of the archway and solidifies into a small, knee-high throne with His Majesty seated upon it. You rise and turn to your right and move around to the southern pair of stones where you pause and face between the stones.

You call your Magical Name.

You adopt a similar attitude of respect and invite Djinn, King of Fire, to attend. The misty form swirls into the solidity of the knee-high throne with His Majesty seated upon it.

You rise and turn to your right and move to the lip of the pool in the west. You repeat your Magical Name and invitation in the same manner, calling for Neksa, King of Water. Once again the mist swirls and he is enthroned before you.

You rise, turn to your right and move to the northern pair of stones where you pause and face between the stones. You repeat your Magical Name and invitation in the same manner, calling for Ghobb, King of Earth. The mist swirls and he is enthroned before you.

You rise, turn to your right and take your place in the center of the horseshoe stones. Dimly through the archway stones you become aware of a strip of cold light edging the distant horizon. Slowly it expands across the eastern edge of the landscape. In the grass about the stones you begin to hear the rustle of small creatures and insects as they stir from their slumbers.

The dawn light grows and the chill breeze blows against you. Suddenly, all movement stops, the breeze drops and the world seems to be holding its breath. Between the archway a sliver of the Sun peeps over the horizon, and a brilliant golden ray of light flashes across the land, through the stones and fans out inside the circle of stones and water, bathing the area in its radiance, neither blinding nor painful.

You raise your arms into the "Y" of glorious salutation to the light. The warmth penetrates your entire being.

The Sun finally clears the horizon and the archway becomes, once again, the portal of total light, blazing like a beacon of brilliance. Everything seems to freeze and time stands still. The light pulses and swirls. A form dimly, gradually, takes shape. It is the one whom you awaited.

He/She has come. You lower your arms and pay your deepest respects and reverence. The one moves out of the light and comes toward you, their eyes piercing into your very being, as though reading your very soul. A gentle smile of acceptance creeps over their face and the light of compassion and forgiveness flows from their eyes. He/She has recognized your humanity, strivings and failings. These, added together, sum up the reality of love.

A soothing voice speaks into your mind, asking who you aspire to be. You reply with your Magical Name.

The voice then asks, "Why are you there?" You respond by stipulating that you have the desire to serve, and therefore require to know in order to so serve.

The voice questions if you really understand what is meant by such service?

You answer *truthfully*. Depending upon this answer, the conversation continues and is totally personal between the two of you.

The one concludes the meeting, turns and moves to mount and stand upon the altar stone where the form gradually dissipates and disappears.

The world breathes again and time restarts. The creatures, insects and birds awaken and continue with their activities. If you have moved from your position, return to the center facing east.

Turning to your left move to the northern stones, pay your respects and thank King Ghobb for his attendance. He then departs.

Turning to your left move to the western waters, pay your respects and thank King Neksa for his attendance. He then departs.

Turning to your left move to the southern stones, pay your respects and thank King Djinn for his attendance. He then departs.

Turning to your left move, via the south of the altar stone, to the archway stones, pay your respects and thank King Paraldar for his attendance. He then departs.

Turning to your left, move via the north of the altar stone back to your central position and pause for a moment.

You return to your room and rest for a moment.

Slowly reawaken your muscles and body, and rise.

POST EXERCISE

Write up your report *immediately*. Write down *exactly* what your conversation was about. Write down your understanding of what has happened. A drink and a snack will bring you back to normal.

POSTESCRIPT

If you have followed these exercises assiduously and devotedly you will have arrived at the point where you are in direct contact with your archmage and will receive *all* further instructions and teachings *directly* from the archmage.

This does *not* mean that you are totally on your own, in a material sense.

You will find in the due course of time that others who have also established contact will gravitate into your environment, and a group *may* form for working together.

There is nothing to gain by comparing notes with each other about how long it took to make the contact. Whether it took one week, one month, one year, ten years or however long is totally irrelevant. It is sufficient that contact has been made—*that* is what it is all about.

Godspeed.

Definitions and Explanations

In a work such as this it is imperative to define and explain what exactly we are trying to present to you. In this "enlightened" age, many words and concepts have been taken into use and their meanings etc., have become confused in overusage and even abusage. We have used many of these terms and ideas, but do you understand what we mean? In order to overcome this problem we present a form of glossary of the terms we have used, with our definitions.

* * *

I ask you to bear in mind that all books are, merely, an attempt to indicate one person's experiences of the subject matter. It doesn't matter what the subject matter is about: physical or mental experiences. What has happened to me, what will happen to you, are totally individualistic experiences that will *never* occur *exactly* the same to any other person.

In the early stages of the Work they can be extremely helpful and useful in determining the definition of symbols/entities as they are presented, with a possible inference of progress being made along your particular path.

* * *

Many may query by what authority we have presumed to publish details of the Work that has been undertaken over the past few years, and still continues even as you read this.

Society demands that we are "pigeon-holed" and given titles to describe our function. Some of those I have worked with have decided, therefore, that I am a magician—a term I do not readily accept.

Like everybody else I have the ability to be both a magician and a medium (see below), and am happier with the title, if I must have one, of "mediator" who does both, as and when required. It is my understanding that a mediator/magician/medium is a form of priest because occultism is a religion, in the truest sense of the word; a way of life.

The task of the priesthood is to offer to every other man/woman the opportunity of being a priest/priestess in their own right, without the necessity for a third party to mediate the individual's wishes to their own conception of Almighty God. Within the context of this work I am, therefore, a priest, thus it is part and parcel of the requirement of my particular path of Work that the information I have gleaned be readily available to every other man/woman, in order that they by themselves may continue the Work in due course.

* * *

Occultism/Magic like all life is evolving. One has only to look at the rappings and table-tilting of the early Spiritualist movement in comparison with the devotional reverence of spiritualists today.

Without the dedication of the early members of organizations such as the Golden Dawn, the Fraternity of the Inner Light, the Servants of the Light, etc., the modern magician would be hard pressed to continue the Work that was started at the turn of the century.

In essence, the early magicians lit the kindling for the liftoff achieved today. Those of you who will follow us will soar to the stars due to the Work we have done today in establishing an Earth orbit.

In analogy we have a situation akin to the building of a house. The excavators arrive and clear the site of the deadwood and underbrush, sink the pilings and depart. Another team arrives to lay the foundations. They subsequently depart and the builders arrive and start on the walls, etc. When they have completed their work and have departed, another team arrives to lay the roof tiles. The tilers could not begin their work without the efforts of the excavators in the first place.

I demean no one in this allusion. All things must evolve or die.

In these pages is the witness of my own efforts in the Work. My start was as a member of a large ritual group, then through solo ritual, through leading a ritual group, to coordinating a mental group Working, each being the product of natural evolution through the various methods of Working.

* * *

There has been a saying in the occult world since, apparently, the beginning of time:

> To know,
> To will,
> To dare,
> To keep silent.

In essence, it has always been understood to mean that you know that there is something to endeavor to reach; you have the will power to apply yourself to go for it; that you dare to do it; that you say nothing about it. Doubtless this last was thought to be extremely prudent during the Inquisition.

I would, however, put a slightly different emphasis on the last part.

To wit:

> To know,
> To will,
> To dare,
> To keep *the silence*.

In other words, the know, will and dare remain the same, but the final caution becomes an instruction to continue with the meditation/contemplation and move even further forward in your task.

* * *

There are many, many schools, colleges, fraternities, etc., throughout the world, all teaching various aspects of the occult/mystical/magical/metaphysical/spiritual matters. Their numbers alone show that there is a deep and intense desire for the knowledge that is available. I have been a member of one sort or another of several of these organizations. Many I admit were false starts, and I left when I realized I had made an error. However, looking at things positively, they were not really mistakes because I learned from the experience; even if it was only that that particular path was not mine.

A tip I will pass on to you is to watch Mammon. If it is going to cost you hundreds, sometimes even thousands, of pounds or dollars to complete the course, be very, very wary. The information available costs absolutely nothing. The cost comes in the dissemination of the information. In the years that I was involved with the *FIL*, at a quick guess, I reckon it cost me less than £250. That includes lessons, books, postage, stationery, train fares, petrol for meetings, etc., less than £1 a week ($1.50) on average.

Being under the tutelage of an organization can be very beneficial. It lays the rod of discipline firmly across the shoulders and helps to keep the nose to the grindstone. The requirement to submit reports on a regular basis is excellent training (without this training it is highly doubtful if my diary, and hence this book, would ever have been written).

Sure, one can kid oneself that to miss the odd day doesn't matter, but it is oh so easy to leave it for a couple of days, then a couple of weeks, until in the end nothing ever gets done.

The necessity of putting pen to paper each month to report what you have achieved goads you into doing it; we all have a conscience.

One of the other positive aspects of allying oneself to an organization lies in the ability to discuss the intricacies of "contact," often far from being straightforward. Much of the input that arrives from "elsewhere" can be in either symbolic images, or unusual ideas welling into the mind. The former can be extremely obtuse, while the latter can be questionable as to the origin. An apparently negative aspect is the need to conform with the group concept of Working which might be found to be at variance with what exactly the individual feels is the way ahead. However, I have been told that there is the need to learn to be a conformist in order that one may be allowed to be a nonconformist at a later stage.

Obviously, there are circumstances which absolutely preclude attendance, even by mail, at such a school or whatever. To cover these situations we decided to include the Practical Section in these pages to meet these eventualities.

It may even be that attempts to find the proper orgnization have failed in your particular case; then please try the exercises. It will not be a waste of time. If anything it will be a good grounding for the day, should it be necessary, when you do find the correct teacher for yourself.

It is, however, strongly emphasized that the exercises are designed *totally* for Working *alone*.

They will work in a group environment, but nowhere as effectively as carried out by yourself, alone. No two people can Work, in this manner, at the same speed. Each is a total individual and must, therefore, proceed at their own rate. Within a group some may shoot ahead of the others, creating dissension, thereby destroying the group. The Work is for unification, *not* destruction.

* * *

It may not have escaped the notice of many, but the published diaries commence at my leaving the Fraternity of the Inner Light. This is by design, not omission; and not because I took an oath, or any other fanciful reason. Oaths and such are unnecessary.

A strong, sure affirmation of intent and the knowledge that one will only be required to fulfill such commitments as you are capable of fulfilling. "They" know, better than you do, what you are capable of, and how much can be expected.

I hold the **FIL** in the highest esteem and would not wish to cast any misconceptions toward the organization, either in the outer or inner worlds. Without their tireless patience and tolerance I would not be in the position I am in today in regard to the Work. Should the **FIL** ever decide that they wish their Work to be published, there are far superior writers than I could ever aspire to be to do it for them. My silence in this is due only to the utmost respect for them. Long may they continue in the Work.

* * *

The Workings in the diary have all been undertaken under the auspices of the Western Mystery Tradition. I feel it is necessary to emphasize this aspect, since so many people seem to have forgotten that we in the West have a tradition of our own. For many years the only paths that seemed to be open were those of the inscrutable East.

Within the Western lodges there is an understanding that "wisdom" comes from the East, and is mediated by the Officer of the Lodge who stands in that position. I believe that this understanding "escaped" into the outside world and became corrupted. Hence, people with a bent toward the Work began looking toward the physical East in their searches.

It cannot be overstressed that the doctrines of the East are designed for the psychological makeup of the Oriental and their environment. I lived in the East for a number of years and experienced the much slower pace and tempo of the lifestyle in those places. Returning to the West and its much increased bustle was a culture shock.

The basis of the Oriental mystical paths is one of living each life in the hope that there may be enough "goodness" stored up in order to escape the wheel of reincarnation and rebirth. It doesn't matter too greatly what this life is like, because the hereafter will be a sufficient reward for the pain and anguish undergone now.

Those who have some experience of these doctrines will appreciate that the chela (student) is expected to spend a tremendous amount of time in passive meditation, letting things rise into the consciousness as they will, and then sitting back and dissecting them in order to try and understand what has been given.

The basis of the Western path is one of life and yet more life. *Now* is the important moment, not some unknown, unguessable, indeterminate time somewhere in the future. The Western path is one of controlling the mind, not letting unwanted things rise up.

There is a predetermined course to be followed and adhered to, without any letup, but with intense discipline. One symbol, when received, leads toward the next. There are some moments of doubt but these are necessary for the strengthening of the individual's faith. Have patience in these moments.

You will find that little hints and nudges will seem to appear out of the blue, just at the right time to emphasize some point or other when there is a question of doubt. For this type of Work one needs to be childlike, but not childish. Have faith in the unseen and often unseeable: the worlds of fairy, angels, etc., and have a child's knowing.

In practical terms, the East operates in a passive role, whereas the West uses an aggressive pattern, a "go for it" philosophy.

* * *

Scattered throughout occult and esoteric literature is the beacon of the Age of Aquarius, and talk of the ending of the Piscean Age. Each Age is deemed to last for a period of approximately 2,000 years.

The symbol of the early Christians was the fish, the astrological sign of Pisces. In the very near future we will be celebrating 2,000 years of so-called Christendom, and the end of the Age of Pisces. The concept of Pisces was "I believe." Note the Apostle's Creed's opening words "I believe in . . . "

Aquarius takes over from Pisces somewhere around the turn of the century. The Sign of Aquarius is the Water bearer. In what is the water carried? An urn, dish or large goblet, depending on the illustrator.

Britain, in common with many others, holds very dear to its heart the Quest for the Holy Grail—a large, sacred goblet or dish.

The concept of Aquarius is "I know." In the context of religious experience and especially metaphysics and philosophy, we have the transfer from "I believe" to "I know." This can only be brought about through experience—personal experience, not what some other person has seen or heard; direct personal experience of things previously hidden from common knowledge, hence the use of the term *esoteric knowledge*. This hidden knowledge is available only to the chosen few. Chosen by whom?

* * *

I disagree with the many who believe that Aquarius will be the vegan/vegetarian Utopia.

From a simple biological point of view, the concept of a carnivorous animal such as a lion becoming a herbivore is totally unacceptable. The stomach is not designed to extract the essentials required of a lion's life from grass and vegetation.

Additionally, I must disagree with those who maintain that Armageddon will herald the New Age, and that all those who are not "spiritually" inclined (in other words, materialists) will be wiped off the face of the Earth. Life is all about balance.

If everybody on Earth decided to be totally engrossed in spiritual matters, who would grow the food, build the bricks into houses, clear away the sewage, provide the electricity, process the energy sources? Everyone would be too busy thinking about Heaven to bother.

* * *

I will stick my neck out at this point and observe that it is very rare that one finds a husband/wife duo Working totally together. My wife Val helps me in the major rituals, but she has her own path to tread. If and when she needs some help, I will be the first to lend a hand.

For many years Val has been my anchor. She has selflessly followed the path of the hearth fire, organizing the home in such a way as to allow me to get on with the Work. When I have felt the desire to "fly off" to airy-fairy realms she has brought me straight back to my senses with a simple statement like, "The electric bill is due." The balance between the two worlds has been maintained—a balance between the spiritual and the physical.

Take all the physical away and the balance is lost. The materialist is as much an essential part of Aquarius as the spiritually inclined.

* * *

This book is the tale of a quest, spanning many years and generations. At the time I was not aware that it was a part of an ongoing saga, nor that others have also been involved and still are.

What is a quest? It is a search, but a search with a difference. A normal search usually has a set objective to be found and possessed.

In our quest we sought something we did not know, an unknown and unknowable goal. The only spur for such was faith in the *necessity* to so seek.

As I began my quest I had absolutely no idea of *where* I was going, nor *why*. There was just an impulse to *do* something. Each Working was undertaken as a separate event.

However, as things progressed, a linking theme became apparent but was only seen in retrospect. It appears that my initial quest was the return of Pendragon and the release of such into my homeland.

* * *

The word *Working* has entered the pages on many occasions and meant to indicate a particular ritual where action was specifically undertaken, either alone or with others, in order to work a major piece of magic, as against the daily minor events. Daily Workings or rituals consist of time being allocated each day to the contacting of those forces that I have aligned myself with. A major Working or ritual is planned for over the preceding period; it may be a few days, weeks or even months.

There are at least two forms of Ritual that I am aware of. There may be others.

The first is pure ritual where the contact is made through movement, sound and smell.

In this manner one physically goes through the actual motions, as if the physical body was in the other realms.

For instance, should one be raising a sword in the other world, then one would raise a physical sword in the physical world. It is a means of duplicating the actions undertaken. It is an aid to the mental activity involved in ritual work.

The second is mental ritual. This is often undertaken in a comfortable chair, at a comfortable temperature. All the actions are undertaken within the mind of the person. This does not mean that "things" are not happening, it merely allows one the ability to Work wherever one may be, at any time, without causing any raised eyebrows on platform five of Euston or Grand Central Station.

There are times and places for both types of ritual, and each can be useful in certain circumstances. On July 28, 1986 the group acted in a mental ritual.

On August 4, 1986 I undertook a physical ritual on the mountain-side in Snowdonia. Rituals are not everyone's cup of tea, I must admit. I am under the impression that 75 per cent of real magic/High Magic/ call it what you will is *confidence*. I can, therefore I will. On the odd occasion it has been necessary for the other world to tell me to do such and such, I can therefore do it, and I do. You never really know until you try.

* * *

I have often used the word *Work* in these pages, and I make no apologies for using it. The task of acting as a catalyst for those on the other side *is* work, often hard work. Like any employment it requires an element of dedication to the common goal of the whole team. Regrettably, many do get involved in the Work and opt out of life by retreating into insular communes, dropping out of society and generally shrugging off their responsibilities and escaping from the rest of the world.

In certain, but very few, circumstances this is necessary. However, I will argue with anyone that accepting the catalytic task does not in any way, shape or form mean a rejection of the responsibilities of home, family and society. It is an *additional responsibility*. A marriage oath, whether taken in church or elsewhere, is totally binding and *must* be honored. Bills must be paid, the family must be fed and clothed and cared for—no matter what.

Time spent with the family, workmates, etc. is as necessary as any time spent with the other side. If something has to be given up, then let it be *your* time, those few minutes each day which you spend in solitude. It does not matter where you *are* at that moment.

Many people that I know get inspiration when standing at the kitchen sink doing the washing up, or having a soak in the bath, and, dare I mention it, even when they are sat on the lavatory. In these circumstances the mind tends to be in neutral and the functions are put on "auto-pilot."

* * *

Magic? It is the most maligned word in the Work.

Crowley tried, with varying degrees of success, to differentiate the difference from conjuring by respelling it as "magick."

Magic is the endeavor to move to other levels to create a cause which will produce an effect on this physical level.

This is brought about by the use of the mind of the magician to transport his will onto the other level and create a situation which will have repercussions, an effect in the physical world. However, the Law of Karma has to be borne in mind at all times, as does Divine Law. *All* magicians, in essence, work in the same manner. They work with the power of the other levels, through the mind.

Be warned, however, that magic does not have magicians prancing around naked having sex orgies, as many (especially the media) would have you believe. From my own experience I have learned that the *absence* of sex is a far greater magical stimulant, due to the tension that builds between the partners in their denial. Physical sex keeps the practitioners very firmly embedded in the physical world (if you will pardon the pun).

I offer a further warning. The question of the use of drugs to "aid" the evolution/quest is perennial. There is a very simple answer: *Don't.*

I cannot emphasize too strongly that the Work is all about control and balance; your control over your actions/experiences.

If you have "surrendered" to the stimulation of a drug you are no longer in control, and therefore can never, in those circumstances, be a magician. A balance is required between the mind and body. All drugs have an effect of some sort on both of these. A body/brain wracked with heroin, etc. is out of balance; one or the other has entered a premature breakdown of the tissue/cells and ceases to be capable of undertaking the rigors of the Work.

* * *

Black Magic? White Magic? What is the difference? A real magician introduces the power in exactly the same way, whatever his/her aim may be. The use he/she makes of that power decides the so-called color of his/her magic.

In simple terms, the power arrives in the magician's hands and is then directed where it is intended to go. Should he/she direct it into, for example, their bank account to boost the balance, carelessly, selfishly, and mindlessly of either the consequences or where the boost comes from, then we have Black Magic. Taking without due regard is theft, on any level. You want it, you earn it, you will get it.

In a similar situation, if the magician directs it into the Earth to cleanse and heal, then we have white magic. The difference lies totally in its usage. For the benefit of others it is white, for motives injurious to another it is black.

* * *

What is a magician? He/she is an active worker with the power, commonly (and erroneously) termed spiritual power, whereas a medium tends to be a passive worker. In short, the magician goes after the power whereas a medium sits and waits for it to come to him/her.

Let us endeavor to define of what *use* a magician is.

In analogy, should you enter a room that is very cold you would turn on the heat. The majority of heating works by convection—the rising of hot air replaced by the cold air, which is then warmed and it too rises. Eventually all the air in the room will have had its temperature raised, but the problem is that it tends to be a very slow process.

Imagine, if you will, that you have entered the same room but this time you carry a fan heater. You plug this in and switch it on. The action of the fan gets the air moving much quicker because it directs the air onto the hot element and expels it into the room under pressure. Consequently, the totality of the air is heated quicker and, naturally, the temprature of the room rises quicker.

In a similar manner, a magician acts as a fan heater for the other levels, speeding things up (metaphorically) by acting as a catalyst on behalf of the other levels.

* * *

Other levels? We physically exist in a physical world, yet we also exist in a mental world, an emotional world, and a spiritual world.

A Cabalist will, quite happily, draw you a diagram to explain and show these various levels (10 of them), and will then go on to show you that each level has yet another four levels. The Cabalist has drawn the Otz Chiim, the Tree of Life.

For those who wish to explore this particular method of understanding I recommend *The Mystical Qabalah* by Dion Fortune.

I digress; let us use the analogy of water. At very low molecular agitation we have a form of H_2O known as ice. Increase the molecular agitation and we have water. Increase it still further and we have steam. Scientists have now produced a still higher molecular agitation that is termed super steam. Basically they are all the same thing molecularly, but differentiated by the often external application of a stimulant.

A similar sort of thing happens with a magician. By the use of his/ her mind they can induce a state of mental molecular agitation to change the level of consciousness and to perceive, through their mind, that other environment. Before the magician can do anything, however, there must be an alliance/acceptance of the "intrusion," a coming to terms with the new environment in conscious terms.

It must be borne in mind, however, that they already exist in that so-called "new" level, but in a nonconscious state of awareness.

Everybody has the right to be there, consciously, but it all depends on the aspiration and intent for being there in a conscious state as to whether they will be eligible to be considered a manipulator/magician.

* * *

The Law of Karma. Tomes have been written on this subject and it has become buried in a mountain of words and phrases which tend to blind rather than clarify.

For the sake of simplification let us accept the idea that our world, the universe and the cosmos are here for a purpose, a part of a Divine Plan. We, as individuals, are also here as a part of that same plan or purpose.

Within the overall concept we are given a tremendous amount of leeway to live our lives under the concept of free will; however, like any other part of creation, we are required to undergo growth, not just physically, but mentally, spiritually, and emotionally.

The Law of Karma demands that we reap what we sow in our freedom to exercise our will. If we create dissension, we reap dissension. If we create peace, we reap the same. Karma is the Law of Cause and Effect. Build a happy, stable home and it will produce a happy, stable atmosphere in that home environment.

You wish to be wealthy? You slave away at your place of employment, with lots of overtime etc. and the money floods in and you become wealthy. The Law of Karma works on all levels.

You have the desire to heal? Two choices are open.

Study medicine and become a doctor or alternative therapist; or, contact the other levels and become a channel for the healing forces to pass through you into those places where healing is requested/required. Both require a degree of dedication and commitment that brings fulfillment in their own way.

Whatever is sown will be harvested. Be very careful, and give a tremendous amount of thought to *what* you are going to do, and *why.*

* * *

Divine Law? Utilizing the same concept of a purpose or plan let us imagine that a particular magician, in a fit of pique, decides to blast the Earth to pieces. Off he or she goes onto another level, winds things up to unleash a thunderbolt of immense proportions at the Earth. However, the Earth, as a part of the plan/purpose, has to be around for the next few millenia. No magician, however powerful, can alter that.

Divine Law cancels that particular thunderbolt, the Law of Karma steps in, the magician had better be able to run fast and be extremely agile in attempting to evade the bolt they have loosed, because it is heading for him/her. Karma.

* * *

We also tend to use the term *Inner Plane Adepti* rather freely.

The inner planes refers to those other levels that we have mentioned earlier: the mental, emotional, spiritual, etc.

Beyond a particular level (exactly where this lies is open to debate, depending upon the school of thought) there exists beings of a nonhuman variety that have a special charge for overseeing various parts of the Divine Plan as it progresses.

Many, but not necessarily all, have passed through the human form at some time or other in the past. They have evolved beyond the need for further incarnatory experience and therefore are referred to as Adepti and reside in the appropriate level to which they have gravitated. Some, but not all, still work in collusion with those of us on the physical plane in order to assist the progression of the plan.

Those of you that wish to delve into this concept should study another book by Dion Fortune, *The Cosmic Doctrine*.

* * *

In the practical section of this book you will see that there is a directive to use your Magical Name. This Name is yours, chosen by you and you alone (?) to symbolize the aspiration you have for the Work. Hence there is an exercise for acquiring such a Name for yourself.

* * *

There is, however, the need for a vehicle with which to travel about the inner planes. Obviously, you have a physical body, but this cannot go on to any level other than the physical; therefore, you need another body. This you "build" in your mind.

Whether you are 19 or 90 makes no difference on the Other Levels. Simply visualize yourself as you would aspire to be. If you are 90 but would like to be in your mid-twenties or thirties, simply visualize yourself as you were at that time. Conversely, if you are 19 but would like to be in your mid-twenties or thirties, try and imagine how you would look at that age, and assume that shape/appearance.

Any handicaps that you possess in the physical could be removed, should you so wish, on the other levels.

Those of you who are housebound or in wheelchairs need not be so on the other levels. It is entirely up to you.

Visualize this "new" body over your existing, physical body. Visualize yourself wearing whatever you would feel comfortable in, or the clothing that you feel is appropriate to the role you are assuming. Each time you set yourself to journey to the other levels make sure that you don this "body," often termed a "Body of Light."

* * *

It will not have escaped many of you that I have found myself working with figures from the Arthuriad.

In essence, the Arthuriad deals with the mythical/legendary exploits of King Arthur and his Knights of the Round Table as they struggled and battled to unite the countries of England, Wales, Cornwall and the Saxon Shores into a cohesive identity, each supporting the other against invasion and internal insurrection; one nation, one king.

Having spent my formative adult life as a soldier, it came as no real surprise to find myself with a patriotic, quasi-military contact. I freely admit that it was not my intention to work with them, however, it happened. One tends to "link" with that particular vibration that is most akin to the nature, attitude, inclination and capabilities of the individual.

Gareth Knight, in his *Secret Tradition in Arthurian Legend* gives an indication of the Path of Progression through the Lesser Mysteries, where all must make a start in their quest.

I have mentioned them, in passing, in my diary. However, it is necessary to offer some simplified explanation of just what each of the three Grades symbolizes. The Grade of Arthur and the Knights of the Round Table, symbolized by the Presentation of the Sword, indicates an acceptance of responsibility; to one's self, family, work, environment and the land as a whole.

The Grade of Merlin, symbolized by the Presentation of the Staff, indicates the knowledge and ability to wield power/forces.

Gareth entitles the third grade as the Grade of Guinevere, but a more suitable name I believe would be the Grade of the Lady of the Lake. This Grade is symbolized by the Presentation of the Cup,

Chalice or Grail (depending on how the individual so honored views the presentation). I believe that this Grade indicates the most important aspect of the Work in general: the wisdom to know *when* and *when not* to wield the power/force.

Nobody can take the matter further into the Greater Mysteries, since one is then Working on a direct one-to-one link with an archetype, and circumstances alter cases. Each must find their own way through these realms.

* * *

A word that crops up continually in the diary is "Force."

Dion Fortune has defined the concept of God as pressure—Cosmic Pressure.

Imagine a fish tank of water. For the purposes of this exercise it is empty of plants, fishes, etc., containing nothing but water.

Just inside one end of the tank we have a plate of movable glass, but there is a seal around the edges which prohibits water from seeping behind it as it moves along. We are now going to move that plate, compressing the water. We are applying pressure. The movement and pressure creates small whirlpools of movement in the water. Some you would see, but others would be either too fast or too small to be spotted. They would react throughout the whole of the water in the tank. The faster the plate was moved, the greater the magnitude of the whirlpools created.

Now let us change the perspective slightly and say that the water in the tank is the totality of the cosmos, bound by the illimitable God.

God "moves," applies pressure and the cosmos responds.

The response is the whirlpools of force, more commonly referred to as vortices. Some we are capable of acknowledging, others we are not.

Each of the entities mentioned in the diary is a representation of one of those vortices of force, a God-created whirlpool in the cosmos. Since we human beings relate more positively to our own kind, we substitute a picture of another human being to act as a "go between" between ourselves and the forces. This is known as anthropomorphism.

The picture is not the force. However, a minute part of the force is sometimes used to assist in the generation of the picture.

Let us take, for example, the force that represents itself to me as Merlin. Without burying ourselves in too much philosophy, accept that Merlin is a part of the overall force of England and Wales (often referred to as Britannia).

However, the Merlin is of such a dimension that no one person can comprehend the whole of it; therefore, a small aspect of the force represents itself on a sufficient scale as to be meaningful.

This means that the concept which I see clairvoyantly as a particularly shaped man may be seen entirely differently by the person standing by my side. He or she may have a different concept of the force/Merlin. Neither of us are "wrong" in our perception of him.

Both of us are "right" in regard to our individual comprehension of something that is completely outside our possible experience. I learned this during the conversation between Merlin and myself in the early days of our liaison, as recorded and published in the diary.

How you will react, respond, etc., when you make contact with your national force, and how it will react and respond to you is entirely a matter of the relationship between the pair of you. From conversations with other people I have discovered that the response comes in the most unexpected manner, which can only confirm the contact. I say this is confirmation because it is unexpected and, therefore, cannot have come from the mind of the neophyte/aspirant.

It will have been noticed that others, such as the Lady of the Lake, have also joined in with the Workings I have undertaken. These were not "called" by me. They were introduced by the Merlin, as and when he felt it was necessary to make such an addition to the effort being expended. For this reason there is a dearth of description in the diary.

I suggest that you concentrate solely upon the initial contact you make. When you have contacted your archetype, he/she will bring in the others when it is necessary. It must be stressed that time is of no consequence; it doesn't matter.

The simple fact that you have made the initial contact means that you are Working. The Work is the important thing. It may not be in the plan for everybody to contact the totality of, shall we say, the Round Table.

There is a trite saying that, "Cleanliness is next to Godliness." The sweeper/cleaner is as essential to the temple as the highest High Priest/High Priestess. The latters cannot function without the aid of the former.

Make the initial contact and leave it in the hands of the other side as to whom else is necessary for your part in the Work. I cannot, nor will not, hazard any guesses how things may go for you. All I can wish you is Godspeed and, based purely on my own experiences, tell you that I have found it to be thoroughly worthwhile in an experiential manner.

* * *

Another point in the diary that may cause a number of questions will, no doubt, be in regard to my Working with crystal. I certainly do not mean a crystal ball.

Let us define what a crystal *is*. It is the physical element of Earth (specifically silicon) that has been subjected to tremendous heat and pressure by the surrounding strata and, as such, has become quartz.

These quartzes, depending on the minerals prevalent in the area of constriction, take on various colors and are then referred to as various types of quartz. For instance there is amethyst, rose quartz, tiger's eye, etc. The list is extensive, but basically they are all types of quartz. (These quartzes are what I am referring to as crystal.)

As I have written in the section on Merlin, Atlantis was fueled by crystal power. Many Atlanteans are currently reincarnating. They all seem to have a natural affinity and love of crystal and like to have some about the home, just as my wife and I do. Many may scoff at this Atlantean connection, however I refer you to my statement about the island kingdom being based on crystal power.

I suggest that they have a look at the power centralization in our modern world. Computers are the seats of the economy of the developed nations. What is the heart of a computer? What am I using right now, typing these words into my word processor to get them onto the pages of this book? Silica—silicon dioxide occurring as quartz crystals, and principal constituent of sandstone and other rocks.

The modern world is, therefore, basing its livelihood on crystal: A new Atlantis? Another new dimension has also entered our world.

In simple terms, if you take a gemstone (another form of crystal) wrap a wire around it, pass an electrical current along the wire, the induced magnetism in the coil of wire reacts on the gemstone and energy streams out of the end of the gemstone. You have a laser.

I was introduced to working with crystal by Manaan and Santoshi from the Crystal Light Center in London. It was quite an experience.

After a brief lecture on the various types of crystal and the esoteric significance of the various types/colors, we were invited to participate in a physical experiment with the crystal. I invite you to carry out this same experiement for yourself, either alone or in a group.

Obtain a piece of natural, unpolished rock quartz, preferably with a natural point on one end. Place this against your sternum (the connecting bone at the front of the rib cage) and sing. Yes, I said "sing." Sing anything you like, it doesn't matter what sort of song it is (except I doubt if heavy metal or similar will really work—but who knows—I may be in error), neither will it matter if you don't know the words; hum it.

Depending upon the size of the quartz, and your tunefulness, you will find that when you strike certain notes, the crystal will start to vibrate, to resonate. Do this a few times, until you are sure that you can spot the sort of note that produces a response, then stop.

Take a few big breaths, relax, and then sing that one note gently. Don't force it. Hold it for as long as you can—if you find that you haven't quite got it right, shift the note slightly until it is right. You will know beyond any shadow of doubt when it is right, I assure you, because the crystal will start to resonate as before, only it will begin to amplify the resonance.

Don't be put off by this particular feeling. It grows on you and becomes both pleasant and relaxing. The vibration will be picked up by your sternum and this will, in due course, set the whole of your skeletal structure vibrating in sympathy. It can be amazing.

Those of you that may have read Anne McCaffrey's *Crystal Singer* will now understand what she meant when she alluded to the singers losing all sense of time and becoming enthralled by the crystal. Here, obviously, is the warning. Like all things, don't become over-enamored of singing crystal in this manner.

Now, forget the singing, take the crystal away from your body and hold it in your active hand (right hand if right-handed, left if left-handed) and then cup your passive hand (the other one) over the top of the point and let this hand go "soft;" let it relax and go very, very gentle. Do not touch the crystal with this passive hand, but keep it about a quarter to half an inch away from the point.

Very gently and lazily move your hand from side to side, always keeping the point under your hand. Assuming you are nicely relaxed you should begin to feel a small, blunt point of something crossing your palm in line with the point. Some feel a form of heat, others a coldness, others something entirely different. What you are in fact feeling is the amplification of raw, cosmic power by the crystal into a jet of force, totally benign. This is only a demonstration of the capabilities of crystal.

Having learned practically of the nature of crystal, let us now turn to the usage of such properties. We have learned of the crystal's ability to respond to a certain wavelength of sound. The case is very similar with light waves, heat radiation, radio waves (some may well remember the old cat's whisker radios at the end of WWII—a crystal set; piece of wire, aerial and headphones) and magic.

If you sing to one piece of crystal, another piece in reasonably close proximity will also resonate in harmony with the original. If you can direct, for instance, healing energies to your piece of crystal, any other piece of crystal will also resonate in harmony. I was singing healing to the Earth, the nation, the people and us all. I was doing it here in southeast England, but crystal throughout the world was acting in sympathetic resonance to my song.

The majority of crystal is, thankfully, still in the Earth. Some of it is somewhere beneath the ground under our home.

This would have tuned in to what I was doing and would then have amplified it, causing other crystal elsewhere to respond as well.

So it would continue around the Earth.

Given that a big enough vibration was set up, there is always the possibility that, for instance, the crystal embedded in the Moon also responded as well, and so on, out into space and the Cosmos. As I mention in the diary, I was informed that diamond a part of the crystal family and reacts in the same way.

My new employment was to be in an office in Hatton Garden, the center of England's diamond market. Singing diamond is the same as singing crystal. That is, invoke healing to a diamond and the rest of the diamonds respond.

* * *

There is much talk, in occult circles, of the temple "built without hands." They are talking of their astral temples, the place where the ritual commences and should finish.

The first exercise in the Practical Section deals with building just such a temple, albeit very simple, but very effective. To my personal knowledge, that temple has been in use since April, 1986. It has been used not just by me, but also by those who have been Working with me. I still use it, and it still works.

Obviously, you do not have to stick to this particular temple, as it may not suit everyone. Using the basic principle outlined in that exercise you are completely at liberty to "design" and "build" whatever shape, size or type of temple you feel most at home in. The only caution I would add is to try not to build too ornate a construction because it must be built, exact detail by exact detail, *every time* you visit it.

Since you may be new to this particular method of Working, don't try and make things so ornate that you have to spend a quarter of an hour each time just "getting ready." When it comes to actually Working, your mind will be somewhat fatigued before you start. Temples can range from a simple grass circle, standing stones, a wattle and daub hut, church, cathedral or even the Temple of Solomon.

While I was writing these pages I received an invitation to participate in a ritual with a group of people in London. The purpose of the ritual was to "build" the Temple of Solomon. We started the Working just after 10 in the morning and finished about 6 in the evening. Of course there were breaks for natural functions, but it was a long day, and I would not recommend such an exercise to anyone who lacks the experience of such Work.

In due course, if you feel that is where you wish to Work, by all means go for it, but not immediately. The whole point of what I am trying to say is, be comfortable. Go where you feel safe and secure, be dressed in the manner you feel fitting for the occasion. There is no compulsion to do anything you feel is out of order. Be yourself.

* * *

In a like manner, many maintain that you should construct a physical temple, setting a room or area aside in your home for the exclusivity of the Work. They also maintain that you should wear certain clothes (robes) whenever you are Working. I would agree with them—up to a point.

From a psychological point of view, the putting on of certain clothes which are only worn for these times tells the mind (especially the subconscious) that a certain set of special operations is about to be undertaken. This sort of thing can be seen, even now, in modern life.

We still have a saying about putting on your "Sunday Best" to go to church, or wherever. This is a suit or dress that was only brought out on special occasions. It tells the subconscious that it is about to be engaged in something out of the ordinary. Donning your robes does the same thing.

From a similar vantage point, having a special room/area for your Work aids this subconscious reaction. Let us assume that you have a space that is only used for mystical/magical Work. Therefore, the only times you will ever enter that space are when you are going to be involved in that Work. The subconscious mind suddenly sits up when you enter that room/area and takes notice.

"We're going to do something." As you progress, you will learn that they are no longer a necessity, and that the room and robes can become an encumberance, stopping you in fact from Working.

As you become more and more involved in the Work you will discover that every moment of your life becomes a part of the Work, and therefore *is* your whole life. We cannot put our robes on and wander about the streets and neglect our daily chores. We cannot spend all our days locked up in our room/area. Life is to be lived.

The art lies in being inconspicuous—a chameleon, able to pass unnoticed and unremarked in the hustle and bustle of daily life. Your unseen presence being the sole circuitry for the flow of occult forces into the world of men/women and matter, stimulating those who pass you by and ignoring you. *That* is where the most Work is carried out.

On a very few occasions it is necessary for a particular person to have a certain amount of publicity thrust upon them, in order to bring the Work to the notice of the general public and to stimulate interest in people Working for themselves.

I must stress that this only happens in the very rarest of occasions. The vast majority of Workers are unknown and unseen, and will remain that way throughout their incarnation, the butchers, bakers, clerks, cleaners, etc., the unsung heroes and heroines of life; their only reward being the silent self-satisfaction that they are following their path to the best of their ability and the sure and certain knowledge that the Work continues.

* * *

Much time and energy is spent in endeavoring to establish some idea of the individual's previous incarnations. It is my understanding that we incarnate in order to learn a specific lesson. Assuming that we have learned the lesson, there is no necessity to revise. It's done and has been absorbed into the psyche, therefore it is of no benefit to go back to try and see what it was all about. It is done and finished with.

I have never consciously spent any time or effort in backtracking. However, there have been a very small number of occasions when it has been essential for me to know and understand certain things from history.

Those I serve deemed it to be so and have orchestrated the input of the information, often at the most unexpected times and in equally unexpected situations. Those "views" were shown for a specific purpose and were necessary for me to understand the cause/reason for current Work.

I cannot overemphasize the importance of *now*. The past and future are of little import in comparison to the *now*. By all means have a dream/vision/aspiration to work toward, but it is the effort *now* that determines whether those will be fulfilled.

* * *

As I sit typing, it is now some two months since Alan suggested we get together for the publication of the diary. In a cheerful tone he happily commented that we would need a description of exactly *what* Pendragon is. I have wracked my brain, dug into tomes, taken the question "upstairs," delved into the complete *Oxford English Dictionary* but just cannot seem to find an adequate explanation. Words that threaten to crush my nasal sinuses (like "chthonic") don't really seem to help.

You will have read Derek's splendid report after the Working of July 28, 1986 and, hopefully may have understood his concept of Pendragon, just as I did. The difference lies in the fact that Pendragon still exists as a total entity for me. I still sit astride him almost every day.

Sure, I can describe him, right down to the size of his claws, but to define *exactly what he is* eludes me. In essence there is the Spirit of Chivalry, the unifying Force of England and Wales, the Banner. All are totally inadequate.

* * *

I have mentioned on numerous occasions that I have Worked with a group, but have made no mention as yet what the essential difference is between a group and solo Workings. Unlike Christine and the Colonel, our groups were not coming together to confirm the actions/incidents taking place elsewhere. Each member of our groups had a specific task to carry out within the concept of the overall Workings.

It would have been possible for me to have carried out all the tasks by myself, however the Working took some 45 minutes as a group, but alone it might have taken four or five hours. Even with the training I have had, I doubt if I could have handled it all by myself and been anywhere near so successful.

In our first attempt in March 1985, each was asked to mediate the energies of a specific member of the Arthuriad and were, in the main, fairly passive. In the Working of July 28, 1986, they were asked to act as envoys to the various Forces we were calling to the Meet. They then became a "front" for the Forces they had escorted, and endeavored to mediate the results back to the Forces for the Force's departure.

We were all endeavoring to be catalysts for the fruition of the Working. Each individual was working on a "one-to-one" basis with those they were escorting. This allows a greater sense of rapport to be established. We all felt we were successful—our successors will confirm, or deny, in the due course of time.

* * *

Another benefit of a group lies in the establishment of a group identity, sometimes referred to as a Group Mind. On a very simple scale, these pages are being put together as a result of a Group Mind.

The Merlin is (hopefully) inspiring me as to what is coming out of my fingertips in my half of this book. Another is (hopefully) inspiring Alan in a similar fashion with his half.

In due course, Alan and I will get together with the red pencils, scissors, our contacts and will try to make some sort of intelligible cohesion appear out of the notes, cigarette packets, envelopes and other assortments of paper that finally make a book. This liaison creates a rapport.

The editor, the publisher, the proofreader, etc., work on the book, and thereby work on the strengthening of the Group Mind. By the time it actually goes to the printer, the Group Mind should be fairly active.

You, the reader, in reading the book become involved with the Group Mind, possibly adding even more strength to it.

A rapport is a force in its own right; some may even prefer to think of it as a form of magnetism between two or more people. As the force "works" and is used, so it grows stronger. It is very similar with the groups I have worked with. The group rapport (force) builds and gains strength and, in the end, becomes an additional "active member" of the group.

However, should the Group Mind be ignored, it will eventually dissipate and cease to exist. As an example, the Golden Dawn has served its purpose and its Group Mind has gone. [I disagree—A.R.] The *FIL*, on the other hand, is still working and its Group Mind is extremely strong.

"Where two or three are gathered together in my name, there shall I be." He was expounding the same sort of concept. The Christ will be with any group, however large or small, that comes together in the name of the Christ. A rapport is established with the Christ Force, as like attracts like, so the Divine Christ Force is contacted.

* * *

This sort of thing does not only apply to us mere mortals, it applies to many other things as well. Take houses, for instance, through a form of evolution. A cottage becomes a part of a hamlet, which becomes a part of a village, which becomes a part of a town, which becomes a part of a city, which becomes a part of a county, which becomes a part of the country. From this analogy it can be seen that the original cottage is an integral part of the group mind of the country.

Not many people seem to be aware that vegetation has an awareness as well. Let us look at trees.

England was once one huge forest that covered the whole land. Remnants still exist today. Regrettably, they are under threat. A copse was once part of a wood, which was once part of the forest. The forest group mind is, unfortunately, gradually being eroded, but for the time being it still exists. Smaller woods have survived, and luckily they have been able to sustain/produce their own group mind.

Within any wood there is more than just trees; there are the ferns, grasses, birds, animals, the worlds of fairy and the elemental kingdoms. Each of these add to the strength of the group mind.

I continuously mention the Lord and Guardian of the Wood in my trips into the local woods. In simple terms, it is the group mind of the wood. Every time we go over the wood we make a mental acknowledgement to it, and say a polite "thank you" when we leave.

* * *

On a slightly different tack, I suggest you accept that you are part of a group mind in your home, wherever you go for rest and relaxation and, just as important, where you carry out any form of employment that you may have. *Wherever* you go make a mental acknowledgement to the Lord of (place).

A job interview coming up? Try and make a preliminary visit, say the day before, just to make sure you know where you are going and how long it will take you to travel; you certainly don't want to be late. You don't have to go in. Simply walk by, and as you do so, cast a mental thought toward the Lord of (firm/organization) and say "Hi, I'm (name/Magical Name), I have an appointment for a job interview tomorrow/whenever."

It is polite, if nothing else. You may even find that you get some form of "response," a feeling, an indication of whether you will be accepted, whatever. Remember, you are doing this mentally, so no one is going to know and wonder about the candidate for the "funny farm."

This sort of thing also applies to going on a vacation, especially abroad. "Hi, I'm (name/Magical Name), I've been coming here on vacation/a business trip for (however long)." You will be surprised how different you find things, simply through a few seconds' politeness to the unseen.

Of course, remember to say "thank you" when you leave. Obviously, this does not mean that you keep a running commentary to every hamlet/wood/field you pass through, over or by on a motorway, interstate highway, railway line. Just pick out the major influences. For instance, my forays into London were always announced, but not to every station we passed through.

The watchword is *discrimination*.

* * *

I have recently discovered that there are a large number of people coming into incarnation who are the forerunners of the Aquarian Age. They have specifically elected to enter the material world at this time in order to prepare the world for Aquarius—it could be suggested that they are a form of Aquarian Vanguard.

They are coming to introduce the change of emphasis with a slackening and rejection of the shackles of establishment authority, as each seeks knowledge/experience for themselves on an individual basis: to make the esoteric, exoteric. It is an integral part of the evolution of mankind.

* * *

At the end of the Workings that have been entered in my diary, and after a rest, the injunction came:

"Come out of your cave, down off the mountain; get out and about."

Ancient Magicks
for a New Age

Part IV

A Temple Not Made With Hands

Introduction

Seymour's essays were originally published in the journal of the Fraternity of the Inner Light, between 1935 and 1939. It was Basil Wilby, the astute editor of the now-defunct magazine *New Dimensions*, who reprinted some of these and kept some of the spark alive. Today, however, the long and wondrous essay "The Old Religion," can be found within *The Story of Dion Fortune* by Carr Collins and Charles Fielding, while the rest of Seymour's work has been collected and edited by Dolores Ashcroft-Nowicki in *The Forgotten Mage*. Reading these it is hard to avoid the conclusion that the old Colonel was, in his own quiet and undemonstrative way, one of the best and wisest writers on magic in this century.

(Because of its length, the followed quoted material, published under the title "The Children of the Great Mother," has not been reduced in size or indented, in order that it will be easier to read.)

The Children of the Great Mother

In these articles on the ancient Mysteries an attempt will be made to show what the Gods of a Mystery Tradition meant to their initiated servers who, being educated men and women, had a practical working knowledge of the technique for the obtaining of religious experience used by their own particular school or schools.

Speaking generally we may say that each of the cycles or systems of the gods had its own Mystery Cult. And we should probably be not incorrect in stating that in most of these cults there were two types of priests, the ordinary priesthood whose members *performed* the rituals, especially the exoteric rituals, and the initiated priests who were selected from the ranks of the ordinary priesthood and were taught how to *work* both the exoteric and the esoteric rites. The student here should appreciate the fact that the terms *to perform*, and *to work* are not synonymous; and that the difference between them is a clue to the difference that existed in the past between the exoteric priesthood who served the God in his earthly temple and the initiated priests who were able to work these rites in "A Temple not made with Hands, Eternal in the Heavens."

Except possibly in Greece and there only after about 600 B.C., education was given, as a rule, only in connection with a temple. The civil servants of Egypt and Babylon, and probably elsewhere, were almost to a man temple-educated as were also the governors, princes, princesses and queens. Later, when the priesthood fell into disrepute and the Temple Mysteries decayed, the training of initiates in the working of rites and ceremonies was carried out in secular schools which were formed eventually (in most cases) into secret brotherhoods. The school of Pythagoras which was started at Crotona in Southern Italy, and from thence, after becoming a brotherhood, spread widely over the Graeco-Roman Empire, is an example of this. The Societies formed by the *Orphikoi* under cover of the official worship of Dionysus, and the schools of Christian and pre-Christian Gnosticism in Syria and Egypt are examples of hieratic and secular attempts to supplement the inadequate spiritual pablum given by official and state religions when in a degenerate condition.

262

In the widely differing Cults of Mithras, Isis, and Serapis, we have examples of a dying religion taking on a new life, sometimes with a new name and a more up-to-date system of external organization. At the same time it must be noted that these cults as a rule retained much of that secret inner knowledge and technique which enabled their trained and initiated members to work the rites in their new form, often, indeed usually, in a new country; for in most of the cults that have been mentioned here the Gods more or less forsook the lands from which they came.

This is a minor point that may be of interest to the many students of esoteric religion who study it by means of the comparative methods that are so popular today. A prophet is not without honor save in his own country and among his own people. So, too, with many of the gods and goddesses: for example, Christianity with Jesus as its divine Savior has flourished except among the Jews. Mithraism died in its own land with the conquests of Alexander, and then, with Mithra as its divine Savior with a new role and a new message it flourished greatly in Asia Minor and Europe for nearly a thousand years.

Isis died in Egypt but was reborn in orthodox Christianity as the Virgin Mary, the Queen of Heaven, the Stella Maris of Christianity, and "the Help of Christians." Briefly, it can be said that the Great Gods never die. Their names may change; the methods of using that power which they represent may change, and the new message their priest-hoods bring may be different in form and substance, but the Great Gods are eternal in a Temple not made with hands which is itself eternal in the heavens. And so, too, in another way, live for many an age the Lesser Gods, the Heroes, and those earthly teachers who ever follow at the tail of the long train of the followers of the Great Cosmic Gods. Man, even if he follows only in the rear of this great procession, is yet a child of the Aeon; he is not ephemeral, as some seem to think.

It may here be objected that the secrets of the Mysteries have been so well kept that the *Mysteria* are not known to history. This objection is a fair one and it must be given full weight; it is in a sense quite true, but it can be explained.

Dr. Angus, in his fair and constructive history of the Ancient Mysteries ("The Mystery Religions and Christianity") very rightly points out that the secrecy to which initiates were pledged forbade those who knew to write the inner history of the cults to which they belonged, and rendered it impossible for those who did not know to divulge the *Mysteria*.

He also points out that, in addition to destroying the temples and literature of the Mysteries, "Christian writers represented, or rather misrepresented, the mystery cults in such a way that one is sometimes compelled to question how these ever exercised such a potent spell over ancient religious minds."

Consider how great some of these minds were from this hymn of the by no means well-known writer, Cleanthes:*

> Lead me, O Zeus, and lead me, Destiny.
> Whither ordained is by your decree.
> I'll follow, doubting not, or if with will,
> Recreant I falter and I shall follow still!

With all the advantages of modern science and modern education, few moderns, escaping in to the freedom of the dogmaless Western Mysteries, could express themselves more clearly and more beautifully, even when with head bowed over the black double cube, they offer their dedication to the Mystery ideal of the Truth, the whole Truth and nothing but the Truth.

The secret of the Mysteries, it is true, is not known to historians, not even to one so sympathetic as that great scholar, Dr. Angus. It is not known to the anthropologists, not even to men of such vast knowledge as the author of *The Golden Bough*. And the explanation is very simple. History deals with facts or supposed facts, with the things of the age that is under consideration. The secret of the Mysteries is not one that concerns facts, symbols, rites, dogmas, rituals or teachings. It cannot be betrayed because it concerns a mode of consciousness. This secret has been trumpeted from the housetops since man became a thinking, tool-using animal, yet it has remained a mystery since the world began. "Behold I show you a mystery," said one of the founders of Christianity and his empty hands showed NO THING. The empty shrine is the supreme Mystery of Mysteries, and it cannot be betrayed because it is a way of thinking, a NO-THING-NESS like its prototype "the Abyss that is beyond all Abysses."

The acquiring of the technique of NO-THING-NESS is the subject matter of the Mysteries, the Mystery technique is not a secret. Pelmanism is a modern adaptation of an ancient mystery usage which was taught in the Lotus Court of the Mystery Temples of Isis. Yet the Isian *Mysteria* have not been divulged. Apuleius gives a long account

---

* Matheson's translation in Bevan. "Later Greek Religion."

of his initiation and adds "Behold, I have told you things of which, although you have heard them, you cannot know the meaning."

The clue lies in this, initiation is NO THING. It is an experience which takes place NOT IN TIME nor in SPACE. Consider this ancient saying: "The Sun is in the macrocosm what Reason is in the microcosm" (Diog.L.VII.139)—which Angus somewhat obviously interprets by saying: "The *intelligent light* of the physical luminary suggested the *intelligible light* of truth" (Angus, "The Religious Quests of the Graeco-Roman World").

This is an ancient word picture of a truth which can be interpreted in a rather less obvious manner when meditated upon by those upon the Path who realize the relationship between Macroprosopos and Microprosopos as shown upon the Tree of Life, and the use that can be made of it.

Once the principles that govern the methods of training used in Western Schools in good repute and in the direct line of succession have been grasped, it is fairly easy to compare, to analyze and to classify the technique that is used in schools of another tradition. For example, the principles that govern the technique that is used in India, Persia and Tibet are *au fond* the same as those that govern the Yoga of the West, though the techniques are in themselves utterly different.

A highly trained initiate of the West can grasp the purport of the technique of almost any Eastern system. This, however, does not mean that such a one can either practice or use a technique that is foreign to his own. Usually and for good reasons he leaves Eastern Yoga severely alone.

At the back of each of the older Mystery systems is a group mind and behind that group mind is the group soul of the nation or the epoch during which it flourished. If, in the past, a student has been a member of, say, the cult of Hathor at Denderah in South Egypt, he will be able by means of the technique that is taught him today in a School of the Western Tradition that is working under authority in London to project himself into the past. His knowledge of the principles taught in this age will enable him to recover from within himself when back in the astral form of The Temple of the Denderah that was built more than three thousand years ago, the principles and the methods that were taught him in that long forgotten past life.

He can then work a ritual of the cult of Hathor for he is still a member of that ancient group mind which is even today a living integral portion of the group soul of Mother Earth. He picks up the trail first within himself, then within Nature's magical memory, and then he very gently draws up from the deeps a forgotten knowledge. This is education in the true sense of drawing forth from within.

But when the initiate strives to pass into a group mind that is alien and into a culture that is also alien, he will find that though he may understand it, he can neither practice nor use the technique he is examining. He is not a member of this group mind; he is alien to it; he is one of the profane.

He must, as a beginner, take his initiation into this, to him, new tradition. This is the reason why so few Europeans are able to use the great Eastern traditions of China, Tibet and India. These do not come naturally to them, and a fresh start has to be made. The would-be initiate has to be vouched for and trained by one who is a competent master in that particular tradition.

Again, you will seldom find that foreigners (even Europeans) can take their full training in schools working with the English group soul. They can be trained up to a point in meditation, in psychology, and in the philosophy and comparative methods of the Mysteries. But when it comes to teamwork in a ritual, it will be found—as a rule— that their practical work is weak. There are exceptions to this rule, plenty of them, but it can, by experience, be proved to be a useful practical guide, and it is almost infallible when dealing with the immature.

The rulers of the group minds described above are the gods and the goddesses of the various cults, the divine Children of the Great Mother. And, if these results of practical work which have been set forth above are of universal application as it is thought they are, then it will be wiser—in the case of beginners—to stick to the Divine Formulations that belong to the tradition into which one has been born. One may take it for granted that the Lords of Karma know what is good for each of us, and place us where best we can profit from the experiences that must come from environment.

If you would drink in the Initiatory Rites of the Cold Waters that flow from the Lake of Memory, remember the Guardians thereof, for these are the great Race Angels of the Orphic Tablet. They will know "who thou art and whence thou art and what thy city is," when thou comest to revive "the memory of the Beginnings."

Build clearly the images that rise into your mind as you brood in meditation upon this translation of the Orphic Tablet:

Thou shalt find on the left of the House of Hades a Well-spring,
And by the side thereof standing a white cypress.
To this Well-spring approach not near.
But thou shalt find another by the Lake of Memory,
Cold water flowing forth, and there are Guardians before it.
Say: "I am a child of Earth and of Starry Heaven;
But my race is of Heaven (alone). This ye know yourselves.
And lo, I am parched with thirst and I perish. Give me quickly
The cold water flowing forth from the Lake of Memory."
And of themselves they will give thee to drink from the holy
                                Well-spring,
And thereafter among the other Heroes thou shalt have lordship.
                        (*The Flaming Door*, Merry.)

The house of Hades is not hell as the untaught of today imagine. It is the bright shining land to which the Celtic heroes voyaged in the *glass* boat of initiation. It is the inner world that lies behind the dark door of the temple sanctuary. The Guardians are the Gods or Race Angels, and the well is in your own soul which is also in the Lake of the Memory of the Earth Mother.

After drinking, you may look for the moon in the crystal cup of pure water. Can you build these images in reverie? Try the experiment.

Celui qui a de l'imagination sans
erudition a des ailes et n'a pas des pieds.*
                                 —Joubert

In the reformulation of an ancient tradition a great deal of historical research has to be carried out in order to build that bony skeleton upon which all the rest has to fit.

It is often thought that when an adept returns to earth from the unseen realms of Hu (the once all potent Divine Lord of Western Celtic mythology) in order to take up his work in the Temple of Ceridwen—that is, in the realms of the soul of this earth-world, he has merely to open up his own communications with the Masters of Wisdom who are on the Inner Planes, and then a School of Initiation springs into being and also into function as Athene sprang fully armed with a great shout from the head of Zeus.

The Masters of Wisdom from the realms of Hu provide the adept with imagination, and they give him at the same time the winged cup of crystal that contains inspiration. But this is not enough. The adept has to use his own feet in order to search among the dusty and forgotten records of the past for the traditional forms into which the contents

---

* He who has imagination without erudition has wings and not feet.

of the winged crystal cup have to be poured. And the quotation at the head of this section is an exact description of the situation of any leader who, relying on imagination alone, and lacking erudition, gives his group emotional stimuli only.

This type of being is well suited to the pacific and, alas, often soporific atmosphere of an "uplift" society, but an occult society in function, with the terminals of its contacts well plugged home in the realms of both the "Here" and the "Yonder," is seldom pacific and even more rarely soporific. Both the society and its members have to be strong in body and soul to stand the strain of the forces that flow through them. There has to be an adequate technique, or disruptive explosions will shake the society and its members.

To put this rather differently, an occult society has to have an outer court for teaching and training if it is safely to carry on the work of initiation. Now it is the formation and functioning of the outer court that calls for the above-mentioned *erudition*.

In the Inner Group of such a society the members look inwards and seek within themselves in silent meditation for the preparation of the three drops that are brewed in "the seething elements" of the Cauldron of Ceridwen. But when "little Gwion" has licked his scalded fingers and has thereby become inspired, he must look outwards if he is to escape the pursuing fury of the Goddess Ceridwen and bring his imagination to fruition by means of a hardly won *erudition*.

It is at this stage that he repairs to the temple of the Gods of Wisdom. For they and they only enable the Children of Hu to bring that light to their brethren who are still in the shadowy realms of Ceridwen.

In the temples of the Gods of Wisdom there are many books of many kinds. But they all have one thing in common: they deal with something that comes from experience—not argument—and this experience comes through Nature to man who is her child. The first and most important book of all that have to be studied is the great book of Nature—i.e. Ceridwen. This book lies ever open before us on the dark double cubed altar of this material universe. Its secrets are not contained in the printed lines upon its bright golden-colored pages but are hidden, so that he who runs may not read. You have to read slowly, a little at a time, and visualize much in quiet meditation. Even those who can be "awake in sleep" know that when studying the lore of Ceridwen you have to read between the lines. A reasoned argument is no help—your staff support is experience, not reasoning.

Here is a hint which Plutarch in his "Isis at Osiris" gives to his friend Clea, a priestess of Dionysus and an Isiac. He is writing about Anubis, the Prince of the West, a god who not only leads the dead man through the Gates of Death and across the stony desert of the West, but also takes the initiate through the Portals of Initiation, which is always a gate in the West.

Plutarch says: "By Anubis they understand the horizontal circle, which divides the invisible part of the world, which they call Nephthys, from the visible, to which they give the name of Isis; and as this circle equally touches upon the confines of light and darkness, it may be looked upon as common to them both." It will here be remembered that, in addition to the physical horizon, there is also the horizon of consciousness. In terms of the latter, certain of the titles of Anubis are explanatory of his role. He is called UP-UAU, i.e. the "Opener of the Roads"; he is also called SEKHEM-EM-PET or "The Power in Heaven." Apuleius (Book XI) mentions him as having two faces, "the one being black as night, and the other golden as the day."

Plutarch also tells us that Osiris (the Lord of Initiation) is the "Common Reason which pervades both the superior and inferior regions of the Universe, and adds later that it is called both Anubis and Hermanubis, the first name expressing relationship to the superior, as the latter to the inferior world. Now both these worlds exist only in terms of consciousness and have nothing to do with solar light or terrestrial darkness. They become manifest as stages in initiation. (See Budge *From Fetish to God*.)

If we now turn to the Celtic Mysteries, we shall find that the God Hu represented the power and glory of the spiritual world, and in this sense he is analogous to Osiris. His *Shakti* was Ceridwen, the Soul of this Universe. In other words she is as the Twin Goddesses of the Ancient Mysteries, Isis-Nephthys. Hu, like Osiris, is the Lord or directing principle, the common Reason of the whole universe. Ceridwen gives, in her dual role of Isis-Nephthys, the powers of the light and the dark wisdom or vision that is not reason. Once again, these things pertain to planes of consciousness which are other than the physical consciousness.

Anubis or Hermanubis is the light and the dark guide into these dual realms of Isis and Nephthys. But he is also Osiris, and there is the White Osiris and the Black Osiris, just as in modern mysticism there are the Christs of evil as well as the White Christs. "Hu, wearing the gold yoke of the sun and the girdle of the Iris of the World, accompanied the human being when he was united with the 'power of vision', out of the Depths, into the Light. He pointed the way to the Light when he revealed himself fully." (*The Flaming Door*, Merry.)

Here we see that Hu unveils himself gradually, just as in the Egyptian Mysteries of initiation and of death the symbolism of the Dark Anubis gives place to that of the Golden Anubis; and again, when the sanctuary is reached, it is no longer Anubis who guides the candidate, but Horus, the Child of the Sun. For Anubis, the guide as the Child of Osiris, has now become Osiris, and He is on the Throne in the East with Isis-Nephthys standing behind him.

Thus, on reaching the Sanctuary, we have the eternal principle of all things that are in manifestation, a Duality that is a Polarity. And it matters not if the manifestation be that of Death (which is a birth) or Initiation (which is a re-birth). Shiva has his dual-formed Shakti; Osiris is seated in his shrine and behind him are Isis-Nephthys; Hu, the Mighty One, is wedded to Ceridwen, who is not only the Universal and Fruitful Mother, but also the "darkly smiling Giantess." And later, in the Greater Mysteries, even Osiris himself will be found to be either the White or the Black "One." In the sanctuary the two halves become the Four Quarters of the Unit of Manifestation.

The Law of Polarity is the first lesson that Anubis, who is Hermanubis and also Osiris, reads to you from between the lines of the ever open book of Nature—that great Goddess, who is the dual natured Ceridwen, Isis-Nephthys, Kali-Durga. That which is solitary is barren. This is true of humans in the flesh and in the spirit. It is true of the Gods. And it is also true of all types of societies. There must be an outer as well as an inner; there must be the hidden as well as the revealed. The first Law of Life is that Shiva cannot function without his Shakti. And its corollary is Shiva, Vishnu, Kali, Durga; or Osiris, Set, Isis, Nephthys and so on through the Pantheons. For, caught in the Law of Manifestation, are first the ONE who has become two, and then the two who are four.

Having studied the open book of Nature, turn to that closed book which is hidden within the soul of man, a book that is even more difficult to read than is the former. It is known today as the Book of Life, Human Life, but the ancients called it the Book of Thoth. We are told that this book was hidden in the center of the Nile at Coptos, in an iron box, within which were a succession of enclosing boxes, of bronze, sycamore, ivory and ebony, gold and silver. Snakes and scorpions guarded it. Where it was, there was light; when it was not present, darkness was; a saying that only becomes clear when we remember

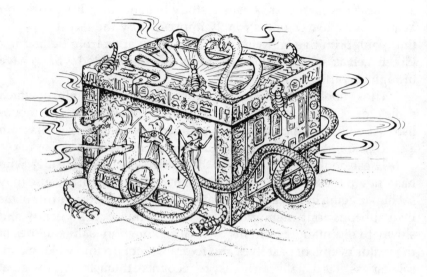

Box Containing the Book of Thoth.

that for the ancients there were earthly, heavenly and human gods. There was the earthly Nile, the heavenly Nile, and the Nile in the human aura. As will be explained later, the ancient seers of the Mediterranean Basin had a system of Yoga not unlike that of Ancient India. (See *Stories of the High Priests of Memphis* by Griffith.)

All the old Mystery rites are hidden in the Memory of Nature that is in the macrocosmic or heavenly Nile. The sea of Coptos is also hidden deep in the heredity of many men who are alive today. But this heredity pertains to the soul and spirit of a man; it has nothing to do with the descent of his physical body. There are many persons in the flesh today who have in the past tended altars in the Temples of Greece, of the Hyperboreans, in Egypt, in Asia Minor and in Chaldea. If such persons can but discover the hidden box that is beneath the microcosmic Sea of Coptos, which is within their own subconscious memory—and there is a technique for doing this—they will be able, later on, to find the macrocosmic Sea of Coptos; the subjective is in this case the key to the objective.

Here are some modern examples that may make this idea of finding the book that is hidden in the center of the Nile at Coptos more easy to understand.

Much the same can be said about books such as *Winged Pharaoh* and *Ancient Egypt Speaks*. Again, a study of some of A.E.'s prose and Yeats' poetry leaves one strongly impressed by the fact that something old, primitive and very real is peeping at us from behind the Green Veil as we muse upon the ideas that these gifted writers have brought to birth within us.

These books are not unique. There are more like them, of which some are good, others not so good. There are also hundreds of unpublished memories which have been recovered by their possessors from a succession of enclosing boxes discovered in the Nile at Coptos.

These books have a value for the trained and careful reader, who has studied the technique that has just been referred to, because they set him tugging gently and very patiently at the delicate tendrils of his own subconscious memories. They enable him ever so gently and slowly to disentangle from his own buried memories the outlines of the major events of past lives and to draw them up into waking consciousness. It is usually fairly easy to recognize them, for it is the great sorrows and tragedies of life that burn themselves into the memory of the soul, and when they come they often release a flood of emotion and of fear that is very painful. It is by this that they can be recognized.

The systems that were used in these ancient temples for reading the records of the Books of Thoth have come down to us in a very fragmentary condition, and much has to be guessed at from modern practical experience. But in countries that were, and probably are still, more civilized spiritually than in England, these ancient systems have come down almost uninjured. Tibet, India, Burma and China have many and varying systems for spiritual development that are coeval with the lost, the shattered, and, at the best, the mutilated, systems of Egypt, Chaldea and Syria.

Under the generic title of Eastern Yoga, the student will find much that throws light upon these lost Mediterranean systems. For example, a student's knowledge of Yoga will be enough to enable one to comprehend the methods of breathing and intoning names that must have been used by the initiate who was working for Mithraic Ritual which is given in *Echoes from the Gnosis*, Volume VI (by G. R. S. Mead).

A knowledge of Eastern Yoga will not only do this but it will also give a clue to the methods of spiritual development that were used by the pre-Christian contemplatives in the wilds of Egypt and Syria. It will throw much light on the accounts given of these heaven storming individuals by Philo and other writers. It may lead, through practical work and personal experience, to knowledge with regard to these mysteries. This knowledge is not the same as belief engendered by a study of historical facts. It reaches beyond facts, and it exchanges beliefs for knowledge.

The Gnostic is called by this name because he knows, and in knowing he discards believing. He has no *credos* in these matters.

The trained initiate of one system can, as a rule, understand without much difficulty the system of another race. "All the gods are one God, all the goddesses are one Goddess" and there is "One Illuminator." The names may vary, and the methods may vary, but the realities that are behind the Veil do not vary because they are purposive mental forces, timeless, ageless, and perfect in their system of working. They are the same yesterday, today and tomorrow. The ever-changing factor is man's conception of these forces and the mental images that he builds in order to reach out to them.

Popular ideology, in the special sense of visionary speculation, as the result of many centuries of narrow teaching, misrepresentation and misconception, is singularly childish, while the wiser teachings of the great modern Greek scholars have been almost unheeded. For example, Gilbert Murray has written in his edition of Hippolytus of Euripides:

> The Aphrodite of Euripides' actual belief, if one may venture to dogmatize on such a subject, was almost certainly not what we should call a goddess, but rather a force of Nature, or a Spirit working in the world. To deny her existence you would have to say not merely: "There is no such person," but "There is no such thing," and such a denial would be a defiance of obvious facts.

Here a great principle, which modern anthropology as a rule neglects, has been clearly set out. But, if Professor Murray had also made it clear that in the heart of every man there dwells this hidden, very potent natural force, personified by the ancients under the name of Aphrodite, and that this Aphrodite within forms a link with its parent Nature force that is without by means of the mental image of the perfect woman, then his statement would have been much more comprehensive.

The personalized form which the Aphrodite Force takes in Greece is not the same as her counterpart, Isis, takes in Egypt, nor is the latter the same as the Isis of savage Nubia. These varying forms for their trained and *conditioned* initiates, act each as a link between the subjective Aphrodite of the microcosm and the objective Aphrodite of the macrocosm. The forces within and without man do not vary. It is the images used for linking them together that vary. Yet the same initiate when trained can get results from all three forms alike when working objectively on the Astro-mental plane, or subjectively in the Astro-mental sphere of consciousness.

For the trained initiate these images are not the Goddess any more than the tap which you turn with your hand is the hot water that comes from the boiler and washes you in your morning bath.

The Christian uses the image of the Master Jesus to touch the Cosmic Christ force. The Ancient Egyptian used the image of Osiris to bring him in touch with that same great spiritual Being. But as the initiate of yesterday, and of today, does not (or should not) identify the metal tap marked HOT with the hot water which cleanses his soul and spirit.

As has already been stated, the initiates of one system, when sufficiently trained, (the word initiate means a beginner), can comprehend the technique of almost any other system. This, however, does not mean that they are competent to work a technique other than their own. They, as a rule, cannot. For you have to take your initiation into a system and to become *conditioned* to its symbols before you can use it. This is a point which many of the junior European initiates of Eastern systems forget.

Each nation has not only its own group soul but also its own group mind. This group mind is the gateway to the group soul, and the group soul supplies the voltage that lights the altar lamps of that tradition. It is true that there is a Common Group Soul to all humanity, and you can touch it and must touch it, if any system is to work for you with power. But this fact does not give you the right of entry into the system of another nation. You have to be tested and conditioned and vouched for by a Yoga-trained Initiate of that nation, and then directly initiated into that national system. This explains why the European Jew, as a rule, is not at home in a Keltic or Nordic system. It is his traditional way of thinking, not the fact that he is physically born a Jew that isolates him.

Yoga was not unknown to the Ancient Egyptians as the directions given in the Tale of Setne Khamuas by the old priest to Ne-nefer-ka-Ptah clearly show:

The Book named (Book of Thoth), it is in the midst of the sea of
Coptos (1) in a box of iron. In the box of iron is a box of bronze, in
the box of bronze is a box of Kete-wood, in the box of Kete-wood
is a box of ivory and ebony, and in the box of ivory and ebony is a
box of silver, within which is a box of gold, wherein is the book . . .
there being an endless snake (2) around the box.

(*Stories of the High Priests of Memphis,* Griffith)

The following notes, written by that fine Oxford scholar, F. H.
Griffith, M.A., will show how impossible it is to think of these stories
as dealing with physical happenings:

(1) "The Sea of Coptos." It takes three days and three nights to row
from the shore to the middle of the "Sea of Coptos" and the "Sea"
comprised one schoenus (six miles ?) of ground swarming with
reptiles surrounding the Book of Thoth. Its name and apparent
size suggest the Red Sea, which was generally approached from
Egypt by the Coptos road; but the identification seems impossible, since it is evident from the narrative that its shore was close to
the city of Coptos,* and that a ship could easily be brought to it
from the Nile. More probably the "Sea of Coptos" was a sacred
lake, perhaps that of the temple of Coptos, or part of the Nile near
Coptos, magically extended when the safety of the Book of Thoth
was in question.

(2) Literally the endless snake is snake of *Zt,* which probably means
the snake of eternity.

(3) In Egyptian, the order of the boxes is exactly the reverse of that
which is given in the above Translation: iron in bronze, bronze in
wood, etc. This curious fact will be commented on later.

The physical geography here given is impossible, but the snake
of Zt gives a clue, as do the three days and three nights spent in
rowing.

In the Temptation in the Wilderness Jesus was taken up into a
high mountain and the devil showed Him all the kingdoms of the
world in a moment of time. Physically this also is an impossibility. Psy-
chologically it is possible. Also the expression—going (or being taken)
up—into a high mountain in the ancient mysteries means a trance
state of deep meditation—another hint to be taken in conjunction
with that of the three days and three nights. It is thus clear that the
journey of Ne-nefer-ka-Ptah to the "Sea of Coptos" was a psychological happening, or a magical experiment, which deals with an inner
plane journey, probably on the Astro-mental Plane, and not an earthly

* The City of Coptos is near Luxor.

journey; also it seems that it is somewhat similar to the experiments described in Virgil's Aeneid Book VI, in Plato's story of Er, in Cicero's Dream of Scipio, and in Plutarch's story of Aridaeus.

There is, indeed, for us who are conditioned to the ancient symbols a great deal more in this story than would appear to the casual reader; for it is told about two of the most famous magicians in Ancient Egypt, Ne-nefer-ka-Ptah and Kha-em-uas; and it explains for those who know about clairvoyance much that is interesting with regard to the methods that were used.

Again, it is a fine example of the curious, and for the profane the misleading methods used in giving a hidden teaching of which the ancients were so fond. We have here a direction for finding the lotus center in the human body that is ruled by the God of Wisdom; for the Nile equates with the spine in the human body and Thoth is the Lord of Death, or Understanding. It was at Coptos that Isis cut off a lock of her hair when she heard that Osiris had been murdered. And as some know, the Death center is at the nape of the neck in the auric envelope. That formerly was the reason why the priest's stole usually had a cross at this point.

Kundalini, the coiled serpent, is the guardian of this knowledge in the symbolism of India, and *She* (the Goddess of cosmic magical power) here appears as the snake of *Zt* coiled round the box, or the base of the spine, the lotus-like source of magical power within the microcosm.

The whole of this story of Kha-em-uas can be considered, as it usually is, to be but a popular tale; yet it can be also a mine of information with regard to the use that was made of the esoteric knowledge of that time, much of which is still contained in the so-called *Book of the Dead* of which the Egyptian name is really *Pert-em-hru* and this means "coming forth by day" or "manifested in the light." This knowledge was intended for the use of the living initiates as well as for their dead, a point which the following footnote taken from page 38 of *Stories of the High Priests of Memphis* clearly shows:

> The Book of the Dead is a collection of magic formulae, some of which were intended to enable the deceased* to travel whither he would. It was by the use of such formulae that Ne-nefer-ka-Ptah, the exceptionally skillful scribe, i.e. magician trained in the use of formulae, succeeded in bringing the ghosts (?) of his wife and child to his own tomb in Memphis, while their bodies remained at Coptos.

---

* Note: The initiated living also could do this astral traveling.

In the *Tibetan Book of the Dead* by Dr. Evans-Wentz, there is the following significant remark:

> Such priestly guiding of the deceased's spirit is for the laity alone, for the spirits of deceased lamas, having been trained in the doctrines of the "Bardo Thodol," know the right path and need no guidance.

On page 22, this great Tibetan scholar points out how similar the Egyptian *Book of the Dead* is to the *Bardo Thodol*, and adds at the end of a list of customs common to both this significant remark: "Both treatises alike being nothing more than guide books for the traveler in the realm beyond death." It is interesting to note that Dr. Evans-Wentz studied for three years the ancient funeral law of the Nile Valley immediately before he went to Tibet. He is looked on as one of the greatest living authorities on these subjects, and his books are published by the Oxford University Press, which is indeed a guarantee of scholarship.

Both these books, the *Pert-em-hru* and the *Bardo Thodol*, as the

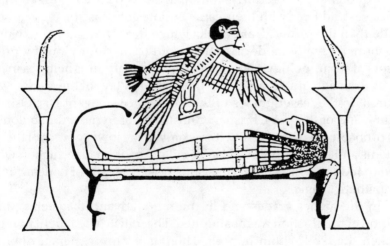

The soul in the form of a bird hovering over the mummy.

Ani and his wife enjoying the delights of Paradise.

above quoted remarks clearly show to those who are able "to see with their eyes and hear with their ears" in states of consciousness more subtle than the physical, are books which deal with initiation. Now initiation, by many modern students of the Mysteries and by professors of anthropology alike, used to be looked upon as being carried out by dramatic rituals rather like the Mystery Plays of the Mediaeval Church. In the lesser grades of the Mystery Systems of Isis, Osiris, Mithra, and of the pre-Christian Gnosticism of Syria and Babylonia this probably was the case. But it was only in the lower grades of these systems and in the primitive Nature cults that dramatized action was used to induce exaltation of consciousness by means of dancing and sympathetic magic.

In the higher grades and in the more advanced systems, this method of ritual action was abandoned. The initiate was taught how to awaken the God within himself. Then, in a purely mental drama, which was carried out in a temple not made with hands, the Thoth-within was connected consciously with that Universal Mind which the Ancient Egyptians called the Lord Tehuti; He who is a personification of the Universal purposive wisdom in Nature. Usually these grades were given in some form of trance which may have been very light indeed, merely the conscious stilling of the bodily senses and the awakening of the initiate's consciousness on those inner planes which are non-physical states of consciousness. But in some of the higher grades, the initiation was given in a very deep trance, a condition so deep that it resembles death, and it might last up to the third day in the tomb, or as long as the three days and three nights in the whale's belly.

In many cases, this initiation had to be given by means of the hypnotic power of the hierophant who presided. But if the Candidate for this initiation was sufficiently developed, he cast himself into this sleep of trance in much the same manner that the modern Indian Yogis do so. And when the candidate was in this condition, the trained initiates in whose care his body remained, followed and checked his experiences in that inner subtler world that in terms of subjectivity, lies just behind the horizon of waking consciousness—the domain of the Anubis-within; or, in terms of objectivity, the domain of the Prince of the West that lies between the realms of the Lady Isis and the Lady Nephthys.

If the reader will experiment patiently with the visualization of these pictures and with the invocation of these names that have here been given to him, much will become clear and real that without such experiments can only dimly be guessed at by the novice. Initiation is empirical and not merely theoretical in its nature.

The ordinary, and certainly the casual, reader will not understand this mass of picture symbolism and these obscure references that are made to Ancient Gods, Goddesses and mythical figures, and he will deem them to be unrealities. And so they are, and so they must remain for him. These things are not real and certainly not actual in any sense of these two words for the untrained conscious mind that receives its impressions through the bodily senses. The initiate has to be conditioned to his symbols through a conscious experience of their power.

The object that is aimed at here is the creating within the soul of the untrained of a great store of images. These images, if quietly brooded upon for a few moments as they are being read, and it is hoped RE-READ, will fall into the darkness of the subconscious mind of the reader, a rich and fruitful country which contains an abundance

Mestha. The Son of Horus.

Qebhsemnuf. The Son of Horus.

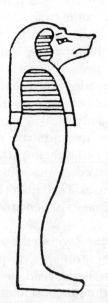

Hapi. A Son of Horus.

Tuantef. Another Son of Horus.

of deep wells that are full of living water. If these images are thus intentionally dropped into this fruitful soil, there is little need to worry about them. They will live and flourish and suddenly ripen into a plentiful harvest. For in the heart of every one of us there dwells a divine husbandman who tends the crops and cares for the vines.

This divine husbandman, while his Lord is in the far country of the conscious mind striving daily with objective phenomena, sits very still in the soft silver light of the Moon Cave. He is the Lord of the Moon Wisdom, and his Kingdom is upon the Astro-mental plane. The Egyptian initiates called him Aah Tehuti, the great god, the lord of heaven, the maker of eternity and creator of everlastingness; the Chaldeans called this god Zinn and he was their Lord of the Moon Wisdom. He is the Lord of the Inner Human Wisdom, he is Merlin in his cave—the moon cave by the still waters of those summer seas that flow and ebb and flow over the drowned lands of Lyonesse. The blue cloak of this divine watcher is still to be seen by the hidden shores of this blue sea. The silver badge of his divine Shakti, whom some call Morgan le Fay, is the full silver moon low in the southeast that throws its long silver bar of glistening rippling light across the darkling sea and then upon the silent figure sitting at the entrance of the moonlit cave. A figure is seated upon a sacred stool. It sits motionless while behind it, with hands placed upon its shoulders, stand two female figures in white and silver robes crowned with the crescent moon and the silver star.

Merlin draws all his power *through* these two, who are the white priestess and the silver priestess. And he loses his rule and his power when he allows the silver priestess to usurp his divine authority. Thus Merlin fell. If we go back into Egyptian myth and legend, we find this same warning given in the tale of Ra and Isis, the silver goddess of the Moon Wisdom that by craft obtained the secret name of Ra, the Sun God, and by so doing became possessed of his power and so his master. Beware of the mastery of the silver priestess. Rule in your own subconscious mind. Tales—fairy tales, just myths and legends—you may say, and with absolute accuracy. Yes, but the myths of this world are but the earthly shadow of a happening in the shining land of the gods of the West, on the verge of the Azure Sea. The fairy maiden sang to Connla:

> It will guard thee gentle Connla of the flowing golden hair,
> It will guard thee from the druids, from the demons of the air;
> My crystal boat will guard thee, till we reach that western shore,

Where thou and I in joy and love shall live for ever more.

(Joyce's *Old Celtic Romances*)

Connla forsook all to follow the fairy maiden and sprang into the curragh in which she stood. The King and his people watched their heir-apparent as he sped over the bright sea to the lands of the Prince of the West.

Some day to someone may come this same call. It is all or nothing then. Death and damnation, hell and purgatory mean little to one who can sit in that moon cave, whither his fairy shakti has brought him in

The Great Sphinx at Gizeh.

the crystal boat that the Prince of the West, the Lord Anubis sends:

> From the land of rest,
> In the golden West
> On the verge of the azure sea!

You are not meant to understand these pictures. If you understand them on reading them, the writer has failed completely in his purpose. These quotations are meant to be incubated in the depths of your unconscious mind. Some day—perhaps under the stress of some great emotional strain of love or hate, or possibly even in that adoration of the ALL which is both love and hate—the inner fountains of your subliminal life will be broken up. These universal images that have worked long and silently in the darkness will spring full grown and powerful for better or for worse into your conscious life. Will you, as lord of the Moon Wisdom, as the initiated Aah-Tehuti, use them, or will they abuse you?

We have made reference to a certain Kha-em-Uaset whose statue is in the British Museum. His name is spelled in various ways— Khamuas or Kha-m-uas, and he is also called Setne Khamuas or Sethon, a corruption of *Sem*, a sacerdotal title.

This Kha-em-Uaset was a son of Rameses II; he was born about 1300 B.C. and died in 1246 B.C., about 10 years before his father. His mother was the Queen Isit-nefert. He was a man of great learning. In his youth he was apparently a soldier, later he became a priest, then High Priest of Ptah, and finally the head of the whole Egyptian hierarchy of his time. He was the most notable of the many progeny of the great Rameses.

His name Kha-em-Uaset has the meaning "manifestation in Thebes" and indicates that he was born in the southern capital, but as a matter of fact he lived mostly in the northern capital which then was Memphis and he died there, his tomb being near the Great Pyramid. Had he outlived his father it is probable that he would have become Pharaoh. At a much later period he played in Egyptian wonder tales, a part very similar to that which Merlin much later again played in the romances of the Middle Ages in England. Even in character there is a strange likeness between these two men.

In order that the reader may visualize the image of this great Initiate more clearly, he is advised to buy a photo of Kha-em-Uaset from the British Museum. If he can go and see the statue, so much the better, for there is magnetic power in it.

For the reader who is not likely to see it, here is a description taken from the British Museum Guide of 1909.

> Flint agglomerate statue of Kha-em-Uaset ... The deceased wears a short heavy wig and a tunic, and holds to his sides with his arms two standards. The standard on the right was surmounted by a mummied form and a figure of the Prince; that on the left by an object which appears to represent the box which held the head of Osiris at Abydos. In front of this object are two Uraei ... The height of the statue including base is 4 feet 8 inches.

The following note may also prove helpful in building an atmosphere about your visualization from the 1930 General Guide to the Egyptian Collection in the British Museum.

> ... Another is the extraordinarily eerie tale (of much later date) preserved in a demotic papyrus, of the magician Setme Khamuas (historically a son of Rameses II), who went down in to a tomb in order to obtain a book of magic reported in it. Khamuas plays draughts with the ghosts, the stake being the precious book ...

The life story of this Magus is well told by Griffith, in his now somewhat rare book (published at the Clarendon Press Oxford, 1900) *Stories of the High Priests of Memphis* and he gives this tale in full in Chapter II under the heading of "The Tale of Khamuas and Ne-nefer-ka-Ptah."

Now as our whole object is to give the reader who is prepared to spend the necessary time, and to take the necessary trouble to master a technique, the chance of *experiencing* the ancient mystery teaching by experimenting for himself, a few notes on the ways of thought habitual to initiates of that time will first be given. They will be followed by a short account of this tale, which the reader should carefully visualize.

So far as historical research has gone, it may be said with reasonable accuracy that the ancient Mysteries in Egypt were divided into two grades. In the first grade were the feminine Mysteries, such as those of Isis (at a late date), of Hathor, of Mut and of Sekhmet, etc. Speaking rather generally and only with regard to the subject matter of these articles it can be said that these particular mystery cults dealt largely with the developing of mediums and mediumship, especially in the young girls who, as the virgins of the Temple, were used for psychic work and who later became the priestly seeresses. These latter very often married into the priesthood, or were married, if they had poor psychical abilities, to laymen selected by the Temple Authorities.

A study of the funeral texts in the British Museum and those given in books dealing with such inscriptions make this theory almost conclusive; more especially if the practices of the other religions of that time are considered.

In these Lesser Mysteries the phenomena, both mental and physical, were much the same as those that are now to be found in that type of Spiritualist Society which seeks to re-awaken religion through the emotions. These Mysteries were not confined to women. But speaking very generally, it can be said that as in spiritualism today, they offered a quick and fairly easy development of the subconscious through the emotions; and for this reason attracted women rather than men. Anthropologists might however explain their attractiveness for women by the theory of a survival, or a recrudescence of the more primitive matriarchal system; but judging from experience the reason is probably psychological rather than social, though both factors may have played a part.

In addition, there was in the outer forms of the Lesser Mysteries a gorgeous ritual with music, song and dance. Here every effort was made to stir up the emotional nature and the subconscious minds of the laity in order to get up what revivalists call a stirring religious atmosphere. These festivals were held usually with reference to the moon periods. The symbolism was that of the moon, of water, and of the form-giving or negative side of Nature. Though the Mother principle of the Macrocosm was the object of this type of worship, which was in reality a joyous worship of the *Life* side of Nature, those who worked these Lesser Mystery cults were the more highly trained priests and priestesses of the Greater Mysteries. The Hierophants who ruled had to be members of that Order which had its colleges at the "Temple of the Net" whose Lord is Thoth, the Great God in Het-Abtit which is situated in Hermopolis, the Greek name for the ancient city of Unnu. Thoth is "the pacifier of the Gods," that is, the ruler over the Chiefs of all the Mystery Schools, and the arbitrator of their disputes.

The Greater Mysteries were (in Egypt but not in Greece) masculine in their nature and the gods were male, and usually were considered to be the Lords of Life, or the Judges in the World-to-come. Male gods such as Osiris, Anubis, Imhetep, Khonsu as Aah Tehuti, and Thoth as the Judge of mankind were human rulers or divine-human saviors. Also they seem to be names for an office that was held by the many Hierophants that ruled over a cult which often existed for centuries. They were the earthly representations of the Lords ruling in the Fields of Aalu (or Aaru) which place was the Egyptian inner plane summerland. It, like the box of Thoth in the Sea of Coptos, was surrounded by a wall of iron, broken by several doors. In other words, iron here stands for the boundary of the material world, as well as for the limit of "the sphere of sensation" in Man. These gods represented what we would now call, in terms of the Mystical Qabalah, the Microcosmic aspect of the Greater Mysteries; that is, they dealt with the salvation of mankind in a purely religious sense.

In addition, the Greater Mysteries had also their macrocosmic aspect. Here the chief gods were Amen, the Hidden One, with a subsidiary yet distinct form as Min or Menu; Ra of many forms; Ptah and Khnemu as cosmic creators. These gods had each a consort of Shakti: Amen had Mut, Ra had Rat, i.e. Isis; Ptah had Sekhmet. It should be noted that the feminine cosmic consorts were often the destructive aspect of the male god. In India this same idea reappears in the relationship between Shiva and Kali-Durga. Most of these gods are personifications of various elemental powers, and often the benevolent Mothers of the Lesser Mysteries become the terrible destroying Mothers of the Greater Mysteries.

Behind these Cosmic Gods were the veiled forms of the Great Abyss personified as Nu (masculine) and Nut (feminine), whence all creation sprang at the command of Khepera. Here is a parallel conception to the modern Indian idea of Shiva and his Shakti, and the "Will to create" which is Shiva-Shakti in action.

In addition there were numerous minor gods who appear to have been the personifications of the Group Minds of cities, temples, religious cults or even local clans. These are conceptions similar in their nature and significance to the modern spiritualist's ideas concerning Guides and Masters.

Controlling all Mysteries, all Gods, saviors, rulers, and hierophants was the Lord of Khemennu, the modern town of Eshmunen. In his colleges were trained selected initiates from the Greater and Lesser Mysteries of all Egypt. Here was the Earthly Order that is behind all the Earthly Orders. In this Order were trained the hierophants skilled in magic, the Kheri Heb or chief priestly magicians. Behind the "House of the Veil," which is the real name of the "Temple of the Net" was, and still is, the Order that is behind and beyond all Orders. A hierophant had to pass through this veil or net, and to take his initiation on the Inner Planes when out of the body; for Initiation is of GRACE and not by a RITE.

The trained priests of the Egyptian Inner Orders (like the trained priests of the Roman Catholic Orders) had spiritual and psychic powers of which modern agnostics and the laity of the Protestant sects have little conception. Excellent descriptions of these powers are scattered throughout books written by Baudouin, Jung, Dion Fortune, Schofield, Ash, Davis, Bramwell, Brown, etc. In addition, there are a host of modern writers who have hastened into print now that E.S.P. (extra-sensory perception) has become respectable. But these latter as a rule take good care to ignore the superstitions of man's benighted past. For unlike the trained initiate these writers, as a rule, have not themselves developed E.S.P. They are usually without either the initiation of "Grace," or the initiation by Rite.

Before we moderns try to look at the experiences of this earthly life through the eyes of the Initiates of Ancient Egypt, a caution must be given. No orthodox anthropologist, nor orthodox priest will allow for one moment that most of the views which have been and are about to be put before you are anything but fancy. One can offer you no proof that they are anything but fancy. But if you will use these ideas as your working hypotheses you can get results which will tend to show you empirically, if you persevere, that these ideas are sound in the main. In other words, while keeping an open mind, say to yourself: "Let me see for myself what is here; at least I am not going to be intolerant."

The ancient initiates who had received their full training, being clairvoyant and clairaudient and having developed extra-sensory perception to a very high degree, were able to function almost at will in states of consciousness other than that of the purely material, the purely physical, the purely sensory; you can call man's earthly experience, as the man in the street meets it, by any one of these three titles.

Again, to use another terminology, you can say these Initiates of Ancient Egypt had by careful training crossed the gulf that divides our normal physical consciousness from supernormal consciousness; (most people can do this even today if they will only spend sufficient time and take sufficient trouble) and had touched, at all events temporarily, worlds beyond the range of our ordinary experience. For them the *seen* had become a reflection of the much greater *unseen*. They had sought and had found *that* world of causes which is behind *this* world of effects—the Platonic *here* and *yonder;* or, as others say, Nature and the Soul of Nature wherein dwell the Divine Henads or the Gods of Proclus; the Children of the Great Mother, the inhabitants of another world. These initiates who knew the lore contained in the books of the "double House of Life" had developed by intensive study and by incessant personal experiment not only objective clairvoyance but also subjective awareness. Their awareness was dual in its nature, and they were fully cognizant of its many possibilities. To widen this range of experience, which is much greater than that of the ordinary person, they sought by very prolonged and thorough training in the quiet of the great temples to develop specially sensitive nervous, vital, emotional and mental mechanisms; and what is just as important, they were careful to build up a physical body capable of standing the extra strain that such psychic work involves.

In these temples were priests who understood the rationale of these psychic experiences and the mechanism of the psychic. Also these men were able to evaluate results on a scientific basis, for, being trained psychics themselves, they had dual vision, dual awareness, and could watch experiments in extra-sensory perception and repeat them in a scientific manner using their pupils as recording or testing instruments. In this way these trained priests had an advantage over the average modern psychic researcher. The latter functions usually on the physical plane, and can see only the mental and emotional phenomena, i.e. the end results of a hidden process. The former could do this and could also see or sense such invisible phenomena as changes in the forms that are used upon the planes that are more subtle than physical matter.

For the fully trained initiate of the Ancient Mysteries the inner worlds were definitely objective on their own planes of consciousness. They knew from experience that in these inner worlds definite forces functioned which wove forms that were seen to be, on their own level, objective. And the trained initiate raised his consciousness to the required level by the use of the cult symbols to which he had been thoroughly conditioned. Yet he never forgot that the Kingdoms of the Heavens were within himself.

By means of these symbols and by the use of the technique he was taught he was able to see as it were objectively on the inner planes and to record what he saw there. That is, he developed as fully as possible what today the Psychic Researchers popularly call by the new name of extra-sensory perception, forgetting that spiritualists and occultists have for long ages known much about E.S.P.

Modern psychical research is only now beginning to take notice of E.S.P. as a recognized part of every man's makeup. But in most men, except sporadically, this extra-sensory perception is and must remain latent and subjective. However, with suitable training it is possible in many cases to turn these usually subjective reactions into experiences that are objective and external. This is the object of most systems of Yoga. And, except under the care of a competent teacher, it is most unwise to attempt development through Yoga of the senses which belong to the etheric, emotional and mental bodies, that is the bodies that form the Aura which psychics see surrounding and exterior to the physical body of a man.

After this brief and very inadequate explanation of the ancient initiate's viewpoint we must return now to the story of Khamuas which will be re-told in such a manner that the reader can use it for training his visualizing imagination.

The first half of the first part of this story has perished, but it has been conjectured by Griffith to be as follows:

> Setne Khamuas, the son of Pharaoh Usermara, being a diligent seeker after divine and ancient writings, was informed of the existence of a book which Thoth, the god of letters, science and magic, had "written with his own hand," and learned that this book was to be found in the cemetery of Memphis, in the tomb of Ne-nefer-ka-Ptah, the son of a Pharaoh named apparently Mer-neb—Ptah. Having succeeded in identifying and entering the tomb, accompanied by his brother Anherru, he finds there the ghosts of the owner, his wife (Ahure) and child, and lying by them the coveted book. But they refuse to give it up to him. Theirs it was, for they had "paid for it with their earthly lives," and its magic power availed them in good stead even within the tomb. To dissuade Setne from taking the book Ahure tells him their own sad story.

Here it is necessary to give an exact definition of what the word Magic means when used by those who have been duly initiated, and the meaning that is given to it here. It has been well defined thus:

> Magic is the art of causing changes to take place in consciousness in accordance with the will.

Using this conception of magic it becomes evident that Khamuas and Anherru visited that tomb by means of that magical (i.e. mental) process that is today called, or rather miscalled, astral projection, for it is much more than astral. That is why they met the ghosts on a footing of equality and were refused possession of the book. And any reader with the necessary qualifications can today do (it has been done) what Khamuas and Anherru did just 3000 years ago, if he will remember that initiation is an experience which takes place NOT IN TIME nor IN SPACE: and if he will realize the full implication of the definition which has just been given of the word magic.

Summary of Ahure's Story

Ahure tells Khamuas and Anherru that her husband, the heir-apparent Ne-Nefer-ka-Ptah, was a man of great learning who, hearing about the Book of Thoth from an ancient priest, determines to get possession of it, having learned that it is hidden in the "Sea of Coptos." Note carefully the following quotation:

> And the priest said unto Ne-nefer-ka-Ptah, "The book named, it is in the midst of the Sea of Coptos, in a box of bronze, the box of bronze in a box of Kete-wood, the box of Kete-wood in a box of ivory and ebony, the box of ivory and ebony in a box of silver, and the box of silver in a box of gold, wherein is the book: there being a schoenus of every kind of serpent, scorpion, and reptile round the box wherein is the book, there being an endless snake about the box named."

Here Griffith very naturally points out that . . .

> In the description of the nesting of the boxes, it is evident that the scribe has reversed the order of things. He should have written "in the box of iron is a box of bronze, in the box of bronze a box of silver (!) etc."

But after all, has the scribe been careless and made a mistake? Iron for the Egyptian as well as the Keltic initiate was a symbol for the material universe, and for the human sphere of sensation.

We know today, and the ancient initiates knew it also, that the physical body is within the etheric body, the etheric body is within the astral, the astral is within the mental, and the mental is within the spiritual; matter being the most condensed (so far as we know) form of spirit. This is a reversal of the ordinary person's way of thinking about his so-called "inner man."

Has the scribe reversed the order of things? Has he made a mistake? Build the tree of life in your aura and see where the Golden Box of Tiphareth comes. The Book of Thoth is in Daath, and Daath is the revealer of all the secrets of the universe. A tree mirrored in water is upside down. So too is the astral when reflected in matter.

Here is a key to this story and indeed to all occultism: *That which is mis-called the inner is outside the outer.*

The subtle is more extensive than the less subtle and it is less contracted. If you do not believe this, and fail to see the implications of this apparent reversal of the normal way of thinking, then look carefully at the diagrams given in Dr. Kilner's book *The Human Atmosphere* (*The Aura*).

You may say questioningly—what is the use of my wasting my time visualizing this story and trying to unravel its subtleties? What do I in this twentieth century get out of these ancient tales of Khamuas?

The answer is direct contact with the minds of the greatest of the magicians in Ancient Egypt—Ka-em-uast and Ne-nefer-ka-Ptah.

Now we have begun the tale of the encounter between the two great magicians Ne-Nefer-Ka-Ptah and Setne Khamwas, and the story of the search for the box containing the Book of Thoth as given by Ahure (the ill-fated wife of the heir-apparent) has been briefly summarized.

The first part of the story, which deals with the finding of the Book, the deaths of the magician's wife and child, and his own subsequent suicide by jumping off the royal yacht into the Nile, is not of very great importance to the student of elementary esotericism. There is, however, much in it that is important to the advanced student for it hints at dangers of which those who explore these ancient byways are well aware; an awareness moreover that is often bought by unpleasant experiences in that curious twilit realm of the Lord Anubis which lies between the boundaries of the realms of the Lady Isis and the Lady Nephthys; realms that we have already described in terms of an ancient symbolism that gives the passway into them and, what is more important, the right of unrestricted return to the Malkuth of Assiah.

Many students think that they can neglect the technique of this return journey, but for such repeated neglect a heavy price has to be paid in a gradually growing ill-health, both psychic and physical.

In the portion of this tale that will now be set forth, Ahure begs Setne Khamwas to leave the book in the tomb, saying "Thou hast no lot in it. Whereas our term of life on earth was taken for it." Setne, however, threatens to "take it by force," and the story runs on as follows:

> Ne-Nefer-Ka-Ptah raised himself on the (funeral) couch, he said "Art thou Setne unto whom this woman hath spoken these vain words and thou hast not hearkened unto her words? The book

named, wilt thou be able to take it by power of a good scribe (magician) or by prevailing over me in playing draughts? Let us play for it at the game of fifty-two points."

And Setne said "I am ready."

They set before them the game-board with its pieces; they played at the game of fifty-two and Ne-Nefer-Ka-Ptah won one game from Setne. He pronounced a spell to him; he supplemented (?) with the draught-board that was before him; he caused him to sink into the floor to his feet. He did the like by the second game; he won it from Setne; he caused him to sink into the floor as far as his middle. He did the like by the third game; he caused him to sink into the floor as far as his ears . . .

Then Setne, feeling that he was beaten, sent his brother Anherru to bring (from the upper world) to the tomb Setne's "Amulets of Ptah and his books of Magic." As soon as the Amulets were on the body of Setne he became free, and he hastened for the light of the upper world, taking with him the Book of Thoth.
    (Quoted from Griffith's *Stories of the High Priests of Memphis*)

Setne did not keep it long, however, for the vengeance of the dead pursued him and he soon returned humbly to their tomb to replace the book with the ghosts of Ne-Nefer-Ka-Ptah, Ahure and their child, Merab.

Suggestions (which are based on experiences of pupils) will now be made to assist the reader in conducting his own experiments:

Picture the Book of Thoth as a roll enveloped in its bright aura of soft pale moonlight. Then, day after day, build and rebuild this story by using the visualizing faculties of the human mind. Get photos of Egyptian tombs in order to visualize clearly the place of Setne Kham-was' adventure, and to reconstruct as vividly as possible these scenes. Try to sense the emotions of the various characters in this tale; try to feel the thick, heavy darkness of these ancient tombs that are hidden deep down in the desert lands on the Western bank of the Nile. Feel in your imagination the soft velvet blackness of the realms of the Lord of the West, the guide Anubis.

Use composition of place as set forth by Ignatius Loyola. That is, first build each scene as if you were trying to arrange it in your own mind before setting it out on the stage of a theater. Picture clearly where each of the actors stands or lies. Imagine in detail what the couch upon which the mummy is laid would look like. See Ne-Nefer-Ka-Ptah raise himself from his couch. Watch this swathed mummy, with its still living, ghostly counterpart, playing draughts with the astral forms of Setne Khamwas and his brother Anherru. See, too, the ghosts of Ahure and the child, Merab—without their mummies—and feel their anxiety, and their subsequent joy as the game progresses in their favor. Experience fear as Setne must have felt fear.

Hear Ahure weeping for the lost Book of Thoth and feel the emotion that pervades—her despairing cry as Setne vanishes with it: "Hail, King Darkness! Farewell, King Light! Every power hath gone that was in the tomb, all!"

Again, sense the power and certainty that fills the great dead magician, Ne-Nefer-Ka-Ptah, as he comforts his ghostly wife, Ahure, in the astral blackness that falls upon them when the light shed by the Book of Thoth has gone. And hear his confident speech: "Be not grieved in heart, I will cause him to bring this book hither, a forked stick (?) in his hand and a censer (?) of fire upon his head."

Later picture the chastised Setne returning, as described above, and saluting a magician greater than himself, for "Setne made salutation to Ne-Nefer-Ka-Ptah: he found it to be as though it were (?) the sun that was in the whole tomb." A sentence easy to understand for we are told that where the Book of Thoth is there is Light. Finally, get a clear picture of the last scene when Setne brings—as an act of repentance—the long dead bodies of Ahure and Merab to join their ghosts in the Tomb of Ne-Nefer-Ka-Ptah.

Once again, you may ask what is the use of going to all this trouble? The answer is—some of those who have, over a long period, experimented with these things have found them to be well worth the great amount of time and labor that has to be spent upon them.

You also, if you are capable of doing this type of mental work in order to train the visualizing imagination, may perhaps find it to be of value; but equally you may find it not to be so. All depends on your capacities and your ability to expend in a wise manner the time at your disposal and the energy that is within you. This type of work is only for the few. It is your energy in function that will determine your status as a magician—that is, as one who is able to employ the art of changing planes of consciousness in accordance with the will.

To the limited extent that man may know them, the forms of the gods are creations of the created. By men's minds are their forms created; but as forces they are children of the Great Mother. And so the most important is the Lord Thoth, who is the common reason of this World's reason, the divine executor of the Unmanifested Divine

Will. The Lord Tahuti is in very deed the combined wisdom of Gods, of men, *and* of all the other Orders in this Universe that are normally invisible to man's physical sight.

The Wise Ibis is thus the common symbol for the Logos (the Word), that is, for the divine ideation; as such Thoth is the Lord of Magic, and that is why these pictures have been given you in such detail. If you can gain the ear of the Lord Tahuti you can work magic, i.e. you can touch the all-pervading mind of the Great Mother whose mental child you are, even as you are spiritually a child of the Cosmos.

In Magic you must work for your play, and play for your work. This is the law of alternating rhythm; and so, for your work, build upon the Egyptian myths—they are magical. For your play build upon the Keltic myths and folklore. They too are magical, but in another way. Get in touch with nature, our Great Mother, if you want to know the Gods who, like you, are her children. Call upon the Gods by the names that stir you most easily. Your mind may give them form; but nature, that Great Goddess, ensouls your created forms with her self-acting forces. For example, try to use magically, for your play, this picture of an English countryside:

It is the first week of June and a cold dry spring has suddenly become warm summer. On the sunlit edge of a beech-wood, bright with the vivid coloring of its new leaves, seated in the short grass of a golden-green meadow are two worshippers of the Great Mother. They are sitting motionless in meditation, seeking conscious communion with Her children; magically they are at play.

The ancient invocations of the Gods have been made. The God desired has been called upon by that wordless adoration that follows the low-toned vibration of the sacred name. He has given them proof that he has heard. His presence is felt.

Ra, having put off his midday cloak of pure brilliance and completed his course through the Eighth House of Death, has now become Toum, and is sinking slowly through the gold and scarlet cusp of the seventh and the eighth Houses of Heaven. Isis, symbolized by a silver-grey half-moon, is now with Him in the House of Unmanifested Life. Between these Two Great Ones is the planet Venus. She is the ruler of the Star Sothis, the Queen of the Thirty-Six constellations that formed the astronomical tables of ancient Egypt; the Isis of Netzach concealing her mighty powers behind a veil of emerald green. She is, and yet is not, the Silver Isis of the Moon. And as Ra becomes Toum, so the bright Green Isis merges into the Silver-Grey Goddess of the dewy evening when the Children of the Great Mother return to their play.

For now the Lord of Tiphareth is about to give place to the Lady of Yesod, the Queen of Starry Night. As the golden summer's day merges into the silver twilight the Children of Isis, The Great Mother, wake yet again from their day-long sleep, and come peering through the blue and mauve and purple shadows that creep across the still sunlit meadow.

"I am Toum, the Setting Sun," chanted the neophyte in ancient times as he prepared to enter the immeasurable and imponderable region that is the realm of the Great Mother that is next to this material Earth. "I am the Silver Isis, the dark-veiled ruler of Night," answered his guide as she closed his eyes in the temple-sleep so that the neophyte might see with the inner eye those Children of the Great Mother that awaited his passing between the pillars of the East and of the West.

Without speaking, the pair watch the warm golden rays that now begin to cast deep violet shadows across the bright sward; and as each patch of darkness swallows the golden light something shadowy seems to start into waking life within its borders.

In those up-slanting rays the higher branches of the beech trees that edge the wood have their every leaf turned into the golden green of the Great Mother's spring color. But their beauty passes almost unnoticed, for in the stillness that falls when the Great God Toum plunges out of sight beneath the Western horizon, bright eyes look out from behind bush and brake, half-seen forms flit through the undergrowth.

Now the sunset hush is broken only by the evening song of birds perched on high. They sing until the golden leaves of the topmost branches have faded into green. Then something happens to the trees. A strange sort of shivering which can only be registered by inner senses that have been carefully trained takes place. The trees have become sentient. The wood is alive.

All the children of the Great Mother are now awake, and their nightly frolic is about to begin.

In meditation, through tightly-closed eyes, can be perceived bright forms that step out of dim shadows in the woods. High above the dark wood is a great swirling gold and silver form. It is the Deva that rules this densely wooded valley; the Cosmic mind that gives life and keeps order; a formless force that man personifies because man's mind cannot do otherwise.

Deeper and deeper the watching pair sink down into the conscious sleep of deep meditation; their aims are one, their methods are one; and by a technique that was taught in Ancient Egypt they have merged consciousness into a single sphere of sensation. Their backs are propped against the rotting trunk of a cut down tree, and their bodily senses are slowly being put out of action.

As dusk comes on, and as conscious sleep grows deeper, a momentary feeling of panic comes—a welcome sign, for this feeling of fear means that power is condensing upon their sphere of sensation. Spasmodically muscles grow taut as if electric charges have swept through an expectant nervous system; then everything quietly goes slack. The Gates of the Invisible loom up behind the tightly shut eyes. And as these gates of Ivory and Horn swing gently open on soundless hinges, the Great God comes. We are in his garden and the Gates of His inner world close silently behind us. We have invoked and He has come—the First-born of the Great Mother, The Master, the recognized shepherd of all her children—excepting modern man. Name him—if you can. Worship him—if you dare. Invoke him—if you are able.

The consciousness of that pair "awake in sleep" is now in Tir-na-n'oge, or as some once called it, the "Fields of Aaru," and an account has been given of a process that will, if persevered in, enable almost anyone to enter therein who is prepared to give the time and take the trouble to develop their Sphere of Sensation. It will take some time to read this description with understanding. It has taken a long time to write it out. But in actual practice it is a matter of moments only—once you have received the blessing of that Great God who is the First-born love of the Great Mother, and have realized the truth of the saying "as a man thinks, so he is."

Tir-na-n'oge is Fairyland. In the very ancient Gaelic tales it is often called Tir Tairngire, the Land of Promise, and it is one of the chief dwelling-places of the Dedannans, who, in Irish history, conquered the Firbolgs. Now the Dedannans are the Children of the Goddess Danna that is the Great Mother. It is said that in the course of their wanderings they spent some time in Greece where they learned magic and other curious arts. Later they were in their turn defeated by the people of Miled or the Milesians, and then they disappeared into the magic world of Fairyland.

They are often called today the Deena-shee (Daoine-sidhe), that is the people of the fairy hills; also Sloo-shee (Sluagh-sidhe), the fairy host.

One of their chiefs was the Gaelic sea-god Mannanan Mac Lir. Angus Oge, who lived at Brugh-na Boyne near the village of Slane, was their great Magician, being to the Irish of that time what Thoth was for the Ancient Egyptians.

In order to go to Tir-na-n'oge use these names, which are "Names of Power," and brood over these ideas. There are many more Celts in England than there are in Ireland, so call upon the Gods with a good heart and in faith. But do not try to rationalize these ideas nor to explain these names of power for they are seed-thoughts to be buried in the subconscious mind and be left to germinate in the dark. Act *as if* they were potent and they will be potent—very potent, if one is patient and persevering. Remember that in true Magic "You are *what* you think you are. You are *where* you think you are."

All one has to do in order to open the gates that lead into these inner worlds is—with intention and strong emotion, daily to call upon the Children of the Great Mother and to picture her woods, her rivers, her mountains and her seacoasts. Call upon Mannanan Mac Lir when you sit by the slow-rolling waves of the West-country sea. The earth, the waters and the airy realms are densely populated by the children of the Great Mother, as A.E. and Yeats have so often proclaimed.

If the poetry of Yeats be thoughtfully read and carefully visualized, the gates of Horn and Ivory will swing gently, silently, and at first very slightly open before you. Slowly, very slowly perhaps, you will learn first of all to peer through them hopefully, and then later, as a reward for your daily toil, these gates will open wide to the common password for all magic "Labor omnia vincit." Then you can stride through them as a free man. Free are you to roam more and more widely through an ever-opening series of worlds that exist with the spacious rolling realms of the mind of the Great Mother. You can thus become unshackled from the trammels of ancient herd-law superstitions through your own efforts if only you will realize fully that ancient proverb: "Leone fortior fides"; in other words, be taught by Ignatius, for the clue is to *act as if*. If you can do this you need not worry about whys or wherefores of the human reasoning mind; gone are the bogies of ancient superstitions; gone are the semi-sacred tabus of the superstitious past. You are free, for now has begun the Age of Aquarius, the Airy sign of the free man who strides across the wide firmament of the boundless realms of the Great Mother, carrying his own burden upon his own shoulders.

The Celtic Spirit of Freedom is now permeating through and through the life, the religion, the philosophy, and even the customs of Great Britain and France. How many of us realize that much of England is as truly Celtic as is Wales and Scotland, and Brittany.

Do the pictures that rise into your consciousness, as you read these lines (given below) by W. B. Yeats, cause a thrill to run through you? If they do, then you are British, i.e. Celtic as regards your subconscious mind, whatever your Anglo-Saxon reasoning mind may think on this point.

Your subconscious mind, and its link with the British racial subconscious mind, is the source of your personal power. The Celtic subconscious is the driving force in the group soul of the British peoples of these islands. Even if you are a Sassenach, experiment magically with this poem of the Gael, after first considering the Saxon name its author bears.

The Hosting of the Sidhe

The host is riding from Knocknarea,
And over the grave of Clooth-na-bare*;
Caolte† tossing his burning hair,
And Niamh†† calling, "Away, come away";
Empty your heart of its mortal dream.
The winds awaken, the leaves whirl round,
Our cheeks are pale, our hair is unbound.
Our breasts are heaving, our eyes are a-gleam,
Our arms are waving, our lips are apart;
And if any gaze on our rushing band,
We come between him and the deed of his hand,
We come between him and the hope of his heart!
The host is rushing 'twixt night and day'
And where is there hope or deed as fair?
Caolte tossing his burning hair,
And Niamh calling, away, come away!

(*The Celtic Twilight*, W. B. Yeats)

If this affects you, O Sassenach, then let your Anglo-Saxon and very Christian consciences beware. You are in the same position as

---

* Pronounced Clu-na-bare
† Pronounced Kilte
†† Pronounced Nia

some two thousand years ago was the heathen King Conn, the Hundred-fighter, who, hearing the banshee call to his son Connla, cried in despair:

> Bring my druid, Coran, to me: for I see that the fairy lady has this day regained the power of her voice.

STAY IN TOUCH

On the following pages you will find listed, with their current prices, some of the books and tapes now available on related subjects. Your book dealer stocks most of these, and will stock new titles in the Llewellyn series as they become available. We urge your patronage.

However, to obtain our full catalog, to keep informed of new titles as they are released and to benefit from informative articles and helpful news, you are invited to write for our bi-monthly news magazine/catalog. A sample copy is free, and it will continue coming to you at no cost as long as you are an active mail customer. Or you may keep it coming for a full year with a donation of just $2.00 in the U.S.A. ($7.00 for Canada & Mexico, $20.00 overseas, first class mail). Many bookstores also have *The Llewellyn New Times* available to their customers. Ask for it.

Stay in touch! In *The Llewellyn New Times'* pages you will find news and reviews of new books, tapes and services, announcements of meetings and seminars, articles helpful to our readers, news of authors, advertising of products and services, special money-making opportunities, and much more.

The Llewellyn New Times
P.O. Box 64383-Dept. 671, St. Paul, MN 55164-0383, U.S.A.

• • •

TO ORDER BOOKS AND TAPES

If your book dealer does not have the books and tapes described on the following pages readily available, you may order them direct from the publisher by sending full price in U.S. funds, plus $1.00 for handling and 50¢ each book or item for postage within the United States; outside U.S.A surface mail add $1.50 per item postage and $1.00 per order for handling. Outside U.S.A air mail add $7.00 per item postage and $1.00 per order for handling. MN residents add 6% sales tax.

FOR GROUP STUDY AND PURCHASE

Because there is a great deal of interest in group discussion and study of the subject matter of this book, we feel that we should encourage the adoption and use of this particular book by such groups by offering a special "quantity" price to group leaders or "agents."

Our Special Quantity Price for a minimum order of five copies of *Ancient Magicks for a New Age* is $38.85 Cash-With-Order. This price includes postage and handling within the United States. Minnesota residents must add 6% sales tax. For additional quantities, please order in multiples of five. For Canadian and foreign orders, add postage and handling charges as above. Credit Card (VISA, MasterCard, American Express) Orders are accepted. Charge Card Orders only may be phoned free ($15.00 minimum order) within the U.S.A. by dialing 1-800-THE MOON (in Canada call: 1-800-FOR-SELF). Customer Service calls dial 1-612-291-1970. Mail Orders to:

LLEWELLYN PUBLICATIONS
P.O. Box 64383-Dept. 671 / St. Paul, MN 55164-0383, U.S.A.

MYSTERIA MAGICA
by Denning and Phillips

For years, Denning and Phillips headed the international occult Order Aurum Solis. In this book they present the magickal system of the order so that you can use it. Here you will find rituals for banishing and invoking plus instructions for proper posture and breathing. You will learn astral projection, rising on the planes, and the magickal works that should be undertaken through astral projection. You will learn the basic principle of ceremonies and how to make sigils and talismans. You will learn practical Enochian magick plus how to create, consecrate and use your magickal tools such as the magickal sword, wand and cup. You will also learn the advanced arts of sphere-working and evocation to visible appearance.

Filled with illustrations, this book is an expanded version of the previous edition. It is now complete in itself and can be the basis of an entire magickal system. You can use the information alone or as the sourcebook for a group. It is volume 3 of **The Magical Philosophy**, the other two books being *The Sword and The Serpent* and *The Foundations of High Magick*. If you want to learn how to do real magick, this is the place you should start.

0-87542-196-2, 480 pgs., 6 x 9, illus., softcover   **$15.00**

THE SWORD AND THE SERPENT: The Magical Structure
of Cosmos and Psyche
Being a revision and expansion of Books III and IV of the first edition.
by Denning and Phillips

This is the comprehensive guide to the Magical Qabalah with extensive correspondences as well as the techniques for activating the centers, use of images and the psychology of attainment.

In this volume, histories from contemporary life together with references to the works of mystics, poets, artists, philosophers and authorities in psychology are cited to illustrate point by point the action and interaction of the functions of the psyche as identified in Qabalistic teaching.

In this book is set forth clearly the real meaning of adepthood: in relation to this, frequent enigmas of occult literature such as the Abyss, the Knowledge and Conversation of the Holy Guardian Angel, and the supernal attainments, are presented in their true meaning and significance. The natural dignity and potential of life in this world is your birthright. In this volume, its splendor and power are made unmistakably manifest.

0-87542-197-0, 512 pgs., 6 x 9, illus., softcover   **$15.00**

BETWEEN GOOD & EVIL
by William G. Gray
If you are seeking Inner Light, read this important new book. *Between Good and Evil* provides new insight that can help you take the forces of Darkness that naturally exist within us and transform them into spiritual Light. This book will help you discover how you can deal constructively, rather than destructively, with the unavoidable problem of Evil. Our lives depend on which way we direct our energy—whether we make the Devil in ourselves serve the God, or the other way around. We must use our Good intentions to understand and exploit the Evil energies that would otherwise prove fatal to us.

In order to confront and control our "demons," Gray has revived a centuries-old magical ritual technique called the *Abramelin Experience:* a practical, step-by-step process in which you call upon your Holy Guardian Angel to assist in converting Evil into Good. By following the richly detailed explanation of this "spiritual alchemy," you will learn how to positively channel your negative energies into a path leading directly to a re-union with Divinity.

The power of altering your future lies in your own hands, and within this unique book you will discover the means to move forward in your spiritual evolution. You will find the principles discussed in this multi-faceted book valuable and insightful.
0-87542-273-X, 304 pgs., 5¼ x 8, softcover $9.95

TEMPLE MAGIC
by William Gray
This important book on occultism deals specifically with problems and details you are likely to encounter in temple practice. Learn how a temple should look, how a temple should function, what a ceremonialist should wear, what physical postures best promote the ideal spiritual-mental attitude, and how magic is worked in a temple.

Temple Magic has been written specifically for the instruction and guidance of esoteric ceremonialists by someone who has spent a lifetime in spiritual service to his natural Inner Way. There are few comparable works in existence, and this book in particular deals with up-to-date techniques of constructing and using a workable temple dedicated to the furtherance of the Western Inner Tradition. In simple yet adequate language, it helps any individual understand and promote the spiritual structure of our esoteric inheritance. It is a book by a specialist for those who are intending to be specialists.
0-87542-274-8, 240 pgs., 5¼ x 8, illus., softcover $7.95

THE MAGICAL DIARY
by Donald Michael Kraig
Virtually every teacher of magic, whether it is a book or an individual, will advise you
to keep a record of your magical rituals. Unfortunately, most people keep these
records in a collection of different sized and different looking books, frequently
forgetting to include important data. *The Magical Diary* changes this forever. In this
neat, spiral-bound book are pages waiting to be filled in. Each page has headings for
all of the important information including date, day, time, astrological information,
planetary hour, name of rituals performed, results, comments, and much more. Use
some of them or use them all. This book was specially designed to be *perfect for all
magicians no matter what tradition you are involved in*. Everybody who does magic needs
The Magical Diary.
0-87542-322-1, 160 pages, 5½ x 8½, spiral bound   **$5.95**

MODERN MAGICK
by Donald Michael Kraig
Modern Magick is the most comprehensive step-by-step introduction to the art of
ceremonial magic ever offered. It will guide you from the easiest of rituals and the
construction of your magickal tools through the highest forms of magick: designing
your own rituals and doing pathworking. Along the way you will learn the secrets of
the Kabalah in a clear and easy-to-understand manner. You will also discover the true
secrets of invocation and evocation, channeling, and the missing information that
will finally make the ancient *grimoires*, such as the **Keys of Solomon**, not only com-
prehensible, but usable. It is not intended to supplant any other book; its purpose is to
fully train and prepare anyone to use other books as he or she wills, with a full
understanding of what the other writers are trying to present, along with what the
other authors omit. *Modern Magick* is designed so anyone can use it, and is the perfect
guidebook for students and classes. It will also help to round out the knowledge of
long-time practitioners of the magickal arts. In short, the clarity of writing will make
Modern Magick the outstanding resource for all magicians for years to come.
0-87542-324-8, 608 pgs., 6 x 9, illus., softcover   **$14.95**

THE NEW MAGUS
by Donald Tyson
The New Magus is a practical framework on which a student can base his or her
personal system of magic.

This book is filled with practical, usable magical techniques and rituals which
anyone from any magical tradition can use. It includes instructions on how to
design and perform rituals, create and use sigils, do invocations and evocations,
do spiritual healings, learn rune magic, use god-forms, create telesmatic images,
discover your personal guardian, create and use magical tools and much more.
You will learn how *YOU* can be a *New Magus!*

The New Age is based on ancient concepts that have been put into terms, or
metaphors, that are appropriate to life in our world today. That makes *The New
Magus* the book on magic for today.

If you have found that magic seems illogical, overcomplicated and not appropriate to your lifestyle, *The New Magus* is the book for you. It will change your
ideas of magic forever!
0-87542-825-8, 384 pgs., 6 x 9, illus., softcover   **$12.95**

THE GOLDEN DAWN
by Israel Regardie
The Original Account of the Teachings, Rites and Ceremonies of the Hermetic Order of the Golden Dawn as revealed by Israel Regardie, with further revision, expansion, and additional notes by Israel Regardie, Cris Monnastre, and others.

Originally published in four bulky volumes of some 1200 pages, this 5th Revised and Enlarged Edition has been entirely reset in modern, less space-consuming type, in half the pages (while retaining the original pagination in marginal notation for reference) for greater ease and use.

Corrections of typographical errors perpetuated in the original and subsequent editions have been made, with further revision and additional text and notes by actual practitioners of the Golden Dawn system of Magick, with an Introduction by the only student ever accepted for personal training by Regardie.

Also included are Initiation Ceremonies, important rituals for consecration and invocation, methods of meditation and magical working based on the Enochian Tablets, studies in the Tarot, and the system of Qabalistic Correspondences that unite the World's religions and magical traditions into a comprehensive and practical whole.

This volume is designed as a study and practice curriculum suited to both group and private practice. Meditation upon, and following with the Active Imagination, the Initiation Ceremonies is fully experiential without need of participation in group or lodge.
0-87542-663-8, 744 pgs., 6 x 9, illus., softcover $19.95

WICCA: A Guide for the Solitary Practitioner
by Scott Cunningham
Wicca is a book of life, and how to live magically, spiritually, and wholly attuned with Nature. It is a book of sense and common sense, not only about Magick, but about religion and one of the most critical issues of today: how to achieve the much needed and wholesome relationship with our Earth. Scott Cunningham presents Wicca as it is today—a gentle, Earth-oriented religion dedicated to the Goddess and God. This book fulfills a need for a practical guide to solitary Wicca—a need which no previous book has fulfilled.

Here is a positive, practical introduction to the religion of Wicca, designed so that any interested person can learn to practice the religion alone, anywhere in the world. It presents Wicca honestly and clearly, without the pseudo-history that permeates other books. It shows that Wicca is a vital, satisfying part of twentieth-century life.

This book presents the theory and practice of Wicca from an individual's perspective. The section on the Standing Stones Book of Shadows contains solitary rituals for the Esbats and Sabbats.This book, based on the author's nearly two decades of Wiccan practice, presents an eclectic picture of various aspects of this religion. Exercises designed to develop magical proficiency, a self-dedication ritual, herb, crystal and rune magic, recipes for Sabbat feasts, are included in this excellent book.
0-87542-118-0, 240 pgs., illus., 6 x 9, softcover $9.95